Weight Training

FOR

DUMMIES®

A Wiley Brand

4th Edition

by LaReine Chabut, Liz Neporent, and
Suzanne Schlosberg

Weight Training For Dummies,® 4th Edition

Published by: **John Wiley & Sons, Inc.,** 111 River Street, Hoboken, NJ 07030-5774, www.wiley.com

Copyright © 2015 by John Wiley & Sons, Inc., Hoboken, New Jersey

Published simultaneously in Canada

For general information on our other products and services, please contact our Customer Care Department within the U.S. at 877-762-2974, outside the U.S. at 317-572-3993, or fax 317-572-4002. For technical support, please visit www.wiley.com/techsupport.

Wiley publishes in a variety of print and electronic formats and by print-on-demand. Some material included with standard print versions of this book may not be included in e-books or in print-on-demand. If this book refers to media such as a CD or DVD that is not included in the version you purchased, you may download this material at http://booksupport.wiley.com. For more information about Wiley products, visit www.wiley.com.

Library of Congress Control Number: 2014913218

ISBN 978-1-118-94074-7 (pbk); ISBN 978-1-118-94076-1 (ebk); ISBN 978-1-118-94075-4 (ebk)

Manufactured in the United States of America

10 9 8 7 6 5 4 3 2 1

Contents at a Glance

Table of Contents

Introduction

*W*hen the first edition of *Weight Training For Dummies* was published, lifting weights was on the verge of becoming a mainstream phenomenon. Women, Baby Boomers, teens — all these groups were starting to get the message: Using weights benefits everyone, not just bodybuilders, and helps you stay fit and healthy for life. Fast-forward almost a decade, and weight training has become more popular than ever. Any health club you may join offers personal training (compared to 66 percent in 1996). In the same period, health club memberships have more than doubled for people over age 55. With people living longer, it's more important than ever to incorporate weight training into daily workouts.

However, just because weight training has become more popular doesn't mean it has become any less intimidating for novices. It's only natural for a beginner to be baffled by the equipment and the lingo. You may look at a barbell and not know the difference between it and a dumbbell (and you may feel like the latter). You may wonder how you're going to lift any weight while remaining on good terms with your lower-back muscles. You may stare at a weight machine and wonder how you're ever going to learn how to use it. You may wonder what it means when a trainer says, "Do three sets of eight reps on the lat pull-down and then super set with the seated row."

Good thing you bought this book, because here we give you the knowledge and confidence to start a weight-training program, either at home or at the gym. We describe exercises suitable for rookies and veterans alike. This new edition has been updated with information on training over a lifetime. We include training tips for kids, teens, prenatal and postpartum moms, and older adults. And we demystify the latest trends in fitness, core training, yoga, and Pilates. This edition is packed with workouts for every circumstance; whether you're on vacation or you only have 20 minutes to spare, you can fit a weight-training workout into your day.

In *Weight Training For Dummies,* we tell you about safe weight-lifting techniques, steer you toward equipment bargains, entertain you with stories about fellow lifters, and inspire you to keep pumping iron when you'd rather spend your Sunday watching sports. In fact, we take care of just about everything except lifting the weights. We save that job for you.

About This Book

Everyone has different reasons for wanting to lift weights. Undoubtedly, many of these reasons have to do with looking better. Sculpted arms and toned abs have become somewhat of a fashion statement among certain age groups. But we can think of more compelling and, ultimately, more satisfying reasons to lift weights. Here's a reminder of how much weight training can benefit you:

- ✔ **Keeping your bones healthy:** The average woman loses about 1 percent of her bone mass each year after age 35. Men are susceptible to brittle bones, too. Lifting weights can drastically slow the rate of bone loss and may even reverse the process. With strong bones, you won't become hunched over as you age, and you'll lower your risk of life-threatening fractures. No matter your age, it's never too late to start strengthening your bones.

- ✔ **Helping control your weight:** When you lose weight through dieting alone or together with some aerobic exercise (such as walking or cycling), you lose muscle along with fat. This can be a problem — when you lose muscle, your metabolism slows down, so you're more likely to regain the weight. By adding weight training to the mix, you can maintain (or increase) your muscle and thereby maintain (or even boost) your metabolism. Although weight training is no magic bullet for weight loss, many obesity experts consider it to be an essential part of any weight-control program.

- ✔ **Increasing your strength:** Lifting more than 10 to 20 pounds may not be among your goals in life, but a certain amount of muscle strength does come in handy. Weight training makes it easier to haul bottles and cans to the recycling bin and carry and put away your groceries. It can also keep you out of a nursing home in your older age and help you maintain your balance and independence. Studies show that even 90-year-olds can gain significant strength from lifting weights and regain the ability to walk and dress themselves.

- ✔ **Boosting your energy:** Forget about hokey dietary supplements. One of the best energy boosters around comes not in a bottle but on a weight rack. When you lift weights, you have more pep in your step. You can bound to the bus stop, sail through your company's annual charity walk-a-thon, and make it to the end of the day without feeling exhausted.

- ✔ **Improving your heart health:** For years, doctors have known that aerobic exercise and cardio workouts such as walking, jogging, and cycling can lower your risk of heart disease and high blood pressure. But new research suggests that weight training may offer these benefits as well. Specifically, studies show that lifting weights can lower your risk of having a heart attack or stroke by lowering your LDL ("bad") cholesterol and reducing blood pressure.

✔ **Improving your quality of life:** Any activity that accomplishes all the above makes you a happier, more productive, and more confident person. (Research suggests that weight training can even relieve clinical depression.) Of course, lifting weights is no instant cure-all, but you'd be surprised how much satisfaction a pair of 10-pound dumbbells can bring into your life, which also benefits the lives of everyone else around you.

In this book, we give you the information you need to reap all these rewards.

No matter what your level of knowledge about weight training, you can always use this book as a reference. Flip to the index or table of contents and look up the specific topic you're interested in today.

Foolish Assumptions

Each of us owns a body, but we don't necessarily understand how best to train it. To write this book and make it truly friendly to anyone new to weight training, we assume that you're completely unfamiliar with weight training. Because of this, some of the information presented may be review for people with more experience.

We also assume that you've been exposed to a number of popular myths about weight training — the "urban legends" of the weight room. We do our best to correct these myths and explain why they aren't true.

Icons Used in This Book

Icons are the small images in the margins of this book. They're designed to draw your attention to specific topics, and they serve as guides to the kind of information being provided.

The Myth Buster icon rescues you from misleading notions, fighting for truth, justice, and a good weight-training workout. For example, this icon may point out that high-protein diets are *not* the key to weight loss and that abdominal training will *not* eliminate your love handles.

This icon reminds you about good technique so that you don't injure yourself. It points out when to keep your shoulders relaxed, your abdominal muscles tight, and your knees bent.

The Remember icon reminds you of key pieces of advice that you should keep in mind even after you've put down this book.

When you see the Tip icon, you know that we're pointing out an especially helpful weight-training hint or giving you a heads-up on an effective strategy.

The Warning icon cautions you of potential dangers to beware of while weight training, including the hucksters lurking at the depths of the fitness industry, hawking useless gadgets like electronic muscle stimulators. We also use this icon to signal mistakes that can cause injury, such as bending your knees too far or lifting too much weight.

Beyond the Book

Check out the new weight training video online at www.dummies.com/extras/weighttraining to try a 20-minute workout from Chapter 17.

You can find a free Cheat Sheet at www.dummies.com/cheatsheet/weighttraining for resources not found in this book. There, we tell you about some extra weight-training equipment you may want to invest in, how to be a good personal-training client, how to talk the weight-training talk, and more.

In addition, www.dummies.com/extras/weighttraining contains related articles such as myths about abdominal exercises and common weight-training mistakes to avoid.

Where to Go from Here

If you're a novice, we suggest you start by reading Parts I and II. These parts get you comfortable with the equipment, the lingo, the safety basics, and the etiquette. Then skip to Part IV, which explains how to design a weight routine that meets your needs. (You may want to refer back to this part every now and then.) Then go back to Part III, which shows you the exercises. In your spare time, like when you're not busy lifting weights, hit Part V.

If you already know free weights are different from dumbbells and barbells, and know that in the weight-training world, a circuit has nothing to do with electrical currents, you can go straight to Part III and find numerous exercises for each body part. You may also want to focus on Part IV, which describes how to combine these exercises into a variety of routines that fit your schedule and your equipment preferences.

Part I

Getting Started with Weight Training

In this part . . .

✔ Discover the benefits of incorporating weight training in your life.

✔ Get an overview of key weight-training terms and important training concepts.

✔ Assess your current level of fitness, set goals, and track your progress.

✔ Get familiar with the weight-training tools — from dumbbells to barbells to weight machines and more.

✔ Get a crash course in safety so you reap all the benefits of weight training without hurting yourself in the process.

Chapter 1

Weight Training for Life

• •

In This Chapter

▶ Discovering why everyone needs weight training

▶ Gauging your fitness level and setting goals

▶ Choosing the right tools to get you in shape

▶ Training safely to enjoy a lifetime of strength and well-being

▶ Deciding which exercises and routines help you best achieve your goals

▶ Finding out how weight training fits into an overall healthy lifestyle

• •

Weight training on a regular basis improves your strength, endurance, confidence, appearance, health, longevity, and quality of life. Beginning a weight-training program is one of the best decisions you can make for your health, well-being, and physical and mental performance. Consistent weight training helps reduce your stress, manage your weight, strengthen your bones, lower your risk of injury, and gives you a competitive edge in all aspects of life.

In this chapter, you find out why weight training benefits all bodies at every age and fitness level; why it's important to assess your fitness and set goals; what tools to use; why safety measures are essential for a lifetime of enjoyable training; how to decide which exercises, routines, and training settings are right for you; and how to achieve total wellness beyond simply lifting weights. If you want to find out more, each section tells you which chapters provide the necessary details.

Weight Training for All Bodies

Modern living provides every convenience except one: a lot of natural physical activity. From young to old, we ride in cars, use remote controls, step into elevators, play on the computer, and shop online. Many activities that required us to get up out of the chair and use our muscles no longer exist. The result: We need to add weight training to our lives to stimulate our bodies and our brains to keep us healthy and strong.

People of all ages — kids, teens, young adults, pregnant women, and older adults — benefit from weight training (see Chapters 20 and 21). The risks of doing nothing are greater than the risks of injury from exercise — even for the frail and elderly. Whether you're a beginner who wants to get started safely or you're already fit and you want to improve your performance, weight training improves your current condition (whatever that is) and helps you achieve your goals of feeling stronger and better about yourself.

Strong muscles help us move better and avoid pain and injury at all stages of life. Weight training provides the following benefits:

- ✔ Increased strength and endurance
- ✔ Improved sleep
- ✔ Reduced stress
- ✔ Enhanced feelings of confidence and well-being
- ✔ Reduced risk of falls
- ✔ Strengthened bones
- ✔ Boosted metabolism for more energy burn around the clock
- ✔ Full, independent living

Because weight training strengthens your muscles and improves your muscular endurance, you'll naturally have more energy to be more active throughout the day. When you're physically tired, you're able to fall asleep more easily and enjoy a deeper, better quality of sleep. As you're more refreshed and energetic, you feel better and accomplish more, which improves your mood and confidence level. In this manner, your consistent training stimulates an upward cycle of well-being.

Don't wait. Absorb everything you need to know from this book to get going with a program that is perfect for you. Keep taking the steps you need to achieve stronger, more toned muscles for a fuller, more enjoyable and active life.

Fitness Testing and Goal Setting for Success

When it comes to weight training, one size doesn't fit all. In order to create a program that best meets your needs, you need to know what your conditioning level is, what you want to achieve with your training, and how to set goals and monitor your progress for success (see Chapter 2).

Fifty percent of all people who begin a new training program quit in the first six to eight weeks. Most people say that the reason for quitting is that they don't have enough time. A research study of prison inmates, who had all the time in the world for their exercise program, showed the same dropout rate. Leading behavioral scientists have concluded that the real reason people don't stick to new exercise programs isn't lack of time — it's because changing your habits for something new is difficult, especially if motivation is lacking.

To keep this from happening to you, we offer strategies to avoid dropping off the weight-lifting wagon in Chapter 2.

Safety First to Enjoy Training

Before beginning any exercise program, ensure that you're both ready and able. Get clearance from a healthcare professional if necessary. Study and apply the safety tips discussed in Chapter 5 to avoid common mistakes that cause injuries.

Take time to discover the correct use of equipment (see Chapter 4) and to perform exercises by using good form and technique (see Part III). Regular weight training improves muscle balance, posture, movement efficiency, stability, and body awareness. All these qualities reduce the likelihood of injury, as well as the onset of typical aches and pains such as those associated with the lower back, knees, shoulders, or hips.

Choosing Your Training Equipment

In fitness magazines, health clubs, and DVDs, you often hear weight equipment referred to as *resistance equipment*. We hate to clutter your brain with jargon right off the bat, but *resistance* is a word you need to know. Resistance is an opposing force, like a weight or gravity; in order for your muscles to get stronger, you must work against resistance. *Resistance equipment* is actually a more accurate term than *weight equipment* because you can build muscle without using weights at all. For example, rubber exercise bands (see Chapter 23) don't weigh more than a couple of ounces, but they provide enough resistance to strengthen your muscles. Throughout this book, we use the terms *resistance training, weight training, strength training,* and *weight lifting* interchangeably.

Keep in mind that understanding how to train your muscles is like studying a new skill. You aren't born with this knowledge, in spite of the fact that you were born with a body. Many people have the misconception that because they live in a body, they know how to train it. You'll benefit significantly by taking the time to study and acquire the skills from qualified professionals.

Finding out how to use equipment properly is an early step in this process. In this book, we do our best to break this information down in a way that is complete and easy to follow. Take your time. Be patient with yourself. Soon, you'll be lifting like a pro. Chapter 4 outlines all the information that you need to know to demystify the weight room. Refer back to Chapter 4 as often as you need. Give yourself time to experience the equipment and absorb the information.

Resistance training equipment falls into many common categories:

- **Free weights:** Free weights include dumbbells, barbells, bars, and weight plates. These come in a variety of shapes, sizes, materials, and weights (see Chapter 4 for more information).

- **Machines:** Weight machines generally include a seat, a cable or pulley, a variety of weight plates for adjustable resistance, and movable bars. Similar to free weights, machines vary widely in design (see Chapter 4). Newer machines come equipped with programming features and provide feedback while you're training.

- **Resistance bands and tubing:** Rubber bands and tubes provide opportunities for strength training any time and any place. Bands are flat and wide; tubes are round. Cheap, lightweight, and portable bands and tubes are the training tool of choice for frequent travelers. Latex-free versions are available for people with allergies. (We discuss bands and tubes in Chapter 23.)

Although not strictly in the category of resistance-training equipment, the following tools provide a means to enhance your weight-training programs:

- **Balls and foam rollers:** Add balls and foam rollers into many exercises to provide an unstable surface on which to work. Incorporating this element of instability increases the difficulty of the exercise by requiring the use of deeper abdominal and back muscles (see Chapter 24).

- **Body weight:** Your body may not feel like a training tool, but use your own body weight to provide effective resistance in a number of exercises such as the squat and lunge (see Chapter 14) and the push-up (see Chapter 10).

- **Yoga and Pilates:** Yoga and Pilates aren't styles of weight training; however, many yoga and Pilates moves involve challenges that strengthen muscles. The particular advantage of many of these exercises is that they also involve flexibility and encourage the development of strength, balance, and coordination through movement patterns (see Chapter 22 for more information on yoga and Pilates).

Selecting the Right Exercises, Routines, and Training Settings

Deciding whether to train at home or at the gym, whether to take a group exercise class or hire a personal trainer, can be difficult. Chapter 6 provides clear guidelines on how to determine whether training at home is right for you and how to set up a home gym. If you decide that working with a DVD at home is best, Chapter 6 also gives you a lot of practical advice for how to follow along.

Chapter 7 helps you select a gym that meets your needs and tells you everything you need to know about how to fit in and follow the rules of gym etiquette. If you're thinking that a personal trainer may be your best option, check out Chapter 7 — it shows you how to pick a trainer to meet your needs. Chapter 7 also tells you how to select a group fitness instructor who makes you feel comfortable.

Getting started with your weight-training program means selecting the right exercises and routines that meet your goals and fit your personality and lifestyle. The perfect program is the one that fits you. Part III describes all the exercises that you need. Part IV offers a variety of workout programs that feature the exercises.

Weight training today is for all bodies, not only the bodybuilders of previous decades. Whether you're a mom supervising your kid's fitness program or an older adult with special needs, find a program that suits you. There's no reason not to get started right away and to enjoy the many benefits weight training has to offer.

Living a Healthy Lifestyle

Weight training is an important key to living a full and healthy life from childhood to older age. We lose muscle mass as we age due to the gradual loss of efficiency in the process of cellular reproduction (the same reason your hair turns gray). Unless you add stimulation to your muscles, such as weight training to maintain or to build muscle mass, you'll lose your current muscle mass. Weight training alone can't provide everything you need to get and stay strong and fit. You need good nutrition, adequate sleep, stress management, and a strong network of good relationships with friends and family for social support.

Pumping up your heart and lungs

Aerobic exercise or cardio training is necessary to keep your heart and lungs healthy and to reduce the risk of diseases such as heart disease, high blood pressure, and diabetes, as you age. The best form of cardio exercise for most people is walking — it's cheap and easy, and walking requires little planning and offers a low risk of injury.

 Make time for 30 minutes of cardio activity at least four days a week. Your efforts count even if you walk only ten minutes at a time, three times a day. To find out more about increasing your cardio activity through walking, read *Fitness Walking For Dummies,* by Liz Neporent (Wiley).

Improving your flexibility

Stretching is one of the most enjoyable, feel-good exercises that improves your ease of movement and reduces your risk of injury. Stretching to improve flexibility is best at the end of your workout when your muscles are warm. See Chapter 16 for up-to-date information on the whys and how-to's of stretching.

Balancing options and training your brain

Like most aspects of fitness, if you don't practice balance, you lose your ability to maintain your balance, and this loss increases your chance of falling. Certain sports, such as skiing, skating, and surfing, also require good balance for effective performance.

Adding a few extra balance challenges to your weight-training routine is easy and makes all the difference that you need to move with greater confidence and skill. Coordinated moves that require concentration and challenge both the mind and body are also good for maintaining a healthy body and mind. Yoga and Pilates offer many valuable exercises that train these aspects of fitness. Read Chapter 22 to discover the latest important information about balance and coordination.

Chapter 2

The Principles of Training: Concepts and Terminology

The focus of this chapter is to help you discover important workout terms and proven training concepts — the ingredients essential to all training routines. Here, you gain the basic understanding of the importance of rest and recovery and the significance of focusing your mind to achieve the best training results possible. Finally, you discover proven training concepts when it comes to the big picture of training.

Defining Weight-Training Jargon

Weight training certainly has its fair share of confusing jargon. You don't need to be fluent in the language spoken at bodybuilding competitions and physiology conferences, but to design an effective workout, you do need to know the basics to better understand your trainer or training materials.

In the following list, we define key strength-training terminology and training principles:

✔ **Endurance:** Muscular endurance refers to how many times you can lift a sub-maximal weight over a period of time. Muscular strength and endurance are related, but aren't the same. Muscular endurance is handy for everyday tasks like carrying a heavy box from your house to the car.

Don't confuse muscular endurance with *cardiovascular endurance,* which is the stamina of your heart and lungs. Muscular endurance affects only the muscle in question and lasts only a minute or two; you improve the staying power of one muscle rather than the stamina of your entire body.

✔ **Failure:** To achieve overload, you need to take your muscles to failure — the level of fatigue where you can't do one more repetition with good form. For instance, when you can't complete the full range of motion, it's time to end your set.

✔ **Overload:** To increase your strength or endurance, you need to train by pushing your muscles to do more than what they're used to. You can overload your muscles by lifting a challenging weight load, doing a lot of reps and sets, or increasing how many times per week you train.

✔ **Progression:** Overloading your muscles by lifting a weight to muscular failure stimulates your muscles to get stronger. This is the principle of specificity in action. To continue to overload your muscles and keep making progress, you need to find new ways to challenge your muscles. This is why you need to change up your program or routine. In general, wait six to eight weeks to see visible results from your training when you're new to lifting weights. Internal changes start to occur immediately in response to your first training session.

✔ **Range of motion and movement speed:** Perform most of your exercises through the fullest range of motion possible of your working joints to stimulate the muscles most effectively. Movement speed should be slow and controlled. Anyone who lifts weight for general fitness should perform four-second repetitions — two seconds to lift the weight, stop the motion, and two seconds to lower it. Stop for a moment at the midpoint of a rep to avoid using momentum, instead of your muscles, to power you through. Don't pause for more than a split second at the end of a repetition — otherwise, it becomes a rest. Each rep should flow seamlessly into the next. Athletes and those who are lifting for extreme strength or bulk may do slower or faster reps depending on their goals.

✔ **Recovery or rest period:** When your muscles reach failure at the end of a set, you need to recover or rest before you can challenge that muscle to work again. This is also referred to as the *rest period.* Similarly, after you've worked a muscle group in your workout, you need to allow it to recover for at least 48 hours before you train it again. We explain why rest and recovery are so important later in this chapter.

✔ **Repetitions:** This term, often shortened to *rep,* refers to a single rendition of an exercise. For example, pressing two dumbbells straight above your head and then lowering them back down to your shoulders constitutes one complete repetition of the dumbbell shoulder press, as shown in Chapter 11.

✔ **Routine:** This term encompasses virtually every aspect of what you do in one weight-lifting session, including the type of equipment you use; the number of exercises, sets, and repetitions you perform; the order in which you do your exercises; and how much rest you take between sets. By varying the elements of your routine — say, decreasing the number of reps or adding new exercises — you can significantly change the results you get from weight training because of the principle of specificity. Your routine (also referred to as your program or your workout) can change from one exercise session to the next, or it can stay the same over a period of weeks or months.

✔ **Sets:** A set is a group of consecutive reps that you perform without resting. When you've done 12 repetitions of the dumbbell shoulder press and then put the weights down, you've completed one set. If you rest for a minute and then perform 12 more repetitions, you've done two sets.

✔ **Specificity:** Your muscles develop specifically in response to how you train them. For example, if you want to get stronger hips and legs, you should do squats, not push-ups. Similarly, if you want to become a better runner, ultimately you need to practice running. Weight training can complement your running program, but it can't replace the hours you need to spend at the track.

✔ **Strength:** Muscular strength is the maximum amount of weight that you can lift one time — also called your *one-rep max.* For example, if you can squeeze out only one shoulder press with 45 pounds, that's your one-rep max for that exercise.

See the Cheat Sheet at www.dummies.com/cheatsheet/weighttraining for a list of terms commonly used in weight training to describe your body's muscles.

Understanding Reps

The number of repetitions, or reps, you perform matters a lot. In general, if your goal is to build the largest, strongest muscles that your genetic makeup allows, perform relatively few repetitions, about four to six (perhaps even as few as one or two). **Remember:** This refers to lifting a heavy enough weight so that by the end of the last repetition, you can't do another one with good form. If you're seeking a more moderate increase in strength and size — for example, if your goal is to improve your health or shape your muscles — aim for 8 to 12 repetitions to failure. This will help improve *muscle endurance,* or your ability to continuously work a muscle over a long period of time.

The American College of Sports Medicine (ACSM) recommends varying repetitions for different people.

✔ **High intensity:** Perform 6 to 12 reps using heavy weights. Higher-intensity training poses a greater risk of injury. This approach to training is suitable for athletes and experienced exercisers.

✔ **Moderate intensity:** Perform 8 to 12 repetitions using moderate weights because this is the ideal number to strike a balance between building muscular strength and endurance and has a lower risk of injury.

✔ **Low intensity:** For older adults, the ACSM recommends doing between 10 to 15 repetitions using light weights at an even lower intensity.

Why does performing 6 reps result in more strength than doing 15 reps? Because the number of reps you perform links to the amount of weight you lift. So, when you perform 6 reps, you use a much heavier weight than when you perform 15 reps of the same exercise. Always use a weight that's heavy enough to make that last repetition a real challenge, if not an outright struggle.

Weight training isn't an exact science so don't take these rep numbers too literally. It's not as if performing six repetitions transforms you into a body-builder, whereas performing ten reps makes you look like Angelina Jolie. Everyone's body responds a bit differently to weight training. Genetic factors play a significant role in determining the ultimate size that your muscles can develop.

Bodybuilders (who aim for massive size) and power lifters (who aim to lift the heaviest weight possible) often train by hoisting so much poundage that they can perform only one or two reps. You may not want to lift hundreds of pounds of weight over your head, so your goals are best served by doing 6 to 15 repetitions. Doing more than 15 reps is generally not effective for building strength, but it can improve muscular endurance.

To focus on increasing muscular endurance, you want to do at least 12 reps or more, but only two to three sets. To increase muscle size, you want to do 6 to 12 reps, but more sets — anywhere from three to six. To increase muscular strength, you want to do fewer reps, no more than six, and anywhere from two to six sets each.

Getting Acquainted with Sets

Beginners should start with one set for each of the major muscle groups listed under "Knowing Weight-Routine Essentials," later in this chapter. That's roughly 11 sets per workout. The ACSM recommends one-set training because most of your gains occur from that first set. Of course, you'll gain more strength and faster results with more sets, but your program takes more time. After a month or two, you may want to increase the number of sets. But then again, you may not. If your goal is to gain moderate amounts of strength and maintain your health, one set may be as much as you ever need to do.

If you want to continue to increase your strength over time, studies show that trained individuals require multiple-set training of at least three or more. A trained person is someone who's been lifting consistently for at least three months. In addition to increasing the number of sets, you should also vary your training volume and intensity over time with periodized training, as explained later in this chapter. Increases in training should be gradual to avoid injury from overtraining.

However, if your goal is to become as strong as you can or reshape an area of your body, you need to perform more than three sets per muscle group. Some serious weight lifters perform as many as 20. (However, they don't do 20 sets of the same exercise; they may do 5 sets each of four different exercises that work the same muscle.)

The principle of specificity of training determines how much rest you should take in between sets. Beginners should take all the rest they need because you're just becoming acquainted with your body and want to avoid injury. New exercisers may take up to twice as long to rest as those who're more experienced. The National Strength and Conditioning Association recommends that your rest period be based on your training goal. If your goal is to increase endurance and you're lifting 12 or more reps, your rest period should be up to 30 seconds. If your goal is to increase size, and you're lifting 6 to 12 reps, you should rest 30 to 90 seconds. If your goal is to increase strength and you're lifting fewer than six reps, you should rest two to five minutes. People who train for pure strength are going for all-out lifts — a very intense approach. Circuit training, which emphasizes muscular endurance or what is sometimes described as *cardio-resistance* (see Chapter 17), involves taking little or no rest between sets.

Knowing Weight-Routine Essentials

If an orchestra were to play Vivaldi's *Four Seasons* minus the string section, the piece would lack a certain vitality and depth. Likewise, if you leave out a key element of your weight workout, you may end up with disappointing results. So, follow the guidelines in this section.

Focusing on major muscle groups

Be sure that your routines include at least one exercise for each of the following muscle groups. (In Part III, we show precisely where each muscle is located.)

✔ Butt or buttocks (glutes)

✔ Front thighs (quadriceps)

- ✔ Rear thighs (hamstrings)
- ✔ Calves
- ✔ Chest (pecs)
- ✔ Back
- ✔ Abdominals (abs)
- ✔ Shoulders (delts)
- ✔ Front of upper arms (biceps)
- ✔ Rear of upper arms (triceps)

In Part III, you have exercises for additional muscle groups, such as the wrist and shin muscles and inner and outer thighs. But for general fitness, the preceding muscles should be your highest priorities. If you neglect any of these muscle groups, you'll have a gap in your strength, and you may set yourself up for injury.

If you avoid training any particular muscle group, you also may end up with a body that looks out of proportion. You don't need to hit all your muscle groups on the same day — just make sure that you work each group twice a week. In Chapter 19, you find out several ways you can split up your workouts.

Sequencing: Doing exercises in the right order

In general, work your large muscles before your small muscles. This practice ensures that your larger muscles — such as your butt, back, and chest — are challenged sufficiently. Suppose that you're performing the dumbbell chest press, shown in Chapter 10. This exercise primarily works your chest muscles, but your pecs do require assistance from your shoulders and triceps. If you were to work these smaller muscles first, they'd be too tired to help the chest.

On occasion, however, you may specifically want to target a smaller muscle group, like your shoulders, because they're lagging behind in development compared to other parts of your body. If that's the case, you may want to design a program where you do shoulder exercises first one or two days a week for several weeks to build them up. In general, follow the rule of training larger to smaller.

In order to perform your exercises in the right order, you need to understand which exercises work which muscle groups. Many people do their routines in the wrong sequence because they don't realize the purpose of a particular exercise (the purpose isn't always obvious). When you pull a bar down to your chest, as in the lat pull-down (see Chapter 10), you may think that you're doing an arm exercise when, in fact, the exercise primarily strengthens your back. So, make a point of understanding which muscles are involved in each move that you do. In addition, studies show that concentrating on the specific muscle that you're working and visualizing it becoming stronger increases the effectiveness of your training. You definitely want to make sure that you're focusing on the right muscles to get the best results.

When choosing the sequence of a workout, imagine your body splitting into three zones: upper, lower, and middle. Within each zone, do your exercises in the following order. Feel free to mix exercises from the upper and lower body. It's a good idea to train your middle body or core stabilizer muscles last because they stabilize your body during all the preceding exercises and help to prevent injury.

Upper body

1. Chest and back (It doesn't matter which comes first.)

2. Shoulders

3. Biceps and triceps (It doesn't matter which comes first.)

4. Wrists

Lower body

1. Butt

2. Thighs

3. Calves and shins (It doesn't matter which comes first, although we prefer to work our calves before our shins.)

Middle body

You can perform your abdominal and lower-back muscle exercises in any order you want.

Appreciating the Value of Rest and Recovery

When it comes to training, like many other aspects of life, more isn't necessarily better. Moderation and balance, as well as gradual progression, are critical to getting the best possible results and avoiding injury. When you train, you stress or overload your muscles. Microscopic tears occur in the muscle fibers. When you rest, your body repairs these tears and your muscles become stronger. Rest and good nutrition, therefore, are just as important to your training as your workouts.

Taking one day of rest for each muscle group

Always let a muscle rest at least one day between workouts. This doesn't preclude you from lifting weights two days in a row; you could work your chest and back one day and then your legs the next. But if you're doing a full-body routine, don't lift weights more than three times a week and don't cram your three workouts into one weekend.

Avoiding overtraining

As unbelievable as it may sound to a beginner, many exercisers become overly enthusiastic after they start getting results and think that if a little is good, even more has to be great. Researchers have dedicated a lot of time to studying this topic and the ACSM even has a comment paper on the subject entitled, "Overtraining with Resistance Exercise."

Overtraining typically occurs in the following scenarios:

- ✔ Training too many times per week
- ✔ Doing too many exercises per session
- ✔ Lifting excessive numbers of sets
- ✔ Lifting too heavy a weight over too long a period of time

Avoid overtraining by following a periodized training program. See the last section of this chapter for more information.

Signs and symptoms of overtraining include, but aren't limited to, the following:

- ✔ Loss of strength
- ✔ Chronic fatigue
- ✔ Poor sleep or eating habits
- ✔ Reduced appetite
- ✔ Excess muscle soreness

- Mood changes
- Loss of interest in training
- Increased frequency of illness combined with slow rate of healing

Be sure to avoid overtraining through the following strategies:

- Use periodized training.
- Avoid monotonous training that lacks variety.
- Don't perform every single set of every exercise of every session to absolute failure without variation.
- Avoid overusing certain muscles or joints.
- Balance your weight training with your other sports activities or cardio training.

Weight training provides so many benefits to your life. The risk of overtraining isn't high, but it's important to mention so you appreciate the importance of variety in your program, of incorporating rest, and of ultimately listening to your body.

Getting enough sleep

Regular training improves the quality of your sleep because you'll be physically tired at night when you go to bed. Current sleep researchers recommend that most people get seven to nine hours per night. Individuals vary, so you need to figure out what's best for you. Many adults are chronically sleep deprived and are compromising their health and well-being because of it. Don't let yourself be part of that group.

Sleep is always important to your health but even more so when you're training your body. Because you're actively stressing your muscles, your cells need time to repair. If you deprive yourself of adequate sleep, you're limiting your opportunity for your muscle tissue to repair itself optimally. Why spend time training only to undermine your hard work by not getting enough sleep? Take care of all aspects of your health for best results.

An important hormone for the maintenance and repair of muscle tissue is human growth hormone (HGH). Your body naturally secretes this hormone when you sleep. You may have heard about people — from your next-door neighbor to pro athletes — supplementing with HGH. But studies show that supplementation isn't beneficial for healthy individuals, so don't go out and buy HGH pills. Focus on getting enough sleep instead.

Maintaining and detraining: When you're too busy to work out

Although you need to make rest a part of your training program, you need to avoid resting too much. Unfortunately, we can't save or store our fitness. Research suggests that detraining occurs slowly. For example, two weeks after training stopped, study subjects maintained most of their strength and power. However, after eight months of no training, study subjects had lost most, but not all, of their training results. This is the good news: Maintaining a reduced program can significantly slow detraining.

When your schedule is exceptionally busy and you find it difficult to do your full routine, remember that something is always better than nothing. Even training one day a week, especially if performed at a higher intensity, can be very valuable to prevent a loss of strength over time.

How Your Mind Helps Your Body

The evidence of the importance of the connection between the mind and body is strong and clear. In other words, your thoughts and feelings have a significant impact on your physical and mental well-being. Physical and mental well-being have an important bearing on weight training.

Concentrating on the mind-body connection

Have you ever had an argument with someone and then been so flustered that you stubbed your toe on a footstool in the room? This example shows how your feelings affect your movements. Because you're upset, your heart is racing, your breath is shallow and rapid, and you may even be sweating. That's an example of your mind-body connection.

When you train your muscles, you tap into your mind-body connection through your neuromuscular system. Before you can contract a muscle fiber, the nervous system must run a communication network from the brain through the spinal column and out to the individual muscle fiber. In the early stages of training, before you start seeing visible external results, your body is laying down this neural network. The more extensive your neural network, the more individual muscle fibers contract.

Studies show that by concentrating on the muscles that you're training, you can get results faster. In one study, a group of people performed a simple exercise, another group of people imagined doing the exercise but didn't actually do it, and a third group served as the control group and didn't do anything. Of course, participants who actually lifted the weight gained the most strength. However, the people who simply imagined doing the exercise had more gains than those who did nothing.

Physical therapists are also conducting studies on the use of motor imagery with patients who've lost neuromuscular control due to stroke or Parkinson's disease. Patients visualize walking with a perfect gait, as well as practice specific gait exercises. Studies show that this visualization helps improve performance. The bottom line: You have nothing to lose and possibly more effective training results to gain by focusing your mind on your target muscles as you do your exercises.

Visualizing yourself strong

Studies also show that using visualization before you perform a weight-training exercise can improve performance for people with at least one year of training experience. Different strategies include the use of imagery, positive self-talk, affirmations, and focusing attention. So, when you're ready to train, clear your mind, see yourself going through your workout smoothly and successfully, visualize your strong and toned body, and believe in your ability to lift your weights. It makes a difference.

Long-Term Training: Seeing the Big Picture

After you've been training regularly for at least three months, you're no longer considered a beginner. Congratulations! You can now attend group exercise classes suitable for intermediate to advanced participants. More important, if you want to avoid hitting a plateau and continue to make gains in strength, you need to progress your program.

Studies show that the most effective method to progress in your program is through a process called *periodization*. Periodization involves varying volume and training intensity and simply means organizing your program into different periods, each lasting about four to eight weeks. Each period has a different theme. For example, one month you may use weight machines, and the next month you may switch to dumbbells and barbells. Or you can change the number of sets, repetitions, and exercises you perform from one period to the next. Athletes use periodization to vary their weight lifting (and other types of training) from their off-season to their competitive season.

Periodization is more than a fun diversion; this strategy gives you better results. The ACSM recommends periodization for experienced exercisers based on the number of research studies that show its benefits. Consider this study of more than 30 women conducted at Penn State University: Half the women did a typical circuit of 12 weight machines (see Chapter 17 for a definition of *circuit*), performing one set of eight to ten repetitions per machine. They continued this workout three times a week for nine months. The second group engaged in periodized training, systematically changing the number of sets, reps, and exercises they performed. Initially, the groups showed comparable strength gains. But after four months, the circuit group hit a plateau. The periodization group continued to make steady progress throughout the nine months.

We recommend that an introductory periodization program include five distinct phases, each lasting about a month. (However, depending on your goals, each phase can be as short as two weeks or as long as eight weeks.) You can repeat this cycle over and over again. Here's a look at each phase:

- ✔ **Prep phase:** During this period, you prepare your body for the challenges ahead with a basic workout. Use light weights, perform one to four sets per muscle, do 12 to 15 repetitions per set, and rest 90 seconds between sets.

- ✔ **Pump phase:** In this phase, you step up your efforts a bit. You lift slightly heavier weight, perform 10 to 12 reps per set, do three to eight sets per muscle group, and rest only 60 seconds between sets. The pump phase is a good time to introduce a few of the advanced training techniques we describe later in this chapter, such as super sets and giant sets.

- ✔ **Push phase:** In this period, you do eight to ten reps per set, resting 30 seconds between sets. You do only two or three different exercises per muscle group, but you do several sets of each so you can use the advanced training techniques, such as pyramids, that we describe later.

- ✔ **Peak phase:** In this phase, you focus on building maximum strength. Do six to eight reps per set, 15 to 20 sets per muscle group, but fewer different exercises. For instance, you may only do one or two leg exercises, but you do multiple sets of each exercise and six to eight repetitions per set. Rest a full two minutes between sets so that you can lift more weight. This phase is your last big effort before you take a break from heavy training.

- ✔ **Rest phase:** In this phase, either you drop back to the light workouts you did in the prep phase, or you take a break from weight training altogether. Yes, that's right, we're giving you permission to stop lifting weights — for as long as two weeks. Resting gives your body (and your mind) a chance to recover from all the hard work you've been putting in. After your break, you move back into your next periodization cycle with fresh muscles and a renewed enthusiasm for your training.

If you're hell-bent on building up your body, you may be tempted to skip the rest phase. Don't. If you never rest, at some point your body starts to break down. You stop making progress, and you may get injured. If you want to get fit, resting is just as important as working out.

Organizing your programs: Periodization

Here's a recap of the five-phase periodization program.

Phases	Weight	Sets Per Phase	Number of Reps Per Set	Rest between Sets
Prep	Light	1–4	12–15	1½ min.
Pump	Moderately light	3–8	10–12	1 min.
Push	Moderately heavy	8–15	8–10	30 sec.
Peak	Heavy	15–20	6–8	2 min.
Rest	Complete rest or light weights	0–2	12–15	1½ min.

This is just one model of periodized training. The possibilities are endless. Depending on your goals, you may want to emphasize or play down a particular phase. For example, if you aim to get as strong as possible, spend more time in the peak phase; if you've been lifting weights for years, shorten the prep phase or skip it altogether. An experienced and well-educated personal trainer can help you design a periodization program to meet your needs.

Chapter 3

Testing Your Strength, Setting Goals, and Tracking Your Progress

. . . .

In This Chapter

▶ Testing your strength and endurance

▶ Setting successful training goals

▶ Tracking your progress in a workout diary

▶ Staying motivated to meet your goals

. . . .

Taking tests from time to time isn't so bad — if you're taking a test for something you really want! Strength tests are particularly important when you begin a weight-training program. You need to know your starting point so you can set realistic goals and design a workout program that reflects your current abilities. As you get stronger, periodic strength testing can be a great measure of your achievements and keep you motivated to train. Some people are simply more data oriented than others, so how often you track your progress varies from person to person. For some people, recording daily details is relevant; for others, keeping records of annual tests is sufficiently motivating.

In this chapter, you discover a variety of strength tests appropriate for beginners, a proven strategy for achieving your goals, and a way to track your progress in a workout diary.

Before you begin strength training, ask yourself a few key questions:

✔ Do you breathe heavily when walking up stairs?

✔ Do you experience chest pains before, during, or after exercising?

✔ Do you have any injuries that would prevent you from following proper form when beginning a new workout?

✔ Do you take prescription medication for heart disease or high blood pressure?

✔ Do you get dizzy when exercising?

If you answered "yes" to any of the preceding questions, ask your doctor before beginning any exercise program.

Identifying Your Fitness Level

Before you begin the weight-training exercises in this book, it helps to get a sense of your fitness level. Here are some key questions to ask yourself:

- **When was the last time you did a sit-up?** Have you been consistently exercising for the past 6 to 12 months, or can you not remember the last time you worked out? If you do work out currently, how many times a week do you exercise?

  If you answered not at all or not consistently in the past 6 months, even if you were an athlete in high school, you're a beginner. If you've been working out three to five times a week for six months, you're in the intermediate category. And if you've been working out consistently, lifting weights three to five times a week, and your progress has slowed or come to a halt, you're in the advanced category.

- **How much cardio do you get?** Aerobic exercise is really important for good circulation and maintaining a healthy heart. Providing oxygen to your blood and pumping blood through your veins keeps everything running smoothly and helps you sleep better, too!

  If you get winded walking up stairs, you're a beginner. If you can maintain your level of energy during aerobic activities, you're in the intermediate category. And if you play a team sport on a large field, you're in the advanced category.

- **How would you rate your strength?** If you've never lifted weights or it's been a while (even if you were an athlete in high school), you're a beginner. If you're familiar with weight-training concepts and you currently lift light to moderate weights on a regular bases, you're in the intermediate category. And if you can lift 100 pounds for eight to ten reps, you're in the advanced category.

- **How flexible are you?** If you do plenty of strength training and cardio, but you don't do any stretching, you're creating an imbalance in your body. To prevent injuries and learn how to maintain balance, regularly do some stretching, yoga, or Pilates. Flexibility plays a big part in overall fitness.

  If you're sedentary and you can't touch your toes, you're a beginner. If you stretch major muscle groups two to three times a week, you're in the intermediate category. And if you can progress through an advanced level of yoga poses or variable stretches, you're in the advanced category.

Having answered these four questions, you should have a general sense of whether you're a beginner, advanced, or in between. If you're in doubt, err on the side of taking it easier in the beginning — you can always work up to a more advanced level, but if you push too hard in the beginning, you may injure yourself.

Here's what each of these categories means in terms of the weight-training exercises in this book:

✔ **Beginner:** If you're at the beginner level, start out doing one set of ten repetitions of the exercises throughout this book (see Chapter 2 for more info on repetitions). You can always add another set of ten reps when you feel you've mastered the proper form. Also, plan on weight training twice a week, and do some form of cardio training (for example, walking, biking, or swimming) three times a week.

Listen to your body and don't move forward until you feel you're ready.

✔ **Intermediate:** If you're at the intermediate level, do one set of 15 repetitions of the various exercises. If you feel confident that you're using proper form and one set is too easy, you can add another set of 15 reps. Otherwise, complete two weeks of training before adding a second set of 15 reps to each exercise.

✔ **Advanced:** If you're at the advanced level, start out with two sets of 20 repetitions. Using a high amount of reps leads to increased muscle endurance rather than strength and size.

Measuring Your Progress

The fitness evaluation in the preceding section is a great way to determine your strength and how many reps and sets of each exercise you should do. The information you gather in this section is a great way to measure your progress over the coming weeks and months.

Start by recording the following information in a fitness journal before you begin weight training:

✔ **Height**

✔ **Weight**

✔ **Resting heart rate:** Ideally, take your pulse first thing in the morning, before you've gotten out of bed and started moving around. Count for a total of 1 minute.

✔ **Blood pressure:** If possible, have your blood pressure measured at your doctor's office. You can also use one of the blood pressure machines you find in drugstores, but those tend to be less accurate.

✔ **Cholesterol levels:** You'll need your doctor to do a blood test to get these numbers.

✔ **Waist measurement:** Using a measuring tape, measure your waist a couple inches above your belly button.

✔ **Body fat percentage:** You can find scales that measure body fat percentage along with weight, and they're pretty accurate.

✔ **Body mass index:** To find your body mass index (BMI), go to www. nhlbi.nih.gov/guidelines/obesity/BMI/bmicalc.htm and enter your height and weight.

✔ **Fasting blood glucose:** You'll need your doctor to do a blood test to get this number.

All these factors are important indicators of your overall health. Recording this information before you start working out helps you track your progress and see proven, documented results, even when you may not be seeing your waistline decrease or biceps increase as quickly as you want.

When you do a weight-training program consistently, you'll see improvement in three areas:

✔ Body composition

✔ Body mass index

✔ Blood pressure

All three of these improvements contribute to your overall health.

Most fitness facilities offer fitness assessments for their members for a fee. Some clubs include these assessments as part of your introductory membership package.

Evaluating Your Strength and Endurance

Knowing how you stack up against others who've taken similar fitness tests can motivate you to work hard. Plus, it can serve as a great measure of how you're progressing as you work out. In this section, we walk you through some tests you can do to measure your strength and endurance. Keep track of your results in a workout log, and retest yourself ever month or so, to see how you're doing.

You'll have better results if you're warm before you attempt these tests.

The term *strength testing* is somewhat of a misnomer. Strictly speaking, your *strength* refers to the maximum amount of weight that you can lift one time — also called your *one-rep max*. For example, if you squeeze out only one shoulder press with 45 pounds, that's your one-rep max for that exercise. In general, it's not such a hot idea to go around testing your one-rep maxes, especially if you're a beginner. Some veterans like to go all out sometimes, but they typically test their one-rep max for just one or two exercises in a given workout. Pushing to the max places a lot of stress on your body parts and can cause extreme muscle soreness even in experienced weight lifters.

Comparing your upper-body strength

A commonly administered test for upper-body strength is the push-up test. Men do military push-ups. Women do modified push-ups (with their knees on the ground). Do as many push-ups as you can until you can no longer do another one with good form. The best way to take the test is with a friend, family member, or training partner who counts your reps out loud for you. Record the date and number for your records.

Check Tables 3-1 and 3-2 to see how your push-up capability measures up with others.

Table 3-1	Push-ups for Men				
	Age 20–29	Age 30–39	Age 40–49	Age 50–59	Age 60+
Excellent	55+	45+	40+	35+	30+
Good	45–54	35–44	30–39	25–34	20–29
Average	35–44	25–34	20–29	15–24	10–19
Fair	20–34	15–24	12–19	8–14	5–9
Low	0–19	0–14	0–11	0–7	0–4

Table 3-2	Push-ups for Women				
	Age 20–29	Age 30–39	Age 40–49	Age 50–59	Age 60+
Excellent	49+	40+	35+	30+	20+
Good	34–48	25–39	20–34	15–29	5–19
Average	17–33	12–24	8–19	6–14	3–4
Fair	6–16	4–11	3–7	2–5	1–2
Low	0–5	0–3	0–2	0–1	0

Comparing your abdominal strength

The crunch test is another commonly used assessment that is easy to do at home with a friend, family member, or training partner. Lie on your back on your training mat with your knees bent and arms resting at your sides, palms facing down. Have your partner mark a horizontal line with masking tape on each side of your body at the end of your fingertips. Place a second piece of tape parallel to the first piece toward your feet — about 2½ inches down the mat.

To begin the test, align your fingertips with the first marking. Crunch upward and slide your fingers along the mat to the second line. Lower completely to the starting position. Continue to do as many reps as you can. Move rhythmically in a smooth, controlled manner. Avoid using momentum and lifting your body up and down rapidly. Record the date and number of reps for your records. Check Tables 3-3 and 3-4 to see how you did.

Table 3-3	Crunches for Men		
	Under Age 35	*Age 36–45*	*Over Age 45*
Excellent	60	50	40
Good	45	40	25
Marginal	30	25	15
Needs work	15	10	5

Table 3-4	Crunches for Women		
	Under Age 35	*Age 36–45*	*Over Age 45*
Excellent	50	40	30
Good	40	25	15
Marginal	25	15	10
Needs work	10	6	4

Goal Setting for Success

Many people set goals. Many of them even set realistic ones. But too often, people don't fulfill their ambitions — for many reasons. Researchers have studied why this process is so difficult for people and identified strategies that ensure greater success. In this section, we fill you in.

Identifying why your goals are important

You're much more likely to stick to a plan of action if you remind yourself often why it's important to you. For example, if you're starting up a strength-training program because you have borderline osteoporosis, increasing your bone density and preventing fractures — not to mention avoiding looking like a hunchback — are huge motivators. You know your life will be better if you don't end up in the hospital with broken bones on a regular basis. Alternatively, you may be weight training because you want to tone up and have more energy to get through each day. The specific reasons need to be individual and relevant to your life.

Whatever inspires you is key to keeping you on track with your training. Remind yourself of all the benefits you want to enjoy as a result of continuing with your weight-training program. Post your goals (and what you gain from achieving them) on your refrigerator, desk, or computer. Or post pictures of good role models of what you want to achieve. Studies show that the best way to keep you motivated is to remind yourself frequently of the benefits, as well as the negative consequences, if you don't stay on track with your plans.

Using S.M.A.R.T. goals

People who use a system of setting S.M.A.R.T. goals (see the following bulleted list for definitions) have a much better chance of success at achieving their goals. This system consists of taking small, specific steps toward a particular goal and focuses on changing your habits gradually.

When you set your training goals, check to see if they meet the following criteria:

- **Specific:** If you're having a tough time with consistent workouts, set a specific goal that you want to achieve that isn't too extreme. For example, set a specific goal to go through your weight-training program each week, taking into consideration any injuries.

- **Measurable:** A measurable goal is one that you can objectively determine whether you met the goal. For example, make a measurable goal be to train at least twice a week for at least 20 minutes per session (see Chapter 18 for 20-minute sessions for the time challenged).

- **Achievable:** If you've been having a hard time finding a spare hour to train, don't plan to do a one-hour workout. Instead, set a more achievable goal for your schedule, such as two 25-minute workouts.

- **Reasonable:** If you're having a tough time training twice a week, don't set a goal to train three times a week. First, master finding time to train twice a week and build from there. If even two times a week is tough, start out with a goal of once a week and build from there. ***Remember:*** You don't have to achieve your fitness goals all in the first month.

- **Timed:** Give yourself a set time to meet your goal. For example, if you set the goal of training at least twice a week for a minimum of 20 minutes per session, decide that you want to achieve this over a two-month period. If two months seems too long to you, start with a goal of one month.

Keeping osteoporosis at bay

Osteoporosis is a very common condition that can occur when the bone tissue in our bodies breaks down faster than our bodies can build it. As a result, the bones become thin and brittle. It strikes 80 percent of women and 20 percent of men. And it's growing fast, with 34 million Americans expected to be at risk of osteoporosis as a result of low bone mass.

Women have less bone mass than men mainly because of hormones and experience an accelerated loss when they go through menopause.

To slow down the process, there are a few things you can do:

✔ Perform resistance exercises regularly. These can be using your own body weight or weights.

✔ Make sure you're getting the right amount of calcium and vitamin D in your diet.

✔ Don't smoke!

✔ Don't drink too much alcohol. The American Heart Association recommends one 8-ounce glass of red wine daily to keep your heart healthy.

✔ Get a bone density test at your doctor's office.

If you're concerned about osteoporosis, talk with your doctor about vitamin and mineral supplements containing vitamin D, as well as prescription drugs you can take to increase bone mass, especially after menopause.

Fifty percent of people typically drop out of a new exercise program within the first six weeks, according to research evidence. Studies also tell us that it takes about eight weeks of doing a new behavior to create a new habit. Know that after you've passed the first eight weeks of consistent training, you're well on your way to successfully achieving your goals and maintaining a lifetime of fitness.

Life happens. If you fall off track, don't waste precious time beating yourself up with negative thoughts. Simply assess what interfered with your regular training, benefit from the experience, and get right back into your program. As the ancient Chinese saying goes, "The journey of 10,000 miles begins with a single step." This wisdom is applicable to your training. Just keep putting one foot in front of the other and believe in yourself.

Logging and Tracking Your Progress

You may find that recording your workout details increases your motivation and helps you keep up with your workout program. Try using the log provided here to record your workouts, or just keep track of everything in a notebook or weight-training diary of your own to see if this method works for you.

Daily Workout Log

Day of the Week			Date	
Goals				
Cardiovascular Training	Time			Distance
Strength Training	Weight	Sets	Reps	Notes
Stretching			Notes	

Recording information in your log

Some people benefit so much from recording their weight routines (and cardiovascular workouts) that they jot down information daily. Other people find the paperwork annoying and prefer to keep a log for, say, one week every couple of months as a reality check. No matter how often you use your log, jotting down many or all the following details is a good idea:

- **Your goals:** At the start of each week, jot down specific workout goals such as, "Push extra hard on back and biceps," or "Complete eight push-ups."

- **The name of each exercise:** We're talking specifics. Don't just write "chest"; write "incline chest fly" or "vertical chest press." This way, you know whether you're getting enough variety. Plus, you're forced to know the name of each exercise. We know people who've worked out for years and still refer to the dumbbell shoulder press as "that one where you push the dumbbells up."

- **Sets, reps, and weight:** Note how many repetitions you performed and how much weight you lifted for each set. Suppose that you did three sets of leg curls — first 12 reps with 30 pounds, and then 10 reps with 40 pounds, and then 7 reps with 50 pounds. You can note this by writing "3" in the set column, "12, 10, 7" in the reps column, and "30, 40, 50" in the weight column.

- **How you're feeling:** We're not asking you to pour out your emotions like a guest on a talk show. Just jot down a few words about whether you felt energetic, tired, motivated, and so on. Did you take it easy, or did you act as if you were in basic training?

- **Your cardio routine:** Record how much cardiovascular exercise you did — whether it was a half-hour walking on the treadmill at 4 miles per hour or 15 minutes on the stair climber at level 6. Also, note whether you did your cardio workout before or after you lifted weights.

- **Your flexibility routine:** Record the amount of stretching time and how your stretches felt. If you're feeling ambitious, you can record the names of the stretches or come up with names for your standard stretching routines.

Analyzing your workout log

Your journal gives you positive reinforcement no matter how often you choose to record your information. Watching your progress over time also gives you a big boost. If two months ago you could barely eke out ten repetitions with 30 pounds on the leg-extension machine and now you can easily perform ten reps with 50 pounds, you know you've accomplished something.

Not only does a diary keep you motivated, but also recording your workouts helps achieve better results. If you're dedicating plenty of time to your weight training but you aren't getting stronger or more toned, your workout diary may offer clues as to why you're not seeing results. Scrutinize your diary and ask yourself the following questions:

- ✔ **Am I getting enough rest?** Maybe you've been lifting weights every other day, but your body actually needs two rest days between workouts. An extra day of rest may give you more oomph when you lift.

- ✔ **Am I working each muscle group hard enough?** Your log may indicate that you've been neglecting a particular muscle group. Maybe you're averaging only four sets per workout for your legs compared to six or seven sets for your other body parts. Perhaps that's the reason your leg strength seems to be lagging.

- ✔ **Am I getting enough variety in my workout?** When you flip through your diary, maybe you see the words *biceps curl* three times a week for the past three months, but you rarely see any other arm exercise. Maybe you've fallen into a rut. Add new exercises or vary the number of sets and repetitions you've been doing. Or mix up the order of your exercises.

- ✔ **Am I lifting enough weight?** Maybe you never write down the words "tough workout." Perhaps picking up the 10-pound dumbbells for your biceps curls has become such a habit that you forgot to notice that those 10-pounders now feel light.

- ✔ **Am I doing my cardiovascular exercise before my weights or after?** Maybe you've been stair climbing for 30 minutes before your weight sessions and, therefore, you're tired out before you even lift a single weight.

Chapter 4

Weight-Training Tools and Equipment

*T*he most intimidating thing about weight training is definitely the equipment. You can examine a weight machine for half an hour — looking it up and down, walking circles around it, touching it, prodding it, even reading the instructional plaque posted on the frame — and still have absolutely no clue where to sit, which lever to push, or what possible benefit you derive from using it. Even a simple metal bar sitting on a rack can leave you scratching your head.

Handling the bewildering nature of weight equipment consists of two points:

✔ First, relax. With a bit of practice, weight-training contraptions are actually easy to operate.

✔ Second, be happy that you decided to take up weight lifting in the 21st century. Back in the 1800s, fitness enthusiasts lifted furniture, boulders — even cows! Although we personally have never tried hoisting farm animals over our heads, we feel confident that today's weight-training devices are a major improvement.

In this chapter, you discover the basic strength-building tools found in health clubs and home-equipment stores. You also receive a detailed account of the pros and cons of each equipment category:

✔ Free weights (dumbbells and barbells)

✔ Machines

✔ Rubber exercise bands and tubes

✔ Sandbags

✔ Kettlebells

And, with a little guidance, you decide which type of equipment is right for you. This chapter also reveals the answers to the big questions:

✔ Should beginners stick to machines?

✔ Do barbells build bigger muscles?

✔ Can you get strong without using any equipment at all?

Getting Comfortable with Free Weights

Free weights are weights, such as barbells or dumbbells, that aren't attached to any pulleys, chains, or other machinery and are raised and lowered by the use of your hands and arms. Free weights consist of metal bars with weighted plates welded or clipped on the ends. *Dumbbells* are short-barred weights that you lift with one hand. *Barbells* are the long bars that you see Olympic weight lifters pressing overhead with both hands.

Some novices think that free weights are only for advanced weight lifters. Not true. Beginners have as much to gain from using free weights as those guys and gals who look like pros. Beginners can become stronger, improve muscle definition, and increase muscle endurance just like more experienced weight trainers.

Knowing the value of free weights

The best approach to strength training combines free weights and machines. Just know that barbells and dumbbells require plenty of concentration. If you follow the safety tips described in Chapter 5, free weight training is perfectly safe. Here are several good reasons to use dumbbells and barbells:

✔ **Free weights are versatile.** With barbells and dumbbells, you can do literally hundreds of exercises that work virtually every muscle group in your body. Flip through Part III of this book, and get an idea of just how handy barbells and dumbbells are. Most weight machines, on the other hand, are designed to perform only one or two exercises.

✔ **Free weights give your muscles more freedom to move.** Suppose that you're lying on a bench pushing a barbell above your chest (this exercise is the bench press, shown in Chapter 10). You can press the weight straight up over your chest, or you can move your arms a few inches back so you're pressing directly above your neck. Or you can position your arms anywhere between. All these movements are perfectly legitimate ways of doing the exercise and working your pecs, and some motions may feel more comfortable to your body than others.

✔ **Free weights involve several muscle groups at once.** For example, chest press movements (shown in Chapter 10) work your chest, shoulders, and triceps. However, when you perform these movements with a barbell, you also call on your abdominal and lower-back muscles to keep your body still and to keep the bar balanced as you press the weight up. With the equivalent weight machine, you don't have to worry about holding the bar still, so your abdominal and back muscles don't get much work.

The more limited action of a machine is sometimes a benefit, as explained in the "Don't Be Afraid of Weight Machines" section, later in this chapter.

Making the choice, knowing the difference: Dumbbells versus barbells

You can perform many movements with both dumbbells and barbells. For example, while sitting on a bench, you can either press a bar overhead (the bench press, as shown in Chapter 10) or press up two dumbbells (the dumbbell shoulder press, performed in Chapter 11). Which is the better option? Actually, both have their benefits.

Dumbbells and barbells both pose a bit more risk than weight machines because you need to stabilize your own body while performing the exercise, instead of relying on the machine to keep your body in the correct position. But if you follow the safety precautions outlined in Chapter 5, you should have no problem.

Choosing dumbbells

Dumbbells come in pairs, and at most health clubs, they're lined up on a rack from lightest (as light as 1 pound) to heaviest (upward of 180 pounds). By the way, the super-heavy dumbbells are mostly for show, considering that about 0.0000001 percent of the population is capable of lifting them.

Dumbbells come in many shapes and materials. Some have hexagonal ends so they don't roll around the floor. Others have contoured handles so they fit more comfortably in your hand. Dumbbells are made of shiny chrome and gray steel. Others have rubber coating, so if some yahoo drops them, the weights won't dig a hole in the floor the size of Australia. Figure 4-1 shows an array of dumbbells.

Figure 4-1:
Gyms rack dumbbells in pairs.

Photograph by Daniel Kron

Dumbbells allow each arm to work independently. If one side of your body is stronger than the other — a common phenomenon — this imbalance is apparent when you're working with dumbbells. Your weaker arm may start wobbling or may poop out sooner than your dominant arm.

Using dumbbells helps correct strength imbalances because each side of your body is forced to carry its own weight, so to speak. By contrast, if you use a bar, your stronger side may simply pick up the slack for your weaker side.

Pumping iron with barbells

Like dumbbells, barbells, also called *bars,* come in a variety of designs. The most popular model is a straight bar. At most gyms, these bars weigh 45 pounds and are 6 or 7 feet long. (However, many gyms have bars in a variety of weights, sometimes as light as 15 or 20 pounds. If you're not sure how much a bar weighs, be sure to check with a staff member.) If you want to lift more than 45 pounds, as most people eventually do, you choose from an array of round plates weighing 45 to 100 pounds and slide them on either end of the bar. (The plates have a hole in the center.) For example, if you want to lift 75 pounds, you slide a 10-pound plate and a 5-pound plate on both ends of the bar.

Some plates have additional holes cut in either side to make them easier to pick up and carry; the holes function like built-in luggage handles. These plates are a brilliant invention and have probably helped prevent many accidents and backaches.

Be sure to use collars, as shown in Figure 4-2, at the gym and at home. *Collars,* cliplike or screwlike devices, temporarily secure weight plates on the bars. The collars prevent the plates from rattling around or sliding off the bar as you push or pull the barbell. Mirrors have shattered from runaway weight plates. Some health clubs require that you use collars.

Figure 4-2:
Using
a collar
prevents
weights
from slipping
or "running
away."

Photograph by Daniel Kron

In addition to straight bars, most health clubs and equipment dealers have a number of exotic-looking bars with various twists and bends in them. The most common is a W-shaped bar about 3 feet long, called the EZ-Curl, which is designed to make certain triceps exercises more comfortable. Some gyms and equipment stores also have an array of straight and EZ-Curl bars with weight plates welded to the ends. These barbells are convenient to use because you don't have to slide weight plates on and off. If you want to switch from 75 pounds to 85 pounds, you simply put the 75-pounder back on the rack and pick up the 85-pounder. No muss, no fuss.

These welded bars are often shorter and less bulky than the traditional bars, so they're more comfortable for many arm and shoulder exercises. However, you typically won't find these fixed-weight barbells weighing more than 150 pounds. For many barbell exercises — particularly certain chest and leg exercises — you may need a lot more weight than 150 pounds. With traditional bars, you can pile on up to 600 pounds (not that we expect you to do this right away).

Some dumbbell exercises just don't *feel* as good as when you use barbells. Any seasoned lifter can tell you that nothing is quite like doing the bench press — the quintessential meat-and-potatoes chest exercise. Many lifters gain a great sense of satisfaction from being able to press so much weight. Even though the dumbbell chest press is a perfectly good exercise, it may not deliver quite the same amount of satisfaction (probably because you can't lift as much total weight). For example, if you can do the dumbbell chest press with a 20-pound dumbbell in each hand, chances are good that you can lift at least a 60-pound barbell because your weaker side always limits you, and it's more difficult to coordinate moving two separate units, instead of one single barbell.

Using a Weight Bench

A weight bench is what you may expect: a sturdy, padded bench that you lie, sit, or kneel on to lift weights. To get the most out of free weights, benches are a must.

Sure, you could lie on the ground and lift free weights, but many exercises come to an abrupt halt when your elbows smack against the floor. As a result, your muscles won't get a chance to work to their fullest through a full range of motion. (Your elbows may not feel so great, either.)

Benches come in a variety of designs. While weight benches come in four different varieties, some benches adjust to serve all four functions.

- **Flat:** A flat bench looks like a long, narrow piano bench, only with padding and metal legs. See the dumbbell chest press exercise in Chapter 10 for an example.

- **Vertical:** A vertical bench looks like a formal chair — with the seat back straight up. You wouldn't want to sit in one of these at the dinner table, but they're quite comfortable for weight lifting. The back support prevents you from straining your lower-back muscles during exercises that you perform while sitting up. The dumbbell shoulder press, shown in Chapter 11, uses this type of bench.

- **Incline:** The seat back of an incline bench adjusts so you can lie flat, sit up straight, or position yourself at any angle in between. (The angle you choose determines which muscles are emphasized.) See Chapter 10 for an example of the bench in action with the incline chest fly.

- **Decline:** A decline bench slopes downward so you're lying with your legs higher than your head. Weight lifters primarily use a decline bench to strengthen the lower portion of their chest muscles.

Most lifters don't do much decline work because getting in and out of the position is awkward, especially when you're holding weights. We describe a few decline chest exercises as "options" in Chapter 10. Keep in mind that you should always use a spotter if you feel that you need extra assistance.

Weight-lifting accessories

People carry a variety of items in their gym bags. Even if you never set foot in a health club, these weight-lifting accessories can make your workouts more comfortable and safe.

✔ **Belts:** The controversy in the fitness community rages on: to wear a belt or not to wear a belt? Proponents of weight-lifting belts maintain that belts protect your lower back. Opponents counter that a belt is like a crutch: If the belt does all the work to keep your body stable, then your abdominal and back muscles won't develop to their fullest potential, and you may end up with back problems down the line.

Who's right? We don't know. But we're not fond of belts. Although many casual lifters swear by them, you don't need a belt unless you're a serious power lifter. Your abdominal and lower-back muscles benefit from the work they do to support you during a lift.

✔ **Clothing:** Wear tight shorts (or at least long ones) for weight training as some of the machines can be awkward with baggy shorts. On your top, wear a T-shirt or tank top. Heavy clothing only traps your sweat and leads to dehydration; layers can also impede your movement and hide mistakes in your posture that you'd be able to see if you weren't overly dressed.

✔ **Gloves:** Weight-lifting gloves have padded palms, and the tops of the fingers are cut off. Gloves prevent your hands from callusing and slipping off a bar. Wearing hand protection also increases comfort when working with bands or tubing and if you have latex allergies, gloves keep your hands from breaking out.

One alternative to gloves that you may want to use is weight-lifting pads — spongy rubber squares or circles (like potholders) that you place in the palms of your hands while you lift. Pads can offer better control than gloves because more of your hand is in contact with the weight. However, lifting pads aren't as convenient as gloves because you have to carry them around as you work out. (Some pads come with clips so you can hook them to your shorts.)

✔ **Shoes:** Wear athletic shoes that have plenty of cushioning and ankle support to protect your feet, your joints, and your balance. On occasion, we see people wearing flip-flops or loafers when they lift weights. If you drop a weight when you're wearing sandals, your toes have *no* protection. And if you wear shoes without rubber soles, your footing won't be secure enough. Some gyms also have policies that prohibit you from training in inappropriate shoes, because it's an accident waiting to happen.

✔ **Towel:** Do you want to lie down in a pool of someone else's sweat? We didn't think so. Be courteous. Use a towel frequently to wipe off your body and the equipment you use.

✔ **Water bottle:** Every gym has a drinking fountain, but you'll drink more water while weight lifting if you have a bottle by your side. If you exercise at home, a water bottle is a must.

✔ **Weight-training log:** Recording your workouts in a journal keeps you motivated and helps you assess your fitness goals. For suggestions on what to write down, see Chapter 3.

Don't Be Afraid of Weight Machines

Attach a few bars onto a large metal frame, add a cable and a pulley or two, weld a seat and a few pads onto your creation, and — presto! — a weight machine is born. Of course, weight-lifting machines are a bit more sophisticated than this definition suggests. Keep reading to find out more.

Making weight machines work for you

Like every machine ever invented, from the Cuisinart to the iPhone, weight machines provide advantages over the low-tech contraptions that came before. Here are some of the ways that weight machines can top dumbbells and barbells:

- ✔ **Weight machines are safe.** Your movement range is limited and the intended pattern is preset, so you need less instruction and supervision than you do with free weights.

- ✔ **Weight machines are easy to use.** Machines don't require much balance or coordination, so you can get the hang of an exercise more quickly. Also, you're more likely to use proper form because the machine provides so much guidance.

  Machines don't guarantee good form. You can still butcher an exercise on a machine, which can lead to injury or at the very least cheat your muscles out of a good workout.

- ✔ **Weight machines enable you to *isolate* a muscle group.** In other words, machines enable you to home in on one muscle group to the exclusion of all others. For example, very few free weight exercises isolate your hamstrings (your rear thigh muscles). Usually, you can't exclude other muscles — such as your front thighs, butt, or lower back — from getting involved.

  On the other hand, numerous machines can isolate your hamstrings. This feature of weight machines is helpful if you have a particular weakness or you're trying to build up one body part.

- ✔ **Weight machines help you move through your workout in minutes.** You put in the pin, do the exercise, and then move to the next machine. This process also makes working out with a friend, who is stronger or weaker, easier — you don't have to load or unload weight plates off a bar. But keep in mind that you do need to adjust each machine to fit your body. In Chapter 5, we explain how to adjust machines.

✓ **Weight machines challenge your muscles throughout the entire motion of an exercise.** Many (although not all) modern-day weight machines compensate for the fact that your muscles aren't equally strong throughout a particular motion. Consider the triceps kickback exercise, shown in Chapter 12. This exercise is relatively easy at the start, but by the time your arm is halfway straightened out, your muscle is being challenged a lot more. By the end, your triceps again have better leverage, so you finish feeling strong.

Use a kidney-shaped gizmo called a *cam* to manipulate the resistance at various points throughout your exercise. When you're at a weak point during the exercise, the cam lightens the load. When your muscle has good mechanical advantage, the cam gives it more work to do. This way, your muscles are working to their fullest throughout the motion. Otherwise, you're limited to a weight you can move only at your weakest point, as you are with free weights.

Examining specific weight machines

Countless ways exist to put the various elements of weight machines together — flip through Part III and see the wild difference in weight machines. Here's a look at the types of machines.

Weight-stack machines

Traditional weight-stack machines have a stack of rectangular weight plates, each weighing 5 to 20 pounds. Each plate has a hole in it; to lift 50 pounds, you stick a metal pin in the hole of the weight plate marked 50. When you perform the exercise — by pushing or pulling on a set of handles or levers — the machine picks up the plate marked 50, plus all the plates above it.

Weight-stack machines save time because changing the amount of weight you're lifting is easier.

Becoming a generic product

Arthur Jones, inventor of Nautilus machines, was the first person to use the cam in exercise machines, and he became a multimillionaire for it. The cam resembled a spiral-shelled nautilus mollusk. Jones sold his first Nautilus machine in 1970. Often, the term *Nautilus machine* is used generically, like *Band-Aid* or *Jell-O* and is now used to refer to any exercise machine that uses cam gear technology. When people refer to Nautilus machines, they may be talking about any one of the major brands, including Body Masters, Cybex, Galileo, Hammer Strength, or Icarian.

Plate-loaded machines

Plate-loaded machines fuse traditional machines and free weights. They have a large frame and protect you from dropping any weight on the floor, but they aren't attached to a stack of weight plates; instead, you place any number of round weight plates onto large pegs.

Some of these plate-loaded machines are gimmicky. They offer no benefits over traditional machines — unless you happen to enjoy carrying weight plates around the gym. However, we do like the plate-loaded machines that let you work each side of your body separately. We also like the varieties that have "free-floating" levers. Instead of forcing you to move through a fixed pathway, the machines let you move any way you want. These machines mimic the feel of free weights (for the most part) while retaining most of the safety benefits of a weight machine.

Hydraulic and air-pressure machines

This machine category doesn't have a weight stack either. Hydraulic and air-pressure machines have a series of pistons that create resistance by pumping oil, gas, or fluid. These machines are fine — some are very well designed — but some exercisers don't feel motivated when they use them because a weight stack isn't moving up and down or steel isn't clanging. (Some people have quirks about working out.) All you hear is a sound that's similar to a can of hair spray in action. Gyms that offer 30-minute circuit programs often use these machines.

Electronic machines

These high-tech contraptions may be the future of weight machines. Some varieties have computers built right in. You swipe an ID card into the machine, which automatically sets the resistance based on your last workout. As you do your set, the machine sends you technique tips. Other electronic systems attach to regular weight-training machines. You punch in a code and the machine retrieves your personal information.

The advantage of electronic machines is the storing of your information. This feature is great for beginners, who may be too overwhelmed to remember how much they lifted last time. These systems also run a variety of extensive reports so you can analyze your training in depth. For instance, you can compare your progress on the leg press to your progress on the leg extension. Serious athletes may find this information useful.

However, what's new isn't always better. Electronic machines slow down the pace of the gym and remove some of the human element involved in working out. Instead of interacting with the staff and other members, you interact with a machine. Also, if the system goes down, the repair process generally takes longer than it does with your basic weight-stack machine. And, the electronic systems aren't connected with free weights, so computer-dependent lifters may be discouraged from experimenting with dumbbells and barbells.

Smith machines

The Smith machine — named for an influential 1970s fitness figure named Randy Smith — features a regular free-weight bar trapped inside a track so that the bar must travel straight up and down. The Smith machine increases the safety of exercises such as bench presses, overhead lifts, and squats because you don't have to worry about the bar wobbling or slipping from your grip. At the same time, the machine retains the feel of free weights. Many Smith machines possess another safety feature: self-spotting pins jutting out from the frame. These pins prevent the bar from being lowered below a certain point, so there's no chance you'll get crushed under the bar if the weight is too heavy.

Smith machines use a traditional 45-pound bar, but in some cases, the bar balances on springs to negate most or all of its weight. The purpose is to add smoothness to the movement. Many lifters don't like this feature because it takes away from the macho spirit of weight lifting. Also, the movement is a bit too smooth, removing all the coordination and extra muscle usage associated with lifting free weights.

Power cages

A power cage is a large steel frame with a series of stanchions affixed to the sides. You stand in the center of the cage and place your bar on the stanchions that are at the right height for your lift. A power cage doesn't offer as much safety as a Smith machine because after you lift the bar from the stanchions, you're on your own. Still, the cage does offer an extra measure of protection during heavy lifts or lifts that require a lot of balance. And if your muscles give out, the stanchions catch the weight before it crashes to the floor.

Cable machines: A different breed

Not all machines use a cam. A class of equipment called cable machines uses a typical round pulley. A *cable machine* is a vertical metal beam, called a *tower,* with a pulley attached. You can adjust the height of the pulley to move it close to the floor, up over your head, or anywhere in between. Some cable machines have two towers (for an example, see the cable crossover exercise in Chapter 10). Cable machines are more versatile than Nautilus-type machines. Clip a new handle onto the pulley and you instantly create a new exercise.

Consider the triceps push-down, described in Chapter 13. Pressing down with a rope feels considerably different from pressing down with a V-shaped bar. You may prefer one attachment to the other, or you may want to use both for variety. See the sidebar "Coming to grips with cable attachments," in this chapter for a rundown of the most popular attachments. In Part III, we recommend certain attachments for certain exercises.

Coming to grips with cable attachments

At most gyms, you see a large heap of metal bars and handles sitting in a plastic container or milk crate. This pile may look like junk but, actually, it's more like a treasure chest. By attaching these handles to a cable pulley, you create an unlimited variety of exercises.

Some people are afraid to go near this pile, so they simply use whatever bar happens to already be attached to the cable. But if you frequently switch the handles, your workout can be more fun. Here's a rundown of the most popular cable attachments:

© John Wiley & Sons, Inc.

© John Wiley & Sons, Inc.

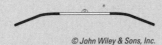

© John Wiley & Sons, Inc.

© John Wiley & Sons, Inc.

© John Wiley & Sons, Inc.

✔ **Ankle collar:** You clip this wide leather ankle bracelet to the pulley to perform exercises such as leg lifts, back kicks, and leg curls. The ankle collar can strengthen your inner and outer thighs while you're standing. We don't use the ankle collar in this book, but a trainer can fill you in on the details.

✔ **Curved short bar:** Some of these are U-shaped and some are V-shaped. Both varieties are used almost exclusively for triceps exercises, such as the triceps push-down.

✔ **Long bar:** These bars come in various lengths and are commonly used for back exercises that involve pulling the bar to your chest, such as the lat pull-down shown in Chapter 11. You can pull these bars with an underhand or overhand grip, and you can place your hands as far apart or as close together as you like.

✔ **Rope:** This attachment is most commonly used for triceps exercises such as the triceps push-down.

✔ **Straight short bar:** This bar is used in triceps exercises, biceps curls, and rows. We especially like to use this bar for the triceps push-down and the seated cable row.

Buckling Down on Bands and Tubing

Giant rubber bands and rubber tubes provide a resistance workout for just pennies. These inexpensive items can't make you as strong or measure your progress as precisely as machines and free weights, but bands do challenge your muscles in different and effective ways. For example, because bands don't rely on weight or gravity for resistance, they provide a challenge during both the up and down motions of an exercise. With most free-weight and weight-machine exercises, on the other hand, you typically feel most of the resistance during the lifting portion of the exercise, because gravity assists in the lowering portion.

Rubber bands and tubes are also convenient and portable. (You can't exactly pack dumbbells in your overnight bag.) If you don't have access to machines, bands are a great supplement to free weights because they allow you to do exercises that aren't possible with dumbbells and bars. Chapter 23 shows you ten exercises that you can perform with bands and tubes.

Lifting your body weight

Why is it that certain exercises can be quite challenging even though you're not holding any weights or using a machine? (The lunge, shown in Chapter 14, is a good example.) In these cases, you're not lifting *zero* weight; you're lifting your body weight. With a number of exercises, moving your own body weight offers plenty of resistance, especially for beginners.

The effectiveness of an exercise without equipment depends on how much of your weight you actually have to move and how hard you have to work to overcome the force of gravity. Consider the push-up, shown in Chapter 10. In the military version of the push-up, you have to push your entire body upward, directly against the force of gravity. The modified push-up, where you're balanced on your knees rather than your toes, factors out the weight of your legs so the exercise is easier. Neither exercise requires you to hold a weight, but both versions can be tough.

Exploring Sandbags for Shifting Weight

Instead of needing dumbbells for weight training, you can now use sandbags! And to make sandbags easier to shift your weight with, a more versatile version has popped up called Sandbells (see Figure 4-3). Now used in gym classes, Sandbells are neoprene-filled pouches filled with sand in the size of a disc, making them perfect for getting a functional workout — meaning a workout that mimics the moves you make in everyday life.

Figure 4-3:
A Sandbell.

Photograph by Nick Horne

The weight of a Sandbell varies anywhere from 2 pounds to 50 pounds. Most gym classes use 8-, 10-, 12-, 15-, and 20-pound versions. The color around the outer rim of the neoprene Sandbells indicates the weight; the pounds are clearly marked on the outside as well.

Sandbells make a simple everyday workout harder because you have to learn a whole new series of movements. Try slamming them onto the floor as you're kneeling. Or get into a sit-up position and shift the Sandbell side to side. It definitely works your abs and back in a whole new way and helps beat boredom.

Keying in on Kettlebells for Weight Training

Kettlebells are the new dumbbells when it comes to classes offered at gyms. A kettlebell looks like a ball of cast iron with a handle on it (see Figure 4-4). The kettlebell works your shoulders and back as it challenges your core.

Figure 4-4:
A kettlebell.

Photograph by Nick Horne

You only use one kettlebell in your workout, so learning how to evenly distribute only one weight instead of two dumbbells can be tricky. Fortunately, there are great gym classes that will show you how the moves are done.

Using a kettlebell allows you to incorporate your butt and thighs to do most of the movements. Bent rows, dead lifts, and front squats can all be done with kettlebells. And your arms will be tired afterward, too!

Chapter 5

Safety First: Protecting Yourself and Preventing Injury

. . . .

In This Chapter

▶ Discovering the safety rules of weight lifting

▶ Perfecting the art of spotting and being spotted

▶ Avoiding injury while lifting weights

▶ Seeking help if you're injured

. . . .

*O*ne of the best reasons to lift weights is to reduce your risk of injury in daily life by strengthening your muscles and bones. Unfortunately, the way in which some people use weight-lifting machines can leave them with minor injuries and intimidated to go back for more. Yes, weight training can be intimidating, but if you use proper form and pay attention to safety guidelines, you can have a lifetime of toned muscles and strong bones.

Follow the safety tips in this chapter, and you'll walk out of the weight room the same way you entered it: in one piece and under your own supervision.

Weight Lifting Safety Rules

We said that weight training is safe and that you can go a lifetime without a minor injury, but with that said, you may feel occasional muscle soreness — especially if you're new to the game or haven't worked out in a while. A little bit of post-workout soreness is okay; chances are, you'll feel tightness or achiness 24 to 48 hours after your workout, rather than right away. (This postponed period is called delayed onset muscle soreness.) But there are ways to reduce your amount of discomfort so you can be a normal, functioning human being after your workout. The following guidelines can help you keep this soreness to a minimum.

Properly warming up before you lift

Before you start your training session, warm up your body with at least five minutes of easy cardio exercise. Walking, jogging, stair climbing, and stationary biking are excellent aerobic warm-up activities for the muscles south of your waistline. But to prepare your upper-body muscles, you need to add extra arm movements to these activities:

✔ Vigorously swing your arms as you walk, jog, or use the stair climber.

✔ When you ride the stationary bike, gently roll your shoulders, circle your arms, and reach across the center of your body.

✔ Use a cardio machine that exercises your entire body, such as a rower, a cross-country ski machine, or a stair machine. (Many gyms have the Cybex Upper Body Ergometer [UBE]; ask a trainer where you can find the UBE.)

Your warm-up increases circulation and the temperature of your working muscles, making them more pliable and less susceptible to injury. Your warm-up also lubricates your joints. The pumping action of your blood at the joints stimulates the release of synovial fluid, which bathes your joints and keeps them moving smoothly, as if you're oiling a mechanical joint. If you have a particularly heavy weight workout planned, warm up for ten minutes.

You can also warm up your muscles by using *active isolated* (AI) *stretching*. AI stretching involves tightening the muscle opposite the one that you're planning to stretch and then stretching the target muscle for two seconds (see Chapter 16). You repeat this process 8 to 12 times before going on to the next stretch.

Warming up with light weights

If you're planning to do more than one set of an exercise, start by performing eight to ten repetitions with a light weight. A warm-up set is like a dress rehearsal for the real thing — a way of reminding your muscles to hit their marks when you go live. Even bodybuilders do warm-up sets. Sometimes you'll see a hunk of muscle bench-pressing with just the 45-pound bar. Just as you're thinking, "What a wimp," he piles on so many weight plates that the bar starts groaning. Then you realize that the first set was just his warm-up.

If you get too confident and head straight for the heavy weights, you risk injuring yourself. With weights that are too heavy for you, you're playing with some risky behaviors:

✔ Losing control of the weight

✔ Dropping the weight on yourself or on someone else

✔ Straining so hard to lift the weight that you tear a muscle

✔ Ending up so sore that you can barely lift your feet up high enough to climb stairs

One or a combination of these accidents can cause a lapse in your workout because you may have to take time off to recover. Be smart and start with lighter weights — weights that you can lift for more reps before you reach fatigue. (Check out Chapter 2 for workout lingo and training concepts.) A personal trainer at the gym can help you target a starting weight for your repetitions.

Lifting weights too quickly doesn't challenge muscles effectively and is a pretty reliable way to injure yourself. When you're pressing, pushing, lifting, or extending at the speed of a greyhound, you can't stop mid-rep if weight plates come loose, you're positioned incorrectly, or something just doesn't feel right. So, take at least two seconds to lift a weight and two to four seconds to lower it. Some experts feel that you should move even more slowly than that. If you're banging and clanging, slow down your pace.

Using your breath

Breathing is often the most overlooked and least understood component of weight training. If you're a competitive lifter, you probably already know that your breathing can either make you or break you come contest time.

We're not suggesting that you're a power lifter, but we also don't suggest inhaling and exhaling with the gusto of a Lamaze student. Relaxed breathing while exercising is the best technique. Don't hold your breath either.

Lifting weights temporarily causes your blood pressure to shoot up, which normally isn't a problem. But when you hold your breath, your blood pressure rises even higher — and then suddenly comes crashing down. Holding your breath creates *intra-thoracic pressure* (pressure in the chest cavity) that stops the circulation of blood from your muscles but can increase blood pressure. When you relax, the muscle relaxes, the blood begins to flow again, and your blood pressure drops. This drastic drop may cause you to pass out and drop your weight. And if you have a heart condition, you could be in serious jeopardy. So, remember: Breathe!

Using proper form

In addition to heeding the general safety tips we present here, be sure to follow the specific tips we give you for each exercise. Even subtle form mistakes, such as overarching your back or cocking your wrist the wrong way, can lead to injury.

The main goal is to adjust your body so that when you move you don't place any undue strain on any of your joints or muscles. It's important that you understand that form is everything in weight lifting. Poor form ultimately leads to injuries.

Before you start building muscle, you need to establish correct form and balance — and especially before you add more weight. When you start using heavy poundage, bad form ultimately leads to injuries to muscles and joints.

Don't get discouraged because form adjustment is something all weight lifters must do. If you start with bad form, you carry that form forward, until you find out the hard way that you've been moving incorrectly. Old habits are hard to break!

Follow these tips:

✔ Don't jerk or bounce any weight around.

✔ Don't be afraid to ask for help while you're in the gym.

✔ Ask gym employees for help if you're having trouble with certain exercises. They're usually helpful and will answer any questions you have — if they're not, you may want to look for a different gym.

✔ Follow a beginner's weight-lifting routine consistently for two to three months before moving on to more challenging exercises. Be patient, you'll eventually start to pile on weight plates; but for now, think form and balance.

Drink water before you get thirsty!

If you feel thirsty during your workout, you waited too long to take a sip of water and you're on your way to dehydration. Drink at least two 8-ounce glasses of water before starting your weight lifting routine and two to four glasses while working out. In order to work your muscles, you need water. Muscle is considered an active tissue, and water is found in the highest concentrations in active tissue. Your muscles are 72 percent water. If your body is only slightly dehydrated, your performance will decline.

Signs and symptoms of dehydration include the following:

✔ Dark yellow urine

✔ Dry cough

✔ Dry mouth

✔ Fatigue

✔ Headache

✔ Lightheadedness

✔ Loss of appetite

You have to train your neuromuscular system before you start increasing muscle tone and size. In other words, you need to improve the connection between your brain and your body so that more muscle fibers will fire with each contraction. This process of developing muscular control simply takes time. Star quarterbacks weren't born throwing touchdown passes in the Super Bowl. Excellent form took many, many years of disciplined practice and training to develop that level of skill and expertise. Training takes time.

Cooling down

If you've done a fairly fast-paced weight workout, complete the workout with five minutes of slow cardio exercise. The cardio cool-down gives your pulse, blood pressure, and breathing a chance to slow down before you hit the showers. If you've been lifting weights at more of a plodding pace, with plenty of rest between sets, a few minutes of stretching suffices as a cool-down. Ending your workout with an easy set also helps you cool down.

Resting your muscles

You can lift weights on consecutive days — just don't exercise the *same muscle* two days in a row. Forty-eight hours is usually the ideal waiting period before exercising the same muscle group again. Lifting weights places stress on the muscle, making the body adapt to the new stress, which in turn makes your muscles stronger.

If you ignore the 48-hour rule, weight lifting may make you weaker rather than stronger. At the very least, your muscles may feel too tired to perform at peak operating levels.

In Chapter 19, we explain how you can lift weights four to six days a week without ever hitting the same muscle group on consecutive days.

Weight-Lifting Safety Tips

Weight lifting is a safe activity that involves a risk of injury. You can minimize your risk of hurting yourself by following the basic common sense tips: Always respect the equipment, stay alert, and focus on your task at hand. You should be able to enjoy a lifetime of training.

Free-weight safety tips

We know a police officer who arched his back so severely over years of bench pressing that he finally was forced to retire. So, keep in mind the following during your free-weight workouts:

✔ **Use proper form when you lift a weight off the rack.** When you lift a dumbbell or barbell off a rack or when you lift a weight plate off a weight tree, always bend from your knees (not from your hips), get in close to the rack, and keep your arms bent. Figure 5-1 shows you how *not* to lift a weight off the rack.

Figure 5-1:
The *wrong* way to lift weights from the rack.

Photograph by Daniel Kron

✔ **Pay attention when carrying weights.** Hold heavier weight plates with *two* hands. Keep the plates close to your body when you carry them. Watch where you're going when you carry barbells — making a U-turn while hauling around a 7-foot bar can cause serious destruction. Keep your elbows slightly bent when carrying a dumbbell in each hand.

✔ **Use collars.** As we explain in Chapter 4, a collar is a clamplike device that you use to secure a weight plate onto a bar. Often, when you perform a barbell exercise, the bar tilts slightly to one side; without a collar, the plates may slide right off and land on somebody's toes or crash into the mirrors on the wall. We know one woman who was knocked unconscious when a collar flew off a guy's weight bar and hit her in the head.

✔ **Don't drop weights on the floor.** After you complete a dumbbell exercise on a bench (such as the chest fly or dumbbell chest press, described in Chapter 10), bring the weights to your chest and then gently rock your-self up into a sitting position.

Some people simply let go of the weights, which is not only unnerving to the other gym members but also unsafe because the weights can land anywhere, roll, and create hazards for others. Weights always need to be controlled.

✔ **Safely return weights to the rack.** When you finish using dumbbells, barbells, or weight plates, don't just lean straight over with locked knees and plunk the weights back on the rack. Instead, bend your knees, pull in your abdominals, and hold the weights close to your body before you release them.

Be careful not to smash your fingers when placing the weights back on the rack. We've done that. Ouch!

Weight-machine safety tips

One of the selling points of weight machines is that they're safer than free weights. And it's true — you're in no danger of being crushed by a 100-pound barbell. The way that machines create a safer environment is that they put your body in the correct position and direct the movement pattern. Still, if you're not careful, you can injure yourself.

Follow these safety tips to keep yourself (and others) out of harm's way:

✔ **Custom-fit each machine.** Some machines require a single adjustment, such as the seat height. Others require two or more adjustments. For instance, with some versions of the leg extension machine exercise, shown in Chapter 14, you have to adjust the back rest as well as the leg bar. Don't worry — you don't need a mechanic's license to adapt these machines to your body. Usually, you just pull a pin out of the hole, lower or raise the seat, and then put the pin back in place. Some machines are so simple to adjust that they don't even involve a pin. With practice, fit-ting the machine to your body becomes second nature.

Don't get lazy about making adjustments. Using a weight machine that doesn't fit your body is like driving a car while sitting in the back seat: uncomfortable, if not downright dangerous. When you strain to reach a handle or sit with your knees digging into your chest, you're at risk for pulling a muscle or wrenching a joint. After you make an adjustment, jiggle the seat or the backrest to make sure that you've locked it securely in place. You don't want the seat to drop suddenly to the floor with you on it.

✔ **Watch your fingers.** Occasionally, a machine's weight stack gets stuck in midair. Don't try to rectify the situation yourself by fiddling with the plates. Instead, call a staff member for help.

We once saw a gym member try to fix a weight stack himself. The stack came crashing down, sandwiching his fingers between the weight plates. We've seen other people get clumps of hair caught in the stacks.

✔ **Buckle up.** If a machine has a seat belt, use it. The belts are there for a reason. Use them! The seat belt prevents you from wasting muscle power squirming around to stay in place as you move the bar or lever of the machine. You're most likely to find seat belts on older models of the inner/outer thigh, pullover, seated leg curl, and triceps dip machines.

✔ **Don't invent new uses for the machinery.** You wouldn't use your favorite sweater to dust the house, right? You wouldn't use your TV as a step-stool to reach the top cupboard. So, don't use a chest machine to strengthen your legs.

People are constantly inventing new — and unsafe — ways to use weight machines. For example: In order to release the chest bar on the vertical chest press machine (described in Chapter 10), you must use your feet to press down on a bar near the floor. Well, we've seen people ignore the chest press altogether and use this floor bar to exercise their thighs or arms. If you dream up new uses for a machine, you may be asking for injuries.

Spotting with a Friend

A *spotter* is someone who stands close by you when you're lifting weights. This person is ready to grab your weights in case your muscles give out. The spotter can be a lifting partner with whom you go to the gym or a stranger in the gym whom you enlist for one or two exercises. If you don't know anyone to be a spotter for you, you can usually ask a staff person who is working on the weight-training floor. If you work with a personal trainer, she'll spot you.

Going to the gym with a friend is a good way to hold each other accountable. You can spot each other during lifting, and while you rest in between repetitions, your partner can perform the same exercise. Friends can encourage you in the last few reps, and keep you motivated. Your regular lifting buddy also knows what you're capable of and when you've had enough.

If you're in the gym lifting weights alone, you may not need a spotter hovering over you for *every* free-weight exercise because you may feel smothered, as if your mom is chaperoning you on a date. But do call on a spotter when you're alone and doing the following:

✔ **Trying an exercise for the first time:** Even if you're not lifting significant weight, the weights may wobble when you perform a new movement. A spotter gently guides you through the motion until you have the confidence and the muscle memory to do it yourself.

✔ **Attempting a heavier weight than usual:** If you've never bench-pressed 100 pounds, try the exercise first in the presence of a spotter. The moment the bar comes crashing down on your chest isn't a good time to find out you weren't ready for the lift (or the time to try gasping for air to yell for help). Lifting heavy weights without a spotter is a lot like a trapeze artist working without a safety net. You may be fine the first nine times, but the tenth time. . . .

✔ **Wanting to eke out extra reps:** Sometimes you're just not sure whether you have one more repetition in you. If you have a spotter, the repetition is worth trying (because there's no danger involved when you have a spotter). A spotter also can help you with machine exercises and assist you, for instance, on the last few inches of a heavy leg curl or arm curl.

Briefing your spotter

Regardless of who your spotter is, prepare him or her for the mission ahead:

✔ **Explain how many repetitions you're aiming to complete.** Consider how many reps you think that you can do before you'll need the spotter's assistance. Be honest! If you think that you may need a spot on the sixth repetition, say so. This way, your spotter can start paying extra close attention around the fourth rep.

✔ **Make it clear to your spotter whether you need help lifting the bar off the rack or getting the dumbbells into position.** Don't try to do something yourself if you know you'll have trouble with it — there's no shame in asking for help. Better safe than sorry.

✔ **Set up a specific plan.** Will the spotter help you *on* the count of three or *after* the count of three? Tiny misunderstandings can lead to big injuries.

✔ **Offer your gratitude both before and after your set.** Don't forget to thank your spotter. An attitude of gratitude makes you a reputable person in the gym.

Being the spotter

When people recruit you as a spotter, you have a big responsibility to perform your job correctly. Be realistic. If you weigh 90 pounds soaking wet, don't attempt to spot someone doing a 350-pound bench press. If you have any doubt you can pull it off, don't take on the assignment. The moment that the lifter's arms give out isn't the moment to realize you're out of your league.

If you do accept the job, pay close attention so you're ready at the precise moment your partner needs help. Step in to help on these situations:

- ✔ The weight stops moving for more than a split second and it's immediately apparent that the person is no longer in control of the movement.
- ✔ The weight begins traveling in the wrong direction.
- ✔ The lifter can't complete a rep.
- ✔ The lifter screams, "Help!"

The do's and don'ts of spotting

When the time comes that you're in the gym and someone calls on you to help with a few exercises, remember the do's and don'ts of being a responsible spotter.

- ✔ **Don't impose a lift-or-die mentality upon your lifting partner.** Just because he may have planned to complete five reps doesn't mean that you should withhold assistance if your partner starts struggling after three.
- ✔ **Don't offer too much help too soon.** This eagerness defeats the purpose of spotting, because the person only needs a spotter because he's trying to test the edge of his limits. If you prevent the lifter from testing that edge, you'll annoy the heck out of him.
- ✔ **Don't lean so close to the lifter that you impede or distract her movement.** Bench pressing isn't enjoyable when someone's face is directly over yours and you can see up the person's nose.
- ✔ **Be a cheerleader!** Put your pom-poms away. You don't have to jump up and do the splits, but people appreciate support — and may even lift more weight — if you offer enthusiastic encouragement: "You're almost there!" or "It's all you! You've got it!"

Exercises that need spotters

Where you stand when spotting someone can make the difference between being helpful and being useless in an emergency. The following list offers spotting tips for a variety of common exercises:

- ✔ **Bench press:** Stand behind the bench with your hands above or underneath the bar but not touching it. When the lifter needs you, lean in and get a quick grip on the bar.

- ✔ **Chest fly and dumbbell chest press:** For these dumbbell exercises (and versions performed on an incline bench), place your hands close to the person's wrists, not close to the weights. (You may see people spot underneath the elbows, which isn't a crime but isn't as safe, either.) When spotting flat-bench chest exercises, kneel on one knee behind the bench and follow the movement with your hands. For incline exercises, you may find it more comfortable to stand with your knees bent.

- ✔ **Barbell squat:** Stand behind the lifter, and be prepared to assist at the hips or underneath the arms. The lifter may not want to be spotted at the hips unless you happen to be that person's significant other. If you're squatting with a particularly heavy weight, you may want two spotters, one standing on either side of the bar.

- ✔ **Pull-up and dip:** Stand behind the lifter and offer assistance by holding his shins or waist and guiding him upward.

- ✔ **Machine exercises:** Spot at the bar or lever of the machine. For example, if you're spotting someone on the cable row, stand slightly behind and to the side of her. Grasp one of the handles and gently assist it the rest of the way.

Never spot machine exercises by placing your hand underneath the weight stack. That's a good way to get a squashed hand!

Common Weight-Training Injuries

Accidents happen, even to careful lifters. So, here's a primer on weight-training injuries in case you do run into one.

When you *strain* or *pull* a muscle, you actually overstretch or tear the *tendon,* the tough, cordlike tissue at the end of the muscle where the muscle tapers off and attaches to the bone. A strain can happen when you push up the bar too forcefully during the bench press or stand up too quickly out of the squat. Strains are often accompanied by a sudden, sharp pain and then a persistent ache.

A *sprain* is something different altogether. This injury happens not to a muscle but to a joint, such as your ankle or wrist. When you sprain a joint, you've torn or overstretched a *ligament,* the connective tissue that attaches one bone to another. You may feel pain and throbbing and notice some swelling and bruising. You can sprain just about any joint in your body; ankles and wrists seem to take the most beating in weight lifting.

Depending on the severity of the injury, the healing process may take anywhere from a couple days to a couple months. If your injury doesn't appear to be healing, see your doctor. Some of the common injuries caused by lifting weights include the following:

✔ **Torn rotator cuff:** The muscles of your rotator cuff (described in Chapter 11) are often injured during bench presses and shoulder presses. You may have torn your rotator cuff if

- You feel a persistent ache or a sharp pain deep within your shoulder at a specific point during the exercise.

- You're unable to raise your arm in front of you and over your head.

If you've injured your rotator cuff

- Stop performing any exercises that cause you pain or soreness in that area.

- Skip all overhead pressing movements for as long as your healthcare provider recommends that you rest. You shouldn't exercise while you have any pain.

- Lighten up your load on the bench press to a weight where you don't feel any pain.

- Limit the distance you move the bar.

- Or skip the exercise altogether.

Review your form: Make sure that you're not bouncing the weights up and down or taking the exercise past your natural active range of motion that you can control.

The rotator cuff exercises shown in Chapter 11 can help prevent injuries to these muscles. These exercises are a must if you lift heavy weights, if you lift regularly two to three times a week, or if you participate in a sport that uses the upper body, such as tennis, rock climbing, or swimming.

✔ **Sore knees:** Pinpointing the source of the problem can be difficult with knee injuries because the injury can come in so many varieties and have so many different causes. Often, the injury is caused by something you did outside the weight room. Still, certain weight-training mistakes, such as those described in Chapter 8, are likely culprits. Runners, walkers, and cyclists can ward off many common knee injuries by performing quadriceps exercises.

- If any leg exercise causes you pain, skip it or modify it by following our instructions. Some people try to protect their knees from injury by wrapping them in yards of bandages. We don't love the idea of knee wraps unless you're into some serious power lifting. A wrapped knee may mask a problem that needs immediate attention.

- To help protect your knees, make sure that you strengthen both your front and rear thigh muscles — the muscles that support your knee joints. Stretching is also helpful to keep all the muscles that surround the knee loose and limber. In Chapter 14, we provide a variety of leg-strengthening exercises to help prevent injuries.

✔ **Sore wrists:** Some people injure their wrist muscles by bending their wrists too much when they lift weights, so pay attention in Part III when we describe the proper wrist position for various exercises.

✔ **Lower back pain:** If you have a history of back problems, you can just as easily throw out your back reaching for an apple in the fridge as you can pumping iron. But because the weight room constantly challenges your ability to stabilize your spine and maintain good form, it increases the risk of triggering an old injury — or developing a new one.

If you have a history of back issues, be sure to study the core exercises in Chapter 15.

Always take precautions for your lower back when you lift weights. One key preventive measure (that we mention repeatedly throughout this book) is to pull in your abdominals. By tightening your abs, you create a natural girdle to support and protect your lower back (see Chapter 15).

Overcoming Injuries

We don't yet have a cure for the common cold, but we do have a reliable remedy for most minor sprains and strains: RICE, an acronym for Rest, Ice, Compression, and Elevation. RICE is most effective if you begin the process within 48 hours of injuring yourself. RICE includes the following four components:

✔ **Rest:** Stop performing activities that aggravate your injury. (Notice that we didn't say stop all activity — that's rarely the solution.) Wait until you've had two completely pain-free days before doing exercises that involve the injured area.

✔ **Ice:** Contrary to popular belief, ice, not heat, helps reduce the pain and swelling of most common injuries. Ice your injury for 15 to 20 minutes, three or four times a day, for as long as you feel pain. You can apply ice with a store-bought pack, a plastic bag full of ice cubes, or even a package of frozen peas. But don't allow ice to sit directly against the skin. (You may end up with ice burns.) Instead, wrap whatever is holding your ice in a thin towel.

Throw out the peas after they've been used as an ice pack a few times. The thawing and refreezing renders them less tasty than they would've been before.

Two areas may not respond well to icing: your neck and back. These injured areas may be so sensitive to the cold that you may tense up. If that's the case, a moist heating pad or wet, warm towel is best for treating the injury and allowing your muscles to relax.

- ✔ **Compression:** Put pressure on the injury to keep the swelling down. Use a damp elastic bandage or buy a special brace or wrap for your knee, elbow, or wrist. Wrap the bandage tightly enough so you feel some tension but not so firmly that you cut off your circulation or feel numb.

- ✔ **Elevation:** Elevating your injured body part drains away fluids and waste products so swelling goes down. If you've hurt your ankle, you don't need to lift it up over your head. You only need to elevate it higher than your hip so gravity assists the blood flow downward. Propping up your ankle on several pillows or books does the trick (pillows will be more comfortable, of course).

Sometimes RICE isn't enough to treat an injury. If the pain is truly excruciating or is bothersome for more than a few days, your injury probably needs more aggressive treatment and possibly medical attention. If you experience excessive swelling, discoloration, or bleeding, you may need a trip to the emergency room. Use your judgment. If you see a bone fragment sticking out of your ankle, don't simply stick an ice pack over it.

Part II
Gaining Weight-Training Wisdom

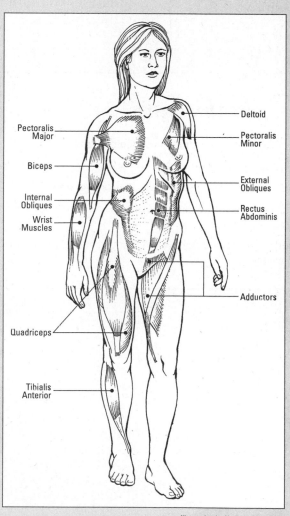

Pectoralis
Major

Biceps

Internal
Obliques

Wrist
Muscles

Quadriceps

Tibialis
Anterior

Deltoid

Pectoralis
Minor

External
Obliques

Rectus
Abdominis

Adductors

Illustration by Kathryn Born, MA

Get tips on setting up your home gym in a free article at www.dummies.com/
extras/weighttraining.

In this part . . .

✔ Set up a home gym for lifting weights on any budget.

✔ Choose a good health club.

✔ Find a personal trainer or group fitness instructor.

✔ Discover weight-training etiquette so you don't offend your fellow gym goers.

✔ Find out about common weight-lifting mistakes and how to avoid them.

Chapter 6

Setting Up Your Own Gym at Home

*I*s lifting weights better at a health club or at home? The answer really depends on your personal needs. There are many great reasons to work out at home. (The new 20-minute video accompanying this book, available at www.dummies.com/extras/weighttraining, may be one of them.) Home workouts can also enhance your gym workouts or can just stand alone. You don't have to choose one or the other.

In this chapter, you discover how to create a training environment at home. A home gym is a great option if you never plan to go to the gym or if you want to complement your gym workouts with a home program. You also discover how to invest in weight equipment, which includes buying gadgets and how much to spend.

Weight Training at Home

Exercising at home is the perfect solution for many people. Here are the main reasons why working out at home makes sense:

▸ **You live too far from a gym.** If you don't live or work within ten minutes of a club, lifting weights at home may be your best option. Or if you can afford it, not only join a club that you can get to on days when you have time, but also invest in some basic weight equipment at home for days when you're too busy to walk, bike, or make the drive (preferably choose an active way to get to the gym — that way you'll already be warmed up).

✔ **Your schedule.** If your club doesn't have childcare or you can't leave the house for some other reason, buying your own equipment makes sense. The same applies if you work unusual hours and the gym's schedule doesn't jibe with yours. If your den is equipped with dumbbells and a bench, you can exercise at 6 a.m. on Sunday if you want.

✔ **You're self-conscious.** If you can't bear the thought of exercising in front of other people — or you just need a little time to get used to what you look like in a pair of athletic shorts — by all means, work out at home. Using DVDs, working out with online videos, or using a personal trainer gives you instruction and helps keep you motivated. However, don't let self-consciousness keep you away from a club for too long if you have other compelling reasons to go. For the most part, health club members are too busy looking at themselves in the mirror to notice what you look like.

✔ **You don't like crowds.** Some people simply like to be alone with their dumbbells.

Setting Up a Home Gym

Exercise equipment lasts a long time, takes up space, and serves a variety of purposes. Put some time and thought into creating your home gym. Keep in mind that this is a long-term commitment. You're investing in a healthy lifestyle and a better quality of life for years to come. You want to create a space that you'll enjoy and look forward to using regularly.

This section deals only with weight-training equipment; you need to consider separately any cardiovascular equipment, such as a treadmill or stationary bike. LaReine uses jump ropes for all her workouts. They're a great way to get your heart rate up, and a jump rope is an inexpensive piece of equipment you can take anywhere. Jumping rope regularly improves endurance, agility, and coordination and helps keep bones strong while burning as many calories as cycling. Quite a bargain for a few dollars!

Before you purchase any equipment, consider the following questions.

✔ **How much space do you have?** If you have virtually no space for weight equipment, your best bet is a set of rubber exercise tubes that come with door-handle attachments. However, we think that you build greater strength and size by using dumbbells and a weight bench, so make room for these gadgets if possible. Conserve space by buying clever dumbbell products such as PlateMate, PowerBlock, or SmartLock, which are all described in the "Nifty dumbbell products" sidebar, later in this chapter.

✔ **What are your goals?** Make sure that you buy equipment that helps you reach your goals. If you're a big guy and you want to build some serious muscle, a couple sets of dumbbells won't cut it. In fact, you may need to buy a dozen pairs of dumbbells and purchase a free-weight bench. Just make sure that your goals jibe with the amount of space you have available: If you live in a tiny apartment but want to live in a body like the Rock, Dwayne Johnson's, you may have to get rid of your bed, coffee table, TV, refrigerator, and stove in order to make space for your weight equipment. (We know people who've done this.) If your goal is to develop moderate strength and muscle tone, your best bet is to buy an adjustable weight bench and several pairs of dumbbells.

✔ **How much money can you spend?** The cheapest (and smallest) weight-training gadget you can buy is a rubber exercise band, which sets you back about $5. On the other hand, you don't need to raid your retirement account in order to build a firm, strong body. For $200 to $500, you can buy an adjustable weight bench and more than enough dumbbells. You may be able to find equipment at an even cheaper price if you search used sporting goods stores or shop on eBay. If you have an extra thousand or two lying around, go ahead and purchase a multigym for variety. By the way, if you're tight on money, don't even think about buying any weight-training gizmo off the infomercials you see on TV. Most of the gadgets are gimmicks that don't offer any training advantages over traditional equipment.

✔ **Will you be using DVDs or working out online?** If you plan to use weight-training DVDs or online videos, we suggest that you invest in dumbbells and an adjustable weight bench (or at least a step aerobics platform, which doubles as a bench) or an exercise ball to sit on. Many DVDs and online videos also use rubber exercise bands, ankle weights, and dumbbells. When you buy new DVDs, make sure that you have (or are willing to buy) the necessary equipment.

Picking Free Weights

If you're just starting out, dumbbells are a more practical purchase than barbells because they're more versatile. You may want to save barbells for your next shopping spree. In terms of quality, where you buy free weights — a sporting goods store, department store, specialty shop, or garage sale — doesn't much matter. A specialty weight shop may offer the best selection, but prices may be higher. For great bargains, check out stores that sell used sports equipment. In many cases, the equipment is almost brand-new.

Before purchasing weights online, be sure to check the shipping price. You may be better off buying products from a local store that includes free delivery or where you can bring the weights home on your own. Shipping costs for weights are usually expensive.

Taking training on the road

If you're looking for an excuse to skip your weight-training workout, vacations and business trips won't cut it. You can keep your muscles strong no matter where you go, whether your destination is Caribou, Maine, or the Mongolian desert.

Although you may not always find a health club with 16 shoulder machines and aromatherapy baths, strength training on the road is well worth the effort. Even fitting in one short workout a week can help you maintain the strength you've worked so hard to build. Here are some tips for getting in a strength-training workout away from home:

✔ **Book a hotel with a gym, if possible.** Some hotel gyms have facilities that rival those at regular health clubs, including personal trainers, towel service, and massage. And these days, even many of the less posh hotel gyms offer a decent array of free weights and weight-training machinery.

✔ **Look for a gym in the neighborhood.** If your hotel doesn't have a gym, ask the concierge, or simply find one online by searching for "health club" or "fitness." Expect to pay $15 to $20. Some upscale Los Angeles and New York clubs charge as much as $35 or more.

✔ **Stick to free-weight exercises and machines that you recognize.** If you're in a gym that's foreign to you, unless you ask someone on staff to help you, this isn't the time to test whether you have a knack for figuring out how weight-training contraptions work. When you work out away from your home club, expect to sign a waiver essentially saying that any torn muscle, broken bone, or smashed toenail you sustain is your fault and yours alone.

✔ **Pack an exercise band.** If you have no access to weight equipment, you can perform dozens of exercises with a single band, which takes up about as much space as your travel toothbrush. See Chapter 23 for band exercises.

✔ **Lift your own body weight as a last resort.** If you get stuck without even a band, you can do equipment-free exercises such as push-ups, triceps dips, crunches, back extensions, squats, and lunges. You can use the coffee table in your hotel room — check out *Core Strength For Dummies,* by LaReine Chabut (Wiley) for a coffee-table workout! Outdoor workouts are also a great way to see the sights and experience local flavor, enjoy the outdoors, and keep up with your fitness program.

Buying dumbbells

The biggest mistake people make when buying dumbbells is investing in a pair of 10-pound weights and then using them for every exercise. We suggest that you start with seven or eight pairs. If that seems overwhelming, buy up to four pairs on the lower end and add the heavier weights as you become stronger.

For women who're beginning lifters, buy dumbbells weighing 3, 5, 8, 10, 12, 15, and 20 pounds. For novice men, buy 8, 12, 15, 20, 25, 30, 35, and 40 pounds. As explained in Chapter 2, to get good results you need to lift precisely the right amount of weight for each exercise.

Look for brands of dumbbells with narrow handles (so you don't have to buy as many weights). This way, you can hold two dumbbells in one hand, for example, a 5-pound weight and a 3-pound weight to create 8 pounds.

If you're short on space or money and buying so many pairs of dumbbells is impossible, consider an adjustable dumbbell kit. You get two short bars and a number of round plates that you clamp on with collars. Just beware: The plates tend to rattle around, and you may find it annoying to constantly pop off the collars and add or subtract weight plates. Making these adjustments can add precious minutes to your workout. Worse, you may be tempted to skip the adjustments and use the same weight for several exercises. See the sidebar "Nifty dumbbell products" for clever alternatives to the ones we discuss in this section.

Figuring the cost

So, what's all this going to cost? The answer depends on how fancy you want your weights to be. Dumbbells cost about 50¢ to $2 per pound ($150 to $300 for the women's set and $300 to $600 for the men's), depending on which part of the country you live in, where you buy them, and whether you catch a good sale. Hexagonal dumbbells (called *hexes* or *hex heads*) tend to be less expensive. Plastic-coated dumbbells are cheaper, but the plastic tends to rip over time.

Liz once owned a pair of dumbbells that started to leak; every time she pressed the dumbbells overhead, a few grains of sand fell in her mouth or eye. The most expensive dumbbells are the shiny chrome ones with contoured handles. You can see your reflection in the ends of the top-drawer ones. You find chrome dumbbells in ritzier health clubs and in home gyms that try to emulate ritzy health clubs.

Storing your equipment

Buy a rack to store your dumbbells. Racks save space, and they keep your house looking tidy so your mother won't have to step over your weights if she stops by unannounced. Also, a rack can save you from injury because you don't have to constantly bend over and lift the dumbbells off the floor. Don't be surprised if a rack costs more than the dumbbells you're storing. A $200 to $300 rack is adequate, but you can shell out up to $800 for a three-tiered, chrome rack.

Nifty dumbbell products

If you're in the market for dumbbells and want to save money and/or space, here are a few inventive gadgets that might suit your needs.

Photograph by Daniel Kron

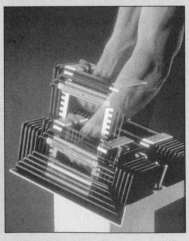

Photograph by Daniel Kron

✔ **PlateMate:** This product is like an oversized refrigerator magnet that you stick on both ends of a dumbbell to increase the weight. Plate mates come in four weights: ⅝ pound, 1¼ pounds, 1⅞ pounds, and 2½ pounds. Prices range from $19 to $28 per pair. PlateMates save you big bucks on dumbbells because you have to buy only half the weights you would otherwise. For instance, transform a set of 5-pounders into 6¼-pound dumbbells or 7½-pounders simply by sticking a PlateMate on each end. PlateMates bond to the weights quite well. Try to shake the dumbbell up and down, and the magnet won't fall off. Removing a PlateMate requires nothing but a quick twist.

✔ **PowerBlock:** These dumbbells are clever and adjustable but strange looking. Each PowerBlock consists of a series of weighted, rectangular frames, each smaller one nesting inside one slightly larger. Holes run along the outside frame: You stick a two-headed pin in the hole that corresponds to the amount of weight you want to lift, and the pin locks in the number of frames you need to lift. PowerBlocks save you time — it's a lot quicker to stick a pin in a hole than it is to clamp on new weight plates. For about $600, you can buy a set that builds up to two 90-pound dumbbells. They fit into a corner of the room and take up no more space than your nightstand. A similar product, Pro-Bell, is easier to use but only goes up to 30 pounds. Pro-Bells usually sell for $299 a pair; their stand costs an additional $149.

Photograph by Daniel Kron

✔ **SmartLock:** SmartLock is a nice improvement to adjustable dumbbells. They're short bars that come with spring-loaded collars that easily pop on and off. The collars lock the plates on the bars so tightly that they don't rattle around or slide off. For less than $200, you can buy a set that builds up to two 40-pound dumbbells.

Buying barbells

You'll probably find it too expensive and too space consuming to buy a whole array of fixed-weight barbells, as recommended with dumbbells. It's more practical to buy an empty bar and clip on the weights yourself. You can buy bars that weigh 15 to 45 pounds, although the most popular bars are the heavier bars used in health clubs.

Figuring the cost

Barbells cost about the same per pound as dumbbells, but if you're lucky, you may find them as low as 5¢ a pound. Most stores sell variety packs, often called *Olympic packs,* which come with a whole assortment of plates weighing a total of 200 to 300 pounds.

We also recommend buying collars to keep the weight plates from sliding off the bar. MCR makes the sturdiest and most user-friendly collars. You slip the collars on the bar and twist a small lever, locking them in place. They cost about $20 a pair.

Storing your equipment

As with dumbbells, we recommend buying a barbell rack. Vertical racks ($100 to $200) take up less space and cost less than horizontal racks ($300 to $700). However, placing a bar on a vertical rack is more awkward. Store your plates on a weight tree — a contraption that has several rungs. Weight trees come in an astonishing variety of shapes and sizes and typically cost $75 to $200.

Buying a bench

If you have a dedicated space for your home gym and want to buy a bench, your best bet is an adjustable incline bench — one that adjusts from a flat position all the way up to vertical. Make sure that the incline mechanism is secure and easy to manipulate. With some cheap brands, the pin that holds the backrest upright tends to slip out or, even worse, break off. The decline feature shouldn't be a high priority because you won't use it very often, if at all. Before you buy a bench, sit on it, lie on it, drag it around, adjust it, and inspect it. Look for a high-quality Naugahyde, leatherlike material used to cover all seat and back pads.

Figuring the cost

Good flat benches start at around $100 and run upwards of $500 for extra-thick padding and high-quality hardware. Adjustable incline and decline benches range from $200 to $600. Good bench brands include Bowflex, Hoist, Icarian, Paramount, Powerline, Tuff Stuff, and York — the brands you're likely to encounter at the gym — along with Body Masters, Cybex, and Galileo.

Storing your equipment

Storing your bench is nearly impossible. Benches that fold up and go under your bed or fit neatly in a closet don't exist. For this reason, you should have a dedicated space for your home gym that's roomy enough for a bench (and all your equipment). If you can only fit in the weights, skip the bench.

Investing in Weight Machines

Obviously, it's not practical to put an entire line of weight machines in your home, unless you're willing to take out a second mortgage to pay for the weights and for the new wing of the house you'll need to build. A more reasonable alternative is a multigym (see Figure 6-1), which combines several weight-lifting stations into one frame. Most multigyms have one or two weight stacks, meaning that one or two people can work out at a time. Good multigyms give your muscles a sufficient workout, although most models don't feel as smooth or as solid as health-club machines.

A decent multigym costs between $300 and $1,000. Buy from equipment specialty stores, not from department stores and certainly not from TV infomercials. Visit several stores to compare prices. If you don't live near a specialty store, call the manufacturers and ask for the dealer closest to you. Most top brands have a dealer in every nook and cranny in the country, as well as in many parts of Europe, Asia, and Africa. In some cases, buying directly from the manufacturer is cheaper. Good multigym brands include California Gym, Hoist, Pacific, Parabody, Paramount, Universal, and Vectra. Here are some tips for buying multigyms:

> ✔ **Look for sturdy and thick padded seats filled with dense foam.** Seats covered with durable material clean easily. The pad is the part of the equipment that has the most body contact, which includes your sweaty body. With a cleanable cover, you can wash away your workout sweat after each use.

✔ **Look for machines that use plastic-coated cables as opposed to chains or giant rubber bands.** Check all cables for imperfections and fraying.

✔ **Try out every exercise station.** Some may feel comfortable, while others make you feel like your arm is about to be ripped out of its socket. Look for a weight stack that moves smoothly up and down. Some machines that move smoothly at heavier weights become wobbly and sticky when you're lifting only one or two plates.

✔ **Make sure that the parts are easy to adjust.** You don't want to waste half your workout fiddling with the arm and seat adjustments to make the machine fit your body.

✔ **Look for free assembly.** Forget about those "easy-to-follow" directions. Trying to put some of these contraptions together yourself is like trying to build a space shuttle with a step-by-step manual.

Figure 6-1:
You can buy
a multigym
to work out
at home.

Photograph by Nick Horne

Purchasing Bands or Tubing

Make sure that you buy bands or tubes specifically designed for exercise, rather than the kind you use to keep your mail together in the office. Office rubber bands aren't strong enough for constant stretching, so you have a pretty good chance of getting popped in the face when one breaks. See Chapter 23 for a complete band workout and helpful tips on using bands and a description of our favorite band products.

Adding health-club features to your home gym

Even if you're not interested in joining a health club, you may want to incorporate aspects of the gym experience into your home workouts. Adding the following health-club features to your home gym boosts your motivation and sense of purpose.

✔ **Mirror:** The purpose of a mirror isn't to develop anxiety over the shape of your body. You need a mirror to check your form, especially when you're doing free-weight and band exercises. Just make sure that you watch where you put your dumbbells and barbells. If you leave them on the floor, they may roll around and crack the mirror. The best way to avoid this problem is to invest in a dumbbell rack. Any mirror suffices, as long as it's big enough for you to see your entire body when you're standing with your arms spread wide.

✔ **Comfortable mat:** A mat is useful for doing strength-training exercises on the floor, such as abdominal crunches and side-lying leg lifts. And, of course, it's useful for stretching and doing yoga or Pilates. You can substitute a towel or blanket, but these substitutions tend to bunch up. Most exercise mats fold or roll up and can be placed in a corner or underneath your weight rack.

A good mat costs $20 to $100. The differences between a cheap mat and a more expensive one are many:

- The thickness and quality of the padding
- The quality of the surface covering
- The antibacterial and antifungal materials
- The size of the mat
- The way the mat rolls up or stores

The mat should be long enough so it fits your body from the top of your head to your tailbone. The padding should be cushy enough so your knees don't dig into the floor when you do the modified push-up and other exercises that require kneeling.

✔ **Rubber floor mat:** A rubber mat, placed under the equipment, looks like the rubber mats on the floor of your car. They help cut down on noise and vibration to the floors below, and they help protect your floors and rugs from sweat and wear and tear. Mats are particularly good to put under equipment that leaks oil, such as multigyms and treadmills. Some mats are custom designed to fit under specific pieces of equipment.

Chapter 7

Exercising Away from Home: Clubs, Trainers, and Classes

. . . .

In This Chapter

▶ Choosing a health club

▶ Finding a qualified trainer

▶ Making the most of your training sessions

▶ Getting the lowdown on group fitness classes

▶ Minding your manners at the gym

. . . .

The gym can be an intimidating setting for the inexperienced. How do you decide which club to choose? And, after you join a club, how do you select a trainer, decide which class to attend, and act in training sessions and around the weight room?

This chapter demystifies the gym environment. You discover whether to invest in a gym membership and how to size up a health club's equipment, staff, atmosphere, and facilities. We explain how to choose a personal trainer or group fitness instructor. We inform you who's qualified to coach you and who isn't and what you can expect to gain from a trainer or a class.

Joining a Health Club

You may feel overwhelmed when you walk into a health club, but don't let feelings of anxiety stop you from signing up. Within a few sessions, your terror of the machines will seem unwarranted, and the club starts to seem as familiar as your own neighborhood. Here are a few reasons to become a health club member:

✔ **Equipment choices:** At a health club, you may have dozens of machines for each muscle group, including the latest contraptions that haven't yet reached the consumer market or are too expensive or too large for home use.

- ✔ **Advice:** A gym that is invested in you has staff members walking around who can remind you how to do the perfect back extension or how to adjust the calf machine.

- ✔ **Safety:** Weight training isn't inherently dangerous, but if you do happen to get stuck underneath a 100-pound barbell, at least you have people around to rescue you. You also have plenty of spotters to choose from.

- ✔ **Motivation:** After you're inside a health club, you eliminate all your excuses not to exercise. Besides, the atmosphere of a club may make you *want* to work out. You see people of all shapes and sizes pumping and pushing and pulling, and you can't help but be inspired to do the same.

- ✔ **Cost:** A typical yearly health-club membership costs between $350 and $2,000, depending on where you live and what type of facilities the club offers. Home weight equipment may cost you less over a period of years, but unless you're a multimillionaire, you probably can't afford to update your equipment as often as health clubs replace their contraptions. In order to stay competitive, many gyms turn over at least some of their equipment every year, if not more often.

- ✔ **Relaxation:** Ironically, a health club may be just the remedy for busy people who say that they don't have time to go to one. At the gym, you're free from stress and distractions. The phone doesn't ring. Your boss can't assign you a last-minute report.

- ✔ **Other facilities:** Weight training is only one component of fitness. At a gym, you have treadmills, stationary bikes, stair climbers, and other elliptical trainers. You may also find a sauna, steam room, swimming pool, vending machine, and even a snack bar (eat the healthy food, of course).

Choosing a Health Club

Many people have no choice. If your neighborhood has only one club, that's the club you probably need to join, even if the facilities aren't top-notch. You're more likely to use the mediocre fitness center around the corner than the first-rate gym that's 45 minutes away. If you have a routine of basic exercises, you can get a good workout in just about any facility that calls itself a gym.

Don't be scared off by the name of a health club or the size of the people who work out there. Among the general public, Gold's Gym franchises seem to have a reputation of catering only to serious bodybuilders. In reality, Gold's clubs — like any other chain clubs — cater to people of all ages and ability levels. We know a 94-year-old woman who is an avid attendee at Gold's Gym in Sacramento. Some gyms attract more serious lifters than others, but believe us, at virtually every gym in America, people like you attend. Besides, you can gather a lot of information from hanging around veteran lifters.

If you're lucky enough to have your choice of clubs, weigh your options carefully. You may want to tour each club to discover the variety of machines and mechanisms offered. You also want to notice if the staff is friendly and helpful. When you tour a club, bring the following checklist for consideration for your membership:

- **Hours of operation:** Some gyms are open 24 hours a day; others close at noon on weekends. Make sure that the hours of operation fit your schedule.

- **The cancellation, freeze, and refund policies:** Many gyms let you put your membership on hold for medical or maternity leave. Some clubs refund your remaining membership if you move more than 25 miles away. Most states have laws that allow you to cancel within three days of joining with a full refund.

- **Qualifications of the staff:** When you visit, ask what the club's requirements are for staff certification. Nationally recognized certification organizations include the American College of Sports Medicine, the American Council on Exercise, the National Strength and Conditioning Association, and the International Sports Sciences Association, among others.

- **Cleanliness:** Make sure that there are no strange growths in the showers. Check the weight benches and equipment for sweat residue. Most gyms have squirt bottles with bleach cleaner and towels handy for cleaning equipment before and after you use it. Remember that you're joining a gym to *improve* your health, not destroy it.

- **Equipment quality:** The quality of free weights doesn't vary much, but it's *not* a good sign if the plates on the dumbbells rattle around or you see lots of "Out of Order" signs scattered around. High-quality weight machine brands include Cybex, LifeFitness, Nautilus, Precor, and Star Trac. Try out a few machines. Do they move smoothly? Is the weight stack rusted? These subtle signs relate to how well the management takes care of the gym.

- **Friendliness of management:** Do the staff at the front desk greet you with a smile, or are they standing in a clique gossiping about the members? If staffers aren't accommodating before they've made a sale, think about how they'll act *after* you sign on the dotted line.

- **Cost:** Cheaper isn't always better. If the club's machinery is always broken or the bathrooms are cleaned monthly instead of daily, you may pay more in doctors' bills for injuries and infections than you do for your monthly membership.

- **Extra conveniences:** Some gyms have hair dryers in the locker rooms, Internet access on the cardiovascular equipment, membership competitions, and special guest instructors — little extras that keep you motivated over the long haul.

- **Affiliation with other clubs:** If you travel a lot, consider joining a club that is affiliated with gyms around the country. Large chains may not have the most qualified staff or offer the most personalized attention, but you can save money on guest passes.

Asking the right questions when joining a gym

Getting the facts you want from a health club often requires persistence and savvy. Here are some tips to prevent you from getting ripped off:

✔ **Stand your ground.** Health-club salespeople may quote what seems like a reasonable price, but by the time you get finished adding in all the options like locker space and towel service, they've doubled the price of admission.

✔ **Ask what the price includes.** If it doesn't include an item you want, such as an extra training session, ask if the salesperson will toss it in to make the sale. Also, don't let the salespeople cheat you out of the advertised price. If you see an ad in the paper, bring it with you to the club. If you heard an ad on the radio, note the station and the time it aired.

✔ **Don't be insulted.** Some salespeople try to assault your self-esteem by telling you how much better you'll look and feel if you lose 10 pounds to get you to join or to sign up for extra training sessions. *Remember:* Many health-club salespeople work on commission, so they say just about anything to make a sale.

✔ **Don't rush into your decision.** The gym will be there tomorrow. And if it isn't, you'll be glad you didn't sign up, right? Take your time.

✔ **Don't pay an initiation fee if you can help it.** An initiation fee is an upfront payment to join and doesn't cover any monthly dues. Some gyms waive this fee during certain times of the year or if you join with a family member — or if you're persistent enough.

✔ **Don't sign up for more than a year.** Many states have laws that forbid lifetime and long-term memberships. Loopholes exist in the law, and even when there aren't these holes, disreputable salespeople may try to snow you. You don't know where you'll be a year from now — and more important, you don't know where the gym is going to be a year from now. Many gyms have monthly memberships that are slightly more expensive than buying a whole year, but these month-to-month deals may be a better deal for you if your life is in flux.

✔ **Join with a friend and ask for a discount.** Know that the best sales are usually in the slower times — all the summer months and right after Christmas. Some clubs give you a rebate or free months if you recommend a friend who joins.

Researching Trainers

This book offers detailed instructions for dozens of exercises and plenty of ideas for designing your own workouts. Still, we think that getting personal instruction at least three times is valuable for anyone who lifts weights. If you join a club, you should automatically get a free training session on top of a fitness evaluation. Ask in advance, and you may even get extra free sessions. If you lift weights at home, you can hire a trainer for a couple sessions to get you up and running.

If a trainer isn't an option for you, a good video or DVD can augment what you gather from this book, although when you're an absolute beginner, a video or DVD is no substitute for hands-on instruction. Online training is the newest thing in fitness. You can find LaReine's exercise videos, along with many other daily workouts, on GymRa (www.gymra.com).

Finding fitness help: What a trainer can do for you

While standing in line at your local grocery store, you read about the stars who spend thousands of dollars on fitness trainers who mold bodies into divas and hotties for upcoming performances. Personal trainers are famous for performing award-winning actions to firm bodies quickly with amazing results for celebrities, but a good fitness trainer can do that for *you* too.

Perfecting your technique

A trainer can offer subtle pointers to improve your weight-lifting form. Even if you do your best to follow instructions like, "Keep your arm parallel to the floor," you may not be able to tell whether your arm is in precisely the right position. After you know what it feels like to correctly perform an exercise, you're likely to keep using good techniques when you're on your own.

Showing you alternatives

A trainer can help you build on the exercises in this book, showing you additional moves that meet your specific needs and preferences. If you're pregnant, a trainer can show you how to perform abdominal exercises without lying on your back and hamstring exercises without lying on your stomach. If you suffer from arthritis, a personal trainer can show you how to stretch and strengthen your muscles while alleviating some pain and fatigue.

Introducing you to the equipment

Each brand of equipment has its own quirks. The seat adjustment for one lat pull-down machine (see Chapter 9 for a description) may work by a different mechanism than it does for another, even though the machines strengthen your back muscles in the same way. A trainer can tell you about the intricacies of each machine in your health club or home gym.

Updating your routine and program

If you wanted to, you could come up with a new routine every day for the rest of your life. A trainer can help you expand on our workout suggestions and design routines that fit your specific schedule, whether you work out three days a week for 20 minutes or twice a week for an hour. Trainers also come in handy if you're working toward a specific goal — preparing for ski season requires a different type of routine than getting ready for a backpacking vacation.

Keeping you motivated

Some people wouldn't even consider getting out of bed, let alone lifting a weight, if they didn't have a trainer standing over them saying, "Okay, ten shoulder presses — now!" Others manage with a motivational boost every month or two, working out on their own the rest of the time. And then some people rely so much on their trainers for inspiration that they actually bring them along on vacation.

Finding a qualified trainer

Fitness trainer is about as meaningful a term as *social-media consultant* or *marketing liaison.* In terms of skills and education, the term doesn't mean a darn thing. We know a group of private trainers who hang a large sign outside their gym that says, "World-Class Personal Trainers." Only one of the group's six trainers is even certified by a single professional organization. Find a trainer you can trust.

Looking for the certification

Although no laws exist on the books requiring trainers to have any particular training or certification, professional organizations and university programs are certifying more and more trainers. Many health clubs now require their trainers to have at least one certification, and as the personal training profession becomes increasingly competitive, many private trainers are obtaining degrees in exercise science in order to stay ahead of the competition.

A number of certifications require several days of seminars taught by fitness experts and a passing grade on a written exam. But beware: We recently came across a certification offered online that involved answering a few questions. You could take the test as many times as you wanted and didn't have to pay until you passed — at which point you would be issued a fancy certificate saying that you're a "Certified Kickboxing Instructor" or "Certified Personal Trainer." The website even bragged "No teaching experience necessary!"

The following organizations are among the most reputable certifying agents:

- American College of Sports Medicine (ACSM)
- National Strength and Conditioning Association (NSCA)
- American Council on Exercise (ACE)

Hiring an experienced trainer

Don't be shy: Ask for references and call a few. Do as good a job screening potential trainers as you'd do checking out potential employees. Ask for a résumé.

Making sure that your personalities mesh

Trainers are human beings, which means that they come in all different personality types. Some are enthusiastic. Some are downright perky. Others are drill sergeants.

Interview a few trainers and choose one who makes you feel comfortable. Your trainer doesn't need to be your best friend. In order to act as an objective professional, your trainer — like your doctor or lawyer — may need some distance from you.

Expecting good teaching skills

Even if your trainer has a PhD in physiology and is friendlier than Tom Hanks, there's no guarantee that he can show you how to perform a push-up correctly. The ability to get a point across is a skill in and of itself. Good trainers speak to you in your native tongue, not in jargon. If you don't understand something, a trainer should be able to find another way of explaining the point. Also, good trainers prepare you to venture out into the world alone. They make sure that you understand not only how to adjust the seat on the leg-extension machine, but also why you're adjusting it that way.

Getting personal attention

Your trainer should shower you with questions about your goals and should thoroughly evaluate your health, strength, cardiovascular fitness, and flexibility. Look for evidence that you're getting a custom-designed routine. Many trainers specialize in certain types of clients, such as seniors, children, pregnant women, multiple sclerosis patients, or ultra-endurance athletes. If you have a specific goal in mind or have special circumstances, it's wise to seek out a trainer who has the training and experience to meet your needs.

Paying a hefty fee

Hollywood stars may pay $400 per weight-training session, but you don't need to. Fees vary widely depending on what part of the country you live in, but in many places, you can find a trainer for about $35 an hour. Expect to pay between $75 and $150 per hour if you live in big cities such as New York, Los Angeles, or Chicago. More experienced trainers generally receive a higher rate. You may spend less money by purchasing five or ten sessions at once, but highly qualified trainers often don't discount their rates. You also can save cash by hiring a trainer who works at your health club, but don't forget that you're also paying the club's monthly dues. Many trainers offer semiprivate sessions for a reduced fee. If you go this route, try to hook up with a buddy whose goals and abilities are similar to yours.

Be sure to weigh all factors when you hire a trainer because the least expensive person may not be the best choice for you, especially if you need someone with extra qualifications. Trainers with additional education in working with people with certain medical conditions or women who're pregnant usually charge higher rates. Yoga and Pilates instructors often charge more, too.

Insisting on liability insurance

Make sure that your trainer carries liability insurance. Of course, we hope you never find yourself in a position where insurance matters. But you do need to face the realities of the modern world. If you get hurt, you may be looking at thousands of dollars in medical bills, even if you have medical insurance. A trainer's liability coverage may foot the bill if you can prove your injury is a direct result of the trainer's negligence. Many insurers award coverage only to trainers who're certified, so liability insurance is often an indication that your trainer has some credentials.

Being on your best behavior

Just as you expect a trainer to meet certain qualifications and protocol, you too need to be up to the standard, aligning your behaviors with a willing participant and one that trainers can work with. Take an active role in your training sessions, especially if you're going to have just a few of them. Follow these tips to get the most out of your training sessions:

- ✔ **Show up on time.** Trainers are professional people with busy schedules and bills to pay, so show them courtesy. Honor your trainer's cancellation policy (and avoid chronic cancellations). Most trainers require at least 24 hours notice when you can't make it to your session. They may let you slide the first time, but they do have the right to charge you for missed sessions.

- ✔ **Have a good attitude.** Your trainer doesn't want to hear you whine about your boss or your latest speeding ticket.

- ✔ **Speak up.** The more questions you ask, the more information you're likely to remember. When you perform the lat pull-down, don't feel stupid about asking why you pull the bar down to your chest rather than to your belly button. A good trainer has coherent answers on the tip of her tongue.

- ✔ **Listen to your trainer.** When you're advised to perform 12 repetitions per set, don't say, "My stockbroker says that it's better to perform 40 repetitions." Trust that your trainer has more experience than you do (or your stockbroker for that matter). Of course, you should always ask questions if you don't understand something and if your trainer's advice sounds out of line. If you don't get your questions answered the way you hope or you have poor results from your training sessions, the time has come to find another trainer who better meets your fitness goals.

Working in a Group: An Introduction to Weight-Training Classes

Some people thrive on one-on-one instruction. Others really respond to the atmosphere of a class, even if they can afford a private trainer. If you're uncomfortable with someone scrutinizing your every move, as a personal trainer does, then taking a class is a good way for you to discover weight-training techniques while still blending into the crowd. And if you're short on self-motivation, your classmates hold you accountable and keep you pumping weights when you'd prefer to go home and watch TV. Even if you're the type of person who enjoys working out alone, you can pick up new moves by taking an occasional class.

Conditioning your muscles

Some buzzwords for weight-training workouts include *circuit training, interval training, muscle conditioning, body sculpting,* and *body shaping.* We think that teachers started these terms because they figured *weight training* would scare away people who're afraid of lifting weights. Some people say, "Oh, I hate weight training, but I love body sculpting," which is like saying that you hate sweet potatoes but love yams. It's all in the delivery!

Group classes use dumbbells and exercise bands, as opposed to weight machines. A class typically lasts between 45 and 60 minutes and works all the major muscle groups in the body. Most clubs also offer 20- to 30-minute classes, such as "Abs Only" or "Lower Back Care," that focus on particular areas of the body. If you take a focused class, just make sure that you don't neglect the rest of your body.

Although we wholeheartedly endorse group training, we do want to point out two flaws that commonly plague these classes: performing too many repetitions and failing to use enough weight. Just because you're in a classroom doesn't mean that the basic rules of weight training go out the window. You still need to lift enough weight for each exercise so that the muscle in question is fatigued by the 15th repetition.

Getting quality group instruction

In general, the quality of instruction has drastically improved in recent years, because most clubs demand certification and because poorly attended classes get dropped from the schedule. If you don't like one instructor, try another one if your schedule permits.

Look for the following when evaluating an instructor:

- ✓ **Certification:** The American College of Sports Medicine, the American Council on Exercise, or another nationally recognized organization should certify your teacher as an exercise instructor. Instructor certifications are different from personal-training certifications. Typically, the exams aren't as difficult in the areas of fitness assessment and individual program design as they are for personal trainers, but the tests focus more on the skills that instructors need for group training situations.

- ✓ **Concern for newcomers:** A good instructor asks whether anyone is new to the class and whether anyone has any injuries or special problems. If you fill the bill, you may want to arrive a few minutes early and explain your situation to the instructor. She may give you a special place to stand so she can keep an eye on you. At the very least, you should get a little extra attention.

- ✓ **Clear instructions:** A good instructor acquaints you with important terminology without overloading you with jargon. We know one instructor who says things like, "Raise up on your phalanges," which in English means, "Stand up on your tiptoes."

- ✓ **Concern for safety:** Don't be afraid to walk out of any class that doesn't feel right. Liz once bailed on a "Step 'n' Sculpt" class because the teacher had class members flying all over the step with weights in their hands. The uncontrolled activity caused a near collision between Liz and the student next to her. Don't worry about hurting the teacher's feelings. Your priority is keeping your body intact.

- ✓ **Motivation:** Instructors shouldn't act like they're on autopilot. Your instructor should be one of the reasons that you look forward to going to class and someone who keeps you interested in your training program. The teacher should model correct form and demonstrate a variety of options for people of different levels in the class. Your responsibility is to choose the correct level. If you're not sure which level that is, ask the instructor.

- ✓ **Individual technique tips:** Instructors can't possibly give a personal-training session to all 20 members of the class, but they should offer some individual tips. They need to let you know if you hold your arms too wide during chest-fly exercises or if you throw your body around when you do biceps curls. If you have questions about any exercises, take the initiative and come to class a few minutes early or speak to the instructor after class. Be courteous. If your instructor is busy that day, ask when a convenient time for you to ask a question is.

- ✓ **A warm-up, cool-down, and relaxation stretch:** Every weight-training class should have a warm-up that consists of at least six minutes of light aerobic exercise to warm up muscles and joints. The class should end with three to five minutes of light movement at a lower intensity to cool down, followed by a five- to ten-minute stretching and relaxation segment.

Take advantage of the instructor-led relaxation and stretches. Focus on deep breathing, releasing muscular tension, and achieving a good stretch. So often, people skip this part of training. More and more evidence from research supports the importance of learning how to relax to improve health and well-being. Enjoy these few moments to relax both your body and mind.

✔ **An intensity check:** During the class, the instructor should check to make sure that people aren't pushing themselves too hard (or taking it too easy to benefit from the workout). The intensity check can be something as casual as "Hey, how's everyone doing so far?"

Class etiquette

Remember that "Gets Along Well with Others" category on your grade-school report card? Well, no one is going to grade your behavior in a weight-training class, but the principle still applies: You must be courteous to your fellow students. Win friends and the teacher's approval in class by following these rules:

✔ **Follow the teacher.** You're not just renting the weights for an hour; you're there to participate with the group. When the class is trying to listen to the instructor's explanation of the shoulder press, you shouldn't be off in your own world doing a set of biceps curls. Your deviation can be distracting to both the class members and the instructor.

✔ **Choose the appropriate class level.** If you're a flat-out beginner, don't venture into the "Monster Muscles" advanced muscle-conditioning class. Your presence isn't fair to the students or the teacher, who is supposed to be challenging the other students, to have to stop to explain the basics to you. (Also, your safety is at risk.) On the flip side, if you're an advanced student slipping into a beginner toning class, know that you won't be as challenged. Don't bother complaining to the instructor that the class is too easy for you.

✔ **Don't disorganize the weights or benches.** We sometimes see class members arrive early, pick through weights to find the ones

they want, and reserve their favorite spot in the class. This behavior wouldn't be a problem if the classmates didn't throw their reject equipment all over the floor. Don't create any hazardous conditions.

✔ **Respect other students' personal space.** Place your equipment far enough from your neighbors so you don't smack into them during the exercises. If the class is too crowded, the teacher is obligated to turn people away or modify the routine so nobody ends up injured.

✔ **Don't show up late.** Most teachers don't let students in after the warm-up period. You shouldn't miss this segment, anyway.

✔ **Respect the teacher's instructions.** A group fitness instructor's most important job is to ensure the safety of everyone in the class. Respect the teacher's exercise instructions, as well as guidance regarding where to position yourself in class and what to wear.

✔ **Bring water and a towel.** Make sure you always have water and a towel when taking a class or doing any workout. Staying hydrated is important. And a towel comes in handy for mopping up the sweat you leave behind — your classmates will appreciate it!

Knowing Weight-Training Etiquette

Even at a health club — a place where tank tops, profuse sweating, and mild grunting are perfectly acceptable — rules of etiquette should be followed. Sure, the social graces expected in a weight room are a bit different from those expected at the symphony or the Louvre, but manners are important just the same. In this section, we explain the rituals and customs unique to gyms. Some habits may seem odd at first, but after you understand how you're expected to act, you'll feel a lot more at home in your club.

 If you witness a flagrant etiquette violation, don't be afraid to inform the club staff. You're not being a snitch. The rules are for everyone, whether you're the Queen of England or one of her loyal subjects.

Sharing equipment

In a gym, weight equipment is considered communal property, so don't sit on a machine while you rest between sets. Especially don't sit there reading a magazine, talking on your cellphone, or rehearsing an opera. (We've witnessed all three.) Instead, stand up and let a fellow gym member *work in* — let the member alternate sets with you. The same rule applies if you're using a pair of dumbbells. When you complete a set, place the weights on the floor so someone else can sneak in a set while you rest.

The only time you should retain possession of weight equipment while you rest is when you're using a barbell stacked with weight plates. Suppose that you're bench-pressing 75 pounds — a 45-pound bar with a 10- and 5-pound weight plate on each side. Someone else, meanwhile, wants to bench-press 225 pounds — the bar plus two 45-pound plates on each side. You can see what a hassle it would be for the two of you to work in with each other; between each set, you'd need to slide eight plates on and off the bar. So you're under no obligation to let the other person work in with you. (However, if people are waiting for the equipment, have the courtesy not to perform 15 sets.)

Unloading your weight bar

After you finish using a bar, leave it completely empty. Don't assume that everyone can lift the same amount of weight you can. Removing weight plates from a bar takes a fair amount of strength, as well as good technique. Don't assume that the next person who comes along has the ability (or desire) to clean up after you.

By the way, this clear-the-bar rule doesn't just apply to heavy lifters. Even if you're using only a 10-pound plate, you still need to clear your bar. If the next person who comes along wants to use 45s, he shouldn't be bothered with removing your 10-pounders.

Don't drop your dumbbells quickly when you're done lifting your set. If you can lift them, you can control them all the way back down to the floor in a safe manner.

Putting weights back where you found them

When you've removed a weight plate from a bar or when you finish using a pair of dumbbells, return the weights to their designated spot on the rack. Typically, clubs have dumbbells sitting in order. On a weight-plate tree, the light plates usually sit on the top rungs, while the heavier ones go on the bottom. When people pile the plates indiscriminately on top of one another, invariably they've made you slide off three 45-pound plates and two 25-pounders just to get to the 10-pound plate (that is, if you're able to lift those weights). You may have to find a trainer to help you, consequently wasting more time.

Never leave dumbbells or barbells on the floor when you're finished using them. Someone may trip on the weights. If you leave dumbbells on the floor between sets, crisscross them or butt them up against the wall or the bench so that they can't roll away.

Wiping down the machines

Carry a towel and wipe off any bench or machine you use. Nothing is quite as gross as picking up a slippery weight or lying down in a stranger's pool of sweat. If you forget to bring a towel, use your sweatshirt or the paper towels provided by the club.

Wipe up the pool of perspiration you may have left on the floor surrounding your machine or bench, too. Otherwise, the next person may inadvertently do a third-base slide into the machinery.

Keeping up with the flow of traffic

Don't block the traffic flow. As we mention earlier, you shouldn't camp out on the equipment while you're resting between sets. However, neither should you clog the pathways between machines or congregate with a dozen of your buddies in the free-weight area. Not only is this inconsiderate, but it can create a hazardous condition. In general, weight rooms are crowded with little room between machines. If you block space, someone may walk around you and inadvertently bump someone who's working out on a machine, causing that person to lose control and drop a weight. This has happened before with serious consequences.

The weight room is for training. If you want to visit with friends, go out into the hallway.

Moving along at the drinking fountain

Don't stand at the drinking fountain trying to catch your breath when the line behind you is longer than the line for World Series tickets. Take a drink and get back in line. Better yet, carry a water bottle in the weight room. For some reason, many people who use a water bottle on the stationary bikes and stair climbers don't think of carrying one around the strength-training area. When you do fill up your bottle, let everyone else in line get a drink first; don't hold up the entire gym membership while you fill a gallon-size water jug.

Don't spit your gum into the drinking fountain — this tip should be obvious, but club staffers report otherwise. Actually, don't spit *anything* into the fountain. No one wants to stick his face into a wad of your spit.

Lugging around your gym bag

Some people carry their bag from machine to machine. You know those large hollowed-out cubes called lockers? That's where you store your gym bag. At most gyms, the machines are only a few feet apart; by dumping your bag on the ground, you're hogging precious floor space. In addition, you're creating a hazardous condition because someone may trip and fall over your bag.

Many gyms forbid members to bring their bags into the weight room because less honest members may walk out with lovely parting gifts, like dumbbells, cable handles, and other small items. Someone recently stole all the collars from a gym that Liz manages, creating a real safety issue until the collars were replaced. (We define collars in Chapter 4.)

Treating the locker room like your own bathroom

Even more so than the weight room, the locker room is the place where your true colors emerge. Women are on equal standing with men in this arena: Men may be more likely to hog dumbbells in the weight room, but women can stand for hours in the only available shower stall with the best of 'em.

Follow these suggestions for locker-room etiquette to maintain good relations with your fellow gym mates:

- **The shower:** Don't take a marathon shower if people are waiting. With the exception of sweat, what you take into the shower should come out with you when you leave. Make sure that you remove all your shower supplies and that little wad of your hair from the drain. When you get out of the shower, stand on a towel to prevent leaving a puddle on the floor. Same goes for the pool if your gym has one.

- **The vanity area:** Don't hog the mirror or the hair dryer. If you brush your hair and 200 strands of hair fall on the counter, wipe them off with a paper towel (and wipe them into the towel or in the trash, not on the floor). When dressing, sit on a towel on the bench. The bench is not a place for bare behinds.

- **The locker area:** Don't take up three lockers and spread your clothing over the entire bench. Share with others. And shut your locker when you leave.

Don't leave your belongings in lockers overnight unless you have permission from your gym to do so. Most gyms empty out unsanctioned lockers at the end of every day and won't guarantee the safe return of your personal items.

If the lockers at your gym require a key, return the key at the end of your workout. Keyed lockers are a convenience to members so they don't have to carry locks of their own. However, members often walk away with the keys, rendering the lockers unusable and creating a big expense for the facility, which has to keep replacing the keys.

- **The laundry and trash areas:** Limit yourself to one or two towels. After you finish using your towels and other paraphernalia, place them in the laundry or trash bin instead of dropping them on the floor.

Chapter 8

Your Muscles and How to Use Them Properly

This chapter is devoted to how to interpret exercise phrases and follow their instructions. This doesn't mean that the instructions are complicated. You won't feel like you're struggling through a tax-prep guide or one of those do-it-yourself manuals. It simply introduces some basic terms used frequently in this book. You also determine what the differences are between the various exercise options.

Understanding the Basic Info

For every muscle group presented in this book (such as back, chest, or shoulders), first we show the nonmachine exercises — moves involving dumbbells, barbells, or no equipment at all. Next are exercises that do require weight machines. Explanations include at least one machine per muscle group (except the abdominals, for reasons we explain in Chapter 13). Figures 8-1 and 8-2 show you the major muscle groups in your body.

If we tried to show you every exercise in existence, this book would be thicker than the unabridged edition of *The Oxford English Dictionary*. So, we've chosen to present the most common, basic exercises — classic moves that are not only safe and appropriate for beginners but also standard moves for experienced exercisers. New to this edition is Chapter 15, which features moves that strengthen the core muscles. Core muscles stabilize the torso, improve posture, and help prevent back pain.

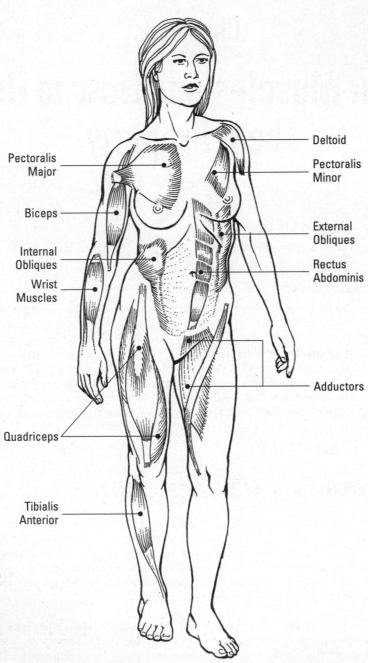

Deltoid

Pectoralis Major

Pectoralis Minor

Biceps

External Obliques

Internal Obliques

Rectus Abdominis

Wrist Muscles

Adductors

Quadriceps

Tibialis Anterior

Figure 8-1:
Your muscles from the front.

Illustration by Kathryn Born, MA

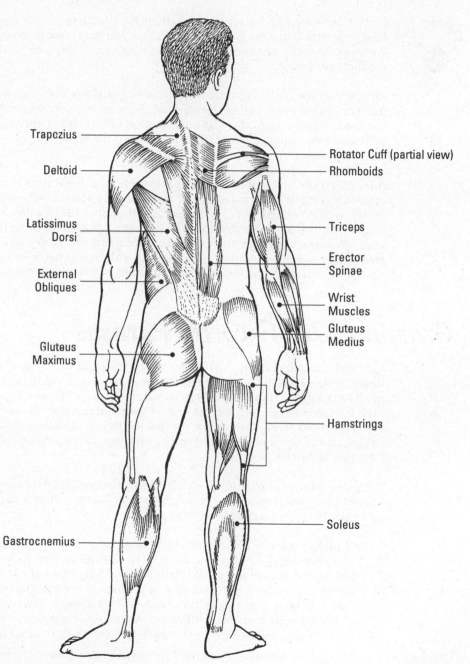

Trapezius

Deltoid

Latissimus
Dorsi

External
Obliques

Gluteus
Maximus

Gastrocnemius

Rotator Cuff (partial view)

Rhomboids

Triceps

Erector
Spinae

Wrist
Muscles

Gluteus
Medius

Hamstrings

Soleus

Figure 8-2:
Your mus-
cles from
the back.

Illustration by Kathryn Born, MA

If you have knee, hip, back, or other orthopedic problems, look for the Warning icon — we use it to alert you to exercises that you may want to avoid or modify. We also provide instructions on how to adjust many of the exercises to work around your issues.

After presenting each exercise, the "Other options" section describes a number of other versions of the workout. Some of the options are easier than the basic version, requiring less coordination or strength. Others are tougher. Some options — neither easier nor harder than the basic version — simply work the muscle from a different angle.

After you feel comfortable with the basic version, expand your horizons by experimenting with the options. You may discover, for example, that you prefer to do the dumbbell exercise explained in Chapter 11 with a barbell instead. Or maybe you enjoy both versions and want to alternate them in your workouts. However, don't get overly enthusiastic and try all options of an exercise in a single workout. Experiment with one or two new versions each time you work out, and concentrate on mastering the movement.

Grasping Our Favorite Phrases

Everyone has pet phrases. Parents like to say "Eat your vegetables!" and "Don't forget to take a jacket!" (even if their offspring are 45 years old). Dentists like to say "Don't forget to floss!" and "Brush in all the corners!" Fitness experts have their favorite sayings, too, such as "Pull in your abdominals!" These phrases aren't meant to annoy you (we'll leave that job to parents and dentists); instead, the goal is to keep your joints and muscles from getting injured and to make the exercises more effective.

Here's a rundown of phrases used repeatedly in Chapters 9 through 24. Chances are, you'll hear these same phrases in exercise videos and classes and when you work out with a fitness trainer:

- ✔ **"Pull in your abs":** Place your hand over your belly button and gently pull your belly button in and away from your hand; that's what it feels like to pull in your abdominal muscles. Don't try to create a vacuum or suck your stomach into your ribs as if someone were going to punch you. Just hold your abs slightly in toward your spine. Tightening your abs helps hold your torso still when you exercise and keeps your back from arching or rounding — mistakes that can lead to back injury.

- ✔ **"Keep your shoulders square":** Keep your head centered between your shoulders, and don't round your shoulders forward. In other words, avoid slouching. Your chest should be comfortably lifted, not forced; you don't have to stand like a soldier at attention. Avoid arching your upper back and pushing your ribs forward.

✔ **"Don't lock your joints":** This phrase refers to your elbows and your knees. *Locking a joint* means straightening it so completely that it moves past the point where it normally sits at rest. For example, you don't usually stand with your quadriceps (front thigh muscles) as tight as can be with your kneecaps pulled up; that's a locked knee. Not only is locking your knees bad news for your knee joints, but it also causes lower-back pain. It can even lead to more serious injuries. One of our friends actually knew someone who passed out when he was singing at a choir concert because he locked his knees — he fell right off the back of the riser. And locking the knees is a way of cheating when you perform exercises in a standing position.

Locking your elbows places excessive pressure on your elbow joints, tendons, and ligaments. Constant elbow locking causes *tennis elbow* (an inflammation of the elbow tendons), even if you've never held a tennis racket in your hand. Locking your elbows also contributes to *bursitis* through the rupturing of the *bursa* (little lubrication capsules) located in your joints. Bursitis results in swelling, pain, and tenderness at the elbow. Snapping your elbows also is a form of cheating because the weight is temporarily shifted off your muscle and on to the bone. When you snap your elbows, your muscles fail to get the proper workout.

✔ **"Keep your neck and shoulders relaxed":** If your shoulders are hunched up near your ears, you need to relax. Hunched shoulders may be linked to holding the phone to your ear or sitting at your computer all day long, absorbing workday stress. If you're prone to hunching, think about lengthening your shoulder blades, as if they're dropping down your back, and try to keep them there as you perform the exercise. Strengthening your shoulder stabilizer muscles, such as the mid-upper back and external rotators, improves your ability to keep your shoulders down.

✔ **"Tilt your chin toward your chest":** Tilt your chin just enough to fit your closed fist between your chest and your chin. This position lines up the vertebrae of your neck with the rest of your vertebrae. (Because your neck is a continuation of your spine, it should stay in the same general line as the rest of your vertebrae.) Don't tilt your chin back or drop it toward your chest the way you do when you sulk. These two movements strain your neck and place excess pressure on the top vertebrae of your spine.

✔ **"Don't let your knees go past your toes":** This phrase and similar phrases are used often when describing butt and leg exercises, such as the squat and lunge (head to Chapter 14 for examples). If your knees are several inches in front of your toes, you're placing your knees under a great deal of pressure. Also, you probably have too much weight distributed on your toes and not enough on your heels, which means that the exercise doesn't strengthen your butt as effectively.

✔ **"Don't bend your wrists":** When you bend your wrists too far inward or outward (that is, when you don't keep your wrists in line with your forearms), you cut off the blood supply to the nerves in your wrists. If you do this frequently enough, you can give yourself a case of carpal tunnel syndrome. The phrases "Keep your wrist in line with your forearms" or "Keep your wrists flat" describe the same position.

✔ **"Maintain proper posture":** *Proper posture* is an all-encompassing phrase that includes everything that we mention in this section. This phrase is used often because good posture is so important — and because people's posture often goes down the tubes when they focus on lifting and lowering a weight.

Good posture isn't automatic for most of us, so give yourself frequent reminders. And if you exercise with correct posture, you'll train your muscles to hold themselves correctly in everyday life. Throughout these chapters, the Posture Patrol icon reminds you to maintain good posture. See Figure 8-3 for an example of good posture.

Figure 8-3:
For good posture, align your ears, shoulders, hips, knees, and ankles.

Photograph by Nick Horne

The Art of Breathing through an Exercise

The exercise descriptions in this book don't include breathing instructions because too many extra instructions amounts to information overload. Nevertheless, proper breathing technique is important, so to spare you the overkill, we're only going to say this once. You'll thank us later. But don't forget to breathe. Promise? Okay. Here are the general rules:

✔ **Inhale deeply through your nose to bring in a fresh oxygen supply during the less difficult part of an exercise (such as when you lower the weight during a bench press).** Inhaling provides the spark of energy for your next repetition.

✔ **Exhale deeply through your mouth during the most difficult part of the exercise, also known as the *exertion phase* or the *sticking point*.** During a bench press, for example, pressing the bar up is the exertion phase, so exhale as the bar travels upward. Exhaling protects your lower back by building up pressure that acts as a girdle to hold your spine in place. Exhaling also ensures that you don't hold your breath so long that you pass out.

Before the hard-core weight-lifting contingency sends irate letters, note that these breathing directions are for *non-maximal lifts*. World-class power lifting isn't discussed here. If you plan to compete in power lifting, you need to use a slightly different breathing technique than the one described here. Because we don't think that many readers of this book plan to enter such a competition (at least not anytime soon), we won't bore you with the details.

Part III
Tackling the Exercises

Photograph by Nick Horne

In this part . . .

- Work your back, chest, and shoulders.
- Tone your arms, abs, butt, and legs.
- Strengthen your core.
- Find out how to stretch as part of your weight-training program.

Chapter 9

Working Your Back

Back pain is your body's way of telling you that your back needs to be strengthened. More than 80 percent of adults experience back pain during their lives. Back pain is the leading cause of disability from work in the United States. With this much back pain going around, you need to be proactive and strengthen your back to prevent pain and injury. Staying healthy and pain free will go a long way toward improving your quality of life. And a strong back is important for many daily activities, including recreation, fun, and work.

This chapter divides the back into two sections: upper back and lower back. Even though these muscle groups reside in close proximity to each other, they have different job descriptions and require different workout routines. Many upper-back exercises involve lifting a fair amount of pounds; lower-back exercises, on the other hand, require more subtle movements, usually without any free weights or machines. You soon realize why you need to perform both types of exercises and which moves get you the best results. We highly suggest you try the weight-training exercises in this chapter as preventive medicine and to help return your body to its natural, pain-free state.

Understanding Upper-Back Muscle Basics

Pull up a chair and let's talk about your upper-back muscles. There. You just used 'em. No, that wasn't a trick. In fact, you use your upper-back muscles whenever you pull anything toward you, whether it's a piece of furniture, a stubborn Golden Retriever on a leash, or the mountain of chips you won at your Thursday-night poker game.

Your upper back consists of several muscles (see Figure 9-1):

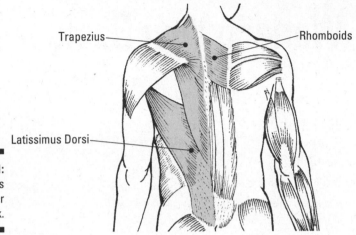

Trapezius

Rhomboids

Latissimus Dorsi

Figure 9-1:
The muscles
of the upper
back.

Illustration by Kathryn Born, MA

✔ **Latissimus dorsi (lats):** The largest muscles in your back run from just behind each armpit to the center of your lower back. Olympic swimmers, particularly those who swim butterfly, have well-developed lats. These muscles give swimmers that V-shaped torso. The main purpose of your lats is to pull your arms (and anything in your hands) toward your body.

✔ **Trapezius (traps):** Above the lats are your two traps. Together, your traps look like a large kite that runs from the top of your neck to the edge of your shoulders and narrows down through the center of your back. Your traps enable you to shrug your shoulders (like when your spouse asks how you could've forgotten to pay the phone bill). More important, your lower traps stabilize your shoulders and help prevent shoulder injuries and your upper traps help you to move your head to the back or side, or to look behind you.

✔ **Rhomboids:** Your rhomboids cover the area between your spine and your shoulder blades. Along with your traps, you use your rhomboids for squeezing your shoulder blades together. You have to call them your rhomboids, because *boids* somehow never caught on. Most people who work long hours at computers or in other seated positions have over-stretched and weak rhomboids.

Strengthening your back muscles has important advantages.

✔ **Real-life benefits:** With a strong upper back, you'll find it easier to drag your kids into the dentist's office or lug your suitcases through endless airport terminals. You'll say goodbye to slouching as your posture improves and get rid of tension in your neck and shoulders.

✔ **Injury prevention:** Strong upper-back muscles play a significant role in keeping your shoulders healthy. Your lats handle most of the work in pulling movements, so you don't overstress your shoulders. For example, well-developed upper-back muscles could save you from injury when unfolding the sofa bed for a houseguest.

✔ **The confidence or the "feel good" factor:** Upper-back exercises make your back broader, which, in turn, slenderizes your lower body. These exercises also improve your posture by helping you stand straighter and taller, open up your chest, and give up slumping as a pastime.

Getting an Upper-Back Workout

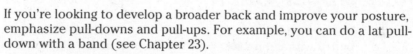

Upper-back exercises fall into three general categories:

✔ **Pull-downs and pull-ups:** With a pull-down, you grab a bar attached to an overhead pulley and pull it down; with a pull-up, you grasp a bar above you and pull yourself up. If you exercise at home, use an exercise band to mimic the pulley machine and do the band lat pull-down (see Chapter 23). Pull-downs and pull-ups are grouped in one category because they work your back in the same way. Both types of exercises involve your lats, traps, and rhomboids, but they also rely heavily on your biceps, shoulders, and chest muscles.

If you're looking to develop a broader back and improve your posture, emphasize pull-downs and pull-ups. For example, you can do a lat pull-down with a band (see Chapter 23).

✔ **Rows:** What we're about to tell you may be shocking, but rowing exercises are similar to the motion of rowing a boat. You may perform rows with a barbell or dumbbell, a set of machine handles, a bar attached to a low cable pulley, or an exercise band. Rowing exercises use the same muscles as pull-downs and pull-ups, except that they don't involve your chest. Rows are particularly helpful if you want to find out how to sit up straighter — to perform a row correctly on a machine, you have to sit up tall.

✔ **Pullovers:** When you do a pullover, your arms move up and down in an arc, similar to when you pull an ax overhead to chop wood. Pullovers rely mainly on your lats, but they also call upon your chest, shoulders, and abdominal muscles. Like the other upper-back exercises, pullovers help with posture. A pullover is an ideal transition exercise from a back workout to a chest workout. In other words, use a pullover as the last exercise of your back workout and as a prelude to your chest exercises because your chest will be warmed up.

Later in this chapter, we provide a variety of exercises in each category. For the most complete upper-back workout, perform at least one exercise from each category — although you don't need to do all these exercises in the same workout.

Whether you're performing pull-downs, pull-ups, rows, or pullovers, remind yourself that these exercises first and foremost strengthen your back muscles, not your arms. Think of your arms merely as a link between the bar and your back muscles, which should do the bulk of the work. Concentrate on originating each exercise from the outer edges of your back. This bit of advice may be difficult to relate to at first, but as you get stronger and more sophisticated, your body awareness improves and you know exactly where you should feel each exercise.

Most of the upper-back exercises in this chapter involve weight machines or cable pulleys. If you work out at home and you don't have a multigym (a home version of health-club machinery, described in Chapter 4), use an exercise band to mimic the pulley machine. See Chapter 23 for an example of a back exercise performed with a band.

Avoiding Mistakes When Working Your Upper Back

The upper back is one area where we see a lot of attempted heroics. With pull-downs and rows, people tend to pile on more weight than they can handle and end up trying to throw their entire body weight into the exercise to move the weight. This sort of behavior won't train your back muscles and may result in injury.

Follow these tips to avoid injury when training your upper back:

- **Don't rock back and forth or wiggle around.** In an effort to pull the weight toward them, many people squirm around to build up momentum, but that's the last thing you want; instead, rely on your own muscle power. If you find yourself shifting around in order to lift and lower the weight, drop down a few plates.

- **Don't lean too far back.** You may be able to lift more weight when you lean way back, but that's because you have better leverage and you're using your body weight to cheat, not because your back muscles get a better workout. A more upright posture ensures that your back muscles are in the prime position to do maximum work. Any time you pull something toward you, slide your shoulders down, squeeze your shoulder blades together, and sit up tall. With pull-downs, you can lean back ever so slightly, but for rows you need to be sitting as tall as you do when your flight attendant demands that you return your seat back to its full upright position with your seat belt fastened and tray table locked.

✔ **Don't pull a bar down behind your neck.** There are endless variations of the pull-down exercise, but one now frowned on by many exercise experts is the behind-the-neck pull-down. Critics of this exercise say that your arms twist so far back that your upper-arm bones get jammed into your shoulder sockets, which could overstretch your ligaments and strain those delicate rotator-cuff muscles we describe in Chapter 11. Unless you're a rock climber, an avid rower, or a swimmer who likes to swim butterfly, front pull-downs will suffice.

Getting Skilled at Upper-Back Exercises

Upper-back exercises that you can do with dumbbells and machines are previewed in this section. You'll move from dumbbell to barbell to machine exercises. Here's a preview of the upper-back exercises shown in this chapter:

✔ One-arm dumbbell row

✔ Dumbbell pullover

✔ Dumbbell shrug

✔ Machine row

✔ Lat pull-down

✔ Cable row

✔ Assisted pull-up

One-arm dumbbell row

The one-arm dumbbell row targets your back, but also emphasizes, your biceps and shoulders.

Be careful with this exercise if you have lower-back problems.

Getting set

Stand in a lunge position, left foot forward, making sure your knee doesn't jut out past your toes. Hold a dumbbell in your right hand with your palm facing in. Let your right arm hang down underneath your right shoulder. Tilt your chin toward your chest so your neck is in line with the rest of your spine (see Figure 9-2a).

Figure 9-2:
One-arm
dumbbell
row.

Photograph by Nick Horne

The exercise

Pull your right arm up, keeping it in line with your shoulder and parallel to the ceiling (see Figure 9-2b). Lift your arm until your hand brushes against your waist. Lower the weight slowly back down.

Do's and don'ts

- ✔ DO remember that, although your arm is moving, this is a back exercise. Concentrate on pulling from your back muscles (right behind and below your shoulder) rather than just moving your arm up and down.

- ✔ DO keep your abs pulled in tight throughout the motion.

- ✔ DON'T allow your back to sag toward the floor or your shoulders to hunch up.

- ✔ DON'T jerk the weight upward.

Other options

Rotation row: As you lift the dumbbell, rotate your arm so your palm ends up facing backward. This position gives the exercise a different feel and places extra emphasis on your biceps.

Barbell row: Place a barbell on the floor and stand about a foot away from it. With your knees bent, bend down and grasp the bar in an overhand grip with your hands a little wider than your shoulders. Pull your abs in tight and don't let your back arch. Keeping your hips bent so that your torso is at a 45-degree angle to the floor, pull the bar toward the lower part of your chest and then slowly lower it back down. You can also perform this exercise with an underhand grip or with your hands a bit closer together.

Dumbbell pullover

The dumbbell pullover is mainly a back exercise, but it also works your chest, shoulders, triceps, and abdominals.

If you have shoulder or lower-back problems, you may want to skip this exercise because the dumbbell pullover requires raising your arms overhead, while stabilizing your spine.

Getting set

Holding a single dumbbell with both hands, lie on a bench with your feet flat on the floor and your arms directly over your shoulders. Turn your palms up so one end of the dumbbell is resting in the gap between your palms and the other end is hanging down over your face (see Figure 9-3a). Pull your abdominals in, but make sure that your back is relaxed and arched naturally.

The exercise

Keeping your elbows slightly bent, lower the weight behind your head until the bottom end of the dumbbell is directly behind your head (see Figure 9-3b). Pull the dumbbell back up overhead, keeping the same slight bend in your elbows throughout the motion.

Do's and don'ts

- DO make sure that you grip the dumbbell securely.
- DO concentrate on initiating the movement from the outer wings of your upper back rather than simply bending and straightening your arms.
- DON'T arch your back up off the bench, especially as you lower the weight.
- DON'T lower the weight too far behind you.

Other options

Barbell pullover: Do this same exercise with a bar, holding the bar in the center with your palms facing up. Another variation on the same theme: Hold a dumbbell in each hand with your palms facing in.

Figure 9-3:
Dumbbell
pullover.

Photograph by Nick Horne

Machine pullover: Many gyms have a machine that mimics the action of a dumbbell pullover while you're in a seated position.

Dumbbell shrug

The dumbbell shrug is a small movement with a big payoff: It strengthens your shoulders and the trapezius muscles of your upper back.

Be careful if you're prone to neck problems.

Getting set

Stand tall and hold a dumbbell in each hand, arms straight down, palms in front of your thighs and facing in (see Figure 9-4a). Pull your abdominals in, tuck your chin toward your chest, and keep your knees relaxed.

Figure 9-4: Dumbbell shrug.

Photograph by Nick Horne

The exercise

Shrug your shoulders straight up toward your ears the same way you do if you don't know the answer to the $500 geography question on *Jeopardy!* (see Figure 9-4b). Slowly lower your shoulders to the starting position.

Do's and don'ts

- ✔ DO keep your neck and shoulders relaxed.

- ✔ DON'T roll your shoulders in a complete circle — a common exercise mistake that places too much stress on your shoulder joints.

- ✔ DON'T move body parts other than your shoulders.

Other options

Barbell shrug: Hold a bar with your hands shoulder-width apart and in front of your thighs, palms facing in. Do the exact same movement as in the basic version.

Shrug roll (harder): Shrug your shoulders upward as in the basic version, squeeze your shoulder blades together, and then lower them back down. This version brings the trapezius and rhomboids (two back muscles) into the mix.

Machine row

The machine row focuses on your back, with additional emphasis on your shoulders and biceps.

Take special care performing this exercise if you've had lower-back or shoulder injuries.

Getting set

Sit facing the weight stack of the machine with your chest against the chest pad.

Adjust the seat so your arms are level with the machine's handles and so that you must stretch your arms fully to reach those handles. This adjustment is important — and one that many people forget to make. If you can't fully straighten your arms when you grasp the handles, you'll end up using your arm muscles a lot more than your back muscles.

Grasp a handle in each hand, slide your shoulders down, and sit up tall (see Figure 9-5a).

The exercise

Pull the handles toward you until your hands are alongside your chest (see Figure 9-5b). As you bend your arms, your elbows should travel directly behind you, not out to the side. At the same time, squeeze your shoulder blades together. Slowly straighten your arms, feeling a stretch through your shoulder blades as you return the handles to their original position.

Do's and don'ts

- ✔ DO sit up even taller as you pull the weight.
- ✔ DON'T lean back so far that your chest comes off the pad as you bend your arms.

   ✔ DON'T round your back or lean forward as you return the handles to the starting position.

   ✔ DON'T stick your neck forward as you pull the weight.

Figure 9-5:
Machine
row.

a   b

Photograph by Nick Horne

Other options

Other machines: Although each manufacturer has its own version of the machine row, the same basic rules apply. Depending on the brand, the handles may be parallel, perpendicular, or diagonal; some machines have all three grips. Experiment with different grips to get a different feel from this exercise.

Advanced machine row (harder): Do this exercise without keeping your chest on the chest pad. Without the support, you have to work harder to sit up straight.

Lat pull-down

The lat pull-down is primarily a back exercise, although your shoulders and biceps also see some action. Try switching grips and attachments to give this exercise a different feel.

When engaging in the lat pull-down, be careful if you have shoulder or lower-back problems.

Getting set

Before you start, sit in the seat and adjust the thigh pads so your legs are firmly wedged underneath the pads with your knees bent and your feet flat on the floor. Stand up and grasp the bar with an overhand grip and your hands about 6 inches wider than shoulder-width apart. Still grasping the bar, sit back down and wedge the tops of your thighs (just above your knee) underneath the thigh pads. Stretch your arms straight up, keep your chest lifted, and lean back slightly (an inch or two) from your hips (see Figure 9-6a).

Figure 9-6:
Lat pull-
down.

Photograph by Nick Horne

The exercise

In a smooth, fluid motion, pull the bar down to the top of your chest (see Figure 9-6b). Hold the position for a moment, and then slowly raise the bar back up.

When you've completed the set, stand up in order to return the weights to the stack. Don't just let go of the bar while you're seated — the sudden release causes the weight stack to come crashing down.

Do's and don'ts

- ✔ DON'T rock back and forth in an effort to pull down the weight.

- ✔ DON'T lean more than an inch or two back as you pull the weight down. Keep that slight lean that you had at the beginning of the movement.

- ✔ DON'T move so quickly that you jerk your elbows or shoulders.

- ✔ DON'T bend your wrists.

Other options

Changing your grip: Experiment with the width of your grip and the orientation of your palms to give this exercise a different feel. For example, use the triangle attachment for a **triangle-grip lat pull-down.** Or use an underhand grip **(reverse-grip lat pull-down)** and hold near the center of the bar for a pull-down that feels similar to a chin-up. Avoid pulling the bar behind your neck (see "Avoiding Mistakes When Working Your Upper Back," earlier in this chapter, for the reasoning). Experiment with other attachments of varying lengths and curves, such as the short straight bar and rope.

Cable row

The cable row strengthens your back, along with your biceps and shoulders.

Be careful with the cable row if you've had lower-back or shoulder problems.

Getting set

Sit on the machine facing the tower with your legs slightly bent and hip-width apart, and your feet firmly planted against the foot plate. Grasp the handle and straighten your arms out in front of your chest (see Figure 9-7a). Sit up as tall as you can, sliding your shoulders down, pulling your abdominals in and lifting your chest.

The exercise

Sitting up tall, pull the handle toward the lower part of your chest, squeezing your shoulder blades together as you pull (see Figure 9-7b). Your elbows should travel straight back, arms brushing lightly against your sides as you go. Without stretching forward, straighten your arms slowly back to the start.

Figure 9-7:
Cable row.

Photograph by Nick Horne

Do's and don'ts

✔ DO feel this exercise in your back, not just in your arms. Concentrate on starting the pull with the outer edges of your back.

✔ DON'T arch or round your back.

✔ DON'T rock back and forth to help you lift and lower the weight.

Another option

Extended row: The basic version of this exercise is excellent for targeting the upper-back muscles. However, you can strengthen your lower back at the same time by leaning forward a few inches at your hips as you stretch your arms out and by leaning back slightly as you pull the handle toward you. Some exercise purists scorn this version because it doesn't "isolate" your upper back, but the extended row works the upper and lower back together and is great for people who do a lot of rowing or activities like weeding, dancing, or climbing. However, skip this version if you have a history of lower-back pain.

Assisted pull-up

The assisted pull-up targets your back, with additional emphasis on your shoulders and biceps.

Be careful if you have lower-back or shoulder problems.

Getting set

Set the weight on the machine according to your own body weight before stepping up on the platform of the assisted pull-up machine (sometimes called a Gravitron). Carefully kneel on the kneepads. (Some versions of the machine require you to stand.) Grab the handles that place your palms facing forward and straighten your arms (see Figure 9-8a). Pull your abdominals in and keep your body tall.

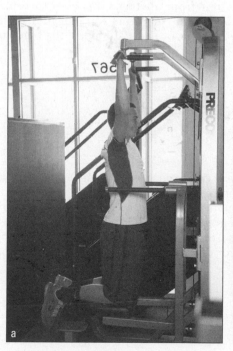

Figure 9-8: Assisted pull-up.

Photograph by Nick Horne

The exercise

Pull yourself up until your elbows point down (see Figure 9-8b), and then slowly lower your body back down.

Do's and don'ts

- ✔ DO relax your shoulders so they don't hunch up by your ears.
- ✔ DON'T rock your body to help move you up and down.
- ✔ DON'T arch your back or round forward.
- ✔ DON'T stall at the bottom of the exercise. Move steadily until you finish your reps.

Other options

Different grips: Some assisted pull-up machines have a choice of wider or narrower grips. Experiment with your hand placement to see which ones you like best.

Bar pull-up (harder): Using a Smith machine or power cage, set the bar so that it's securely resting against the stops set in the center of the frame. Grasp the center of the bar with your hands a few inches apart and palms facing you. Kick your legs out in front of you so that your torso forms a 45-degree angle with the floor. Bend your arms and pull yourself upward until the top of your chest touches, or nearly touches, the bar. Slowly lower to the start position.

Understanding Lower-Back Muscle Basics

Your lower-back muscles have two main jobs: bending your spine backward and bracing your torso when you move some other part of your body. (Your lower-back muscles perform this stabilizing job in tandem with your abdominal muscles, located directly in front of them.) The main lower-back muscles you need to know about are the erector spinae (see Figure 9-9). Feel along either side of your spine just above your hips and you have a handle on your lower erector spinae.

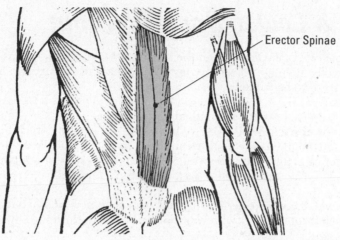
Erector Spinae

Figure 9-9:
The muscles
of the lower
back.

Illustration by Kathryn Born, MA

Getting a Strong Lower Back

Most lower-back exercises — particularly those appropriate for beginners —
don't involve free weights or machines. Usually, it's just you and the floor.
Here's what you can accomplish without any equipment at all:

✔ **Real-life benefits:** Sitting puts your spine under a lot of pressure,
much more pressure than if you stood all day, and it particularly compresses your lower spine. That's why your lower back feels sore after
a day in front of the computer. When your back muscles are weak, you
tend to slouch or arch your back, which places the spine under even
more stress.

In addition to strengthening and stretching your lower back on a regular
basis, you should get up a few minutes every hour when you're sitting
throughout the day.

✔ **Injury prevention:** Ironically, even people with chronic lower-back
pain tend to neglect lower-back exercises, often because they're afraid
of inflicting even more damage. Also, while people have gotten the
message that abdominal exercises help alleviate back pain, many don't
realize that lower-back exercises are equally important in this pursuit.
When one of these sets of muscles is stronger or more flexible than the
other, your posture is thrown off kilter, and you're more prone to back
pain. This scenario is common.

✔ **The "feel good" factor:** Strengthening your lower back helps you stand up
straight, which, in turn, makes you look taller, makes you look as much as
5 pounds slimmer, and gives you a more confident, commanding presence.

Getting a Lower-Back Workout

People often take for granted the role that the lower-back muscles play in everyday mobility. So, while your lower-back muscles need to be strong, they also need to be flexible.

This balance between strength and flexibility is particularly important with your lower back. That's why we include the pelvic tilt, which both strengthens and lengthens the muscles attached to your spine. With the widespread incidence of lower-back pain among adults, everyone should practice this exercise. The same goes for back-extension exercises.

However, if you're experiencing back pain right now or you have a history of back trouble, check with your doctor before performing any extension exercises.

When you do a lower-back exercise, you should feel a mild pull or pressure build within the muscle, *not* a sharp pain. If you do feel a piercing pain, back off. Review the exercise description to make sure that you haven't pushed your body too far and then try the movement again. If you still feel pain, seek medical advice before proceeding.

You may feel a dull ache in your back a day or two after you've worked your lower back. This is normal. But if the pain is sharp and so debilitating that your most upright posture looks like you're trying to duck under a fence, either you pushed yourself too far or you have a back problem.

Avoiding Mistakes When Working Your Lower Back

Few people make mistakes when they do lower-back exercises. That's because few people actually take the time to do these exercises, which is a big mistake in itself. Here are a few other common errors:

✔ **Bending too far back:** On back extensions, raise your body just a few inches, and lengthen out as much as you can. With pelvic tilts, the point is to isolate your lower-back muscles while keeping your back planted on the floor.

✔ **Performing back exercises quickly:** Always perform your back exercises slowly and carefully. If you race through them, you may cause the very back problems you're trying to prevent.

Trying Floor Exercises for the Lower Back

In this section, you follow two lower-back exercises, along with several variations of the exercises:

- ✔ Pelvic tilt
- ✔ Back extension

Pelvic tilt

The pelvic tilt is a subtle move that focuses on your lower back but also emphasizes your abdominals. This is a good exercise to do if you have a history of lower-back problems. The pelvic tilt restores mobility to tight or stiff muscles and heightens body awareness of the muscles of the lower back. It's also a great warm-up exercise for more strenuous core training.

Getting set

Lie on your back with your knees bent and feet flat on the floor about hip-width apart. Rest your arms wherever they're most comfortable (see Figure 9-10a). Start with your pelvis in a level position with the natural curve in your lower spine.

The exercise

As you exhale, draw your abdominals in toward your spine and gently press your back down, tilting your pelvis backward. Don't tilt your head up and back or hunch your shoulders (see Figure 9-10b). As you inhale, return your pelvis to a level position. This is a small move that you feel as you tilt your pelvis.

Do's and don'ts

- ✔ DO keep your head, neck, and shoulders relaxed.
- ✔ DON'T lift your lower back off the floor as you tilt your pelvis up.
- ✔ DON'T arch your back off the floor when you lower your hips back down.

Other options

Chair tilt (easier): Lie on your back and place your heels up on the seat of a chair with your knees bent at a right angle and thighs perpendicular to the floor. Then perform the exercise exactly as the basic version.

Bridge (harder): At the top of the pelvic tilt, continue peeling your spine off the floor until only your shoulder blades and shoulders remain on the floor. Work hard to keep your abdominals pulled inward to prevent your back from sagging. Hold a moment and slowly lower your body downward.

Figure 9-10:
Pelvic tilt.

Photograph by Nick Horne

Back extension

The back extension strengthens your lower-back muscles. Performing this exercise on a regular basis may help reduce lower-back pain.

Use caution if you have a history of back problems or if your lower back is bothering you right now.

Getting set

Lie on your stomach with arms straight out in front of you, palms down, and legs straight out behind you. Pull your abs in, as if you're trying to create a small space between your stomach and the floor. Your forehead can be slightly lifted off the floor keeping your gaze straight down toward the floor (see Figure 9-11a).

Rest your forehead on the floor in between repetitions to relax your neck.

Figure 9-11:
Back
extension.

Photograph by Nick Horne

The exercise

Lift your right arm and left leg a couple inches off the floor and stretch out as much as you can (see Figure 9-11b). Hold this position for five slow counts, lower back down, and then repeat the same move with your left arm and right leg. Continue alternating sides until you've completed the set.

Do's and don'ts

- ✔ DO exhale as you lift and inhale as you lower.
- ✔ DO pretend as if you're trying to touch something with your toes and fingertips that's just out of reach.
- ✔ DO pay special attention to how your lower back feels.
- ✔ DON'T lift your arms or legs more than a few inches.
- ✔ DON'T arch your lower back.

Other options

Sequential back extension (easier): If the basic version of the back extension bothers your lower back, lift and lower your right arm, and then lift and lower your left leg.

Kneeling opposite extension (easier): Kneeling on your hands and knees, extend your right arm out in front of you and your left leg out behind you. This version places less stress on the lower back and is an excellent modification for those new to lower-back training and those who feel lower-back discomfort when doing back-extension exercises.

Same-side back extension (harder): Do the same exercise while lifting your right arm and right leg at the same time.

Chapter 10

Working Your Chest

*W*hen it comes to chest exercises, you want to find a happy medium between strengthening and toning your pecs. In this chapter, you discover the importance of chest exercises and why these exercises won't transform you into Pamela Anderson or Arnold Schwarzenegger. You also get tips on choosing the order to perform your chest exercises, and avoid the most common mistakes people make when working their chest muscles.

Grasping Chest-Muscle Basics

The technical name for chest muscles is the *pectorals,* but you can shorten the term to *pecs.* You have two pec muscles:

✔ **Pectoralis major:** The pec major is a skeletal muscle that draws the arm inward and rotates it. This muscle enables you to give hugs. Whenever you pledge allegiance, your hand is covering the meat of the pectoralis major.

✔ **Pectoralis minor:** The pec minor moves the scapula forward and down and also raises the ribs. This muscle resides underneath the pec major.

Figure 10-1 shows the location of your pectorals. With the help of other muscles, such as your shoulder muscles and triceps, your pecs are in charge of a variety of pushing and hugging movements.

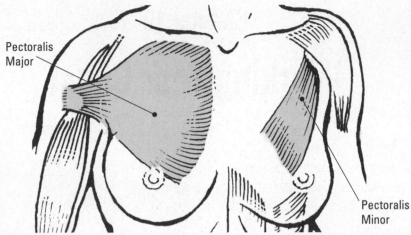

Pectoralis
Major

Pectoralis
Minor

Figure 10-1:
The pectoral
muscles.

Illustration by Kathryn Born, MA

Benefitting from Strong Pecs

This chapter may be the first time you've given your chest muscles any thought, but you've been depending on them your whole life to push things around. Now that you'll be performing chest exercises, you can be pushier than ever. Here's how you profit from training your pecs:

✔ **Real-life benefits:** You get more oomph when you push a lawn mower or a full shopping cart with two kids hanging off the end — or when you wrap your arms around your spouse.

✔ **Injury prevention:** Your chest muscles attach to your shoulder joint. So, with strong pecs, you're less likely to injure your shoulders while rearranging your furniture or picking up your kids or grandkids.

✔ **The feel-good factor:** Chest exercises may make a woman's breasts appear perkier, although keep in mind that these exercises won't transform any woman from an AA cup to a DD cup or vice versa. As for men: Pec training makes your chest fuller. However, both sexes need to maintain realistic expectations about chest exercises.

Getting a Chest Workout

You can change the feel and focus of many chest exercises by adjusting the angle of the bench you use. (See Chapter 4 for descriptions of various benches.) Performing chest exercises on a flat bench emphasizes those fibers in the center of your chest. When you adjust the bench a few degrees to an incline position, you shift the focus of the exercise to the fibers in your upper chest and shoulder muscles. Doing the opposite — adjusting the bench to a decline position — concentrates the work on the lower fibers of the chest. By the way, decline exercises are probably the least important category of chest exercises because they work a relatively small portion of the pecs.

We won't be showing you how to operate one popular chest machine: the pec deck. You sit with your arms spread apart, each arm bent and placed on a pad. You push the pads toward each other, as if you're clapping in slow motion. We think the pec deck should be renamed the "pec wreck" or, more accurately, the "shoulder wreck." Pec decks place an enormous amount of pressure on the shoulder joint and rotator cuff and frequently lead to injury. What's more, they don't actually do much for your pec muscles. A safer and more effective alternative to the pec deck is the dumbbell chest fly (refer to Figure 10-5).

Because your chest muscles are among the largest in your upper body, we suggest that you perform more sets of exercises with these muscles than with the smaller muscle groups of your arms. In general, we recommend:

- **Performing 3 to 12 sets of chest exercises per workout:** True beginners should start with one set.

  By the way, when we say 12 sets, we don't mean a dozen sets of the same exercise. You may want to do three or four (or more) different exercises. And, if you're like most people who sit during the day, you need to do more sets of back exercises than chest exercises to address any muscle imbalances and prevent slouching and a collapsed chest.

- **Beginning each exercise with an easy warm-up set:** Even power lifters who bench-press 500 pounds often warm up with a 45-pound bar.

Which chest exercises should you do first? Experts argue this point, but let personal preference be your guide. Here are our recommendations:

- **Perform free-weight exercises when you're fresh.** These exercises require more concentration, strength, and control.

- **Execute flat-bench exercises before incline or decline exercises.** Experiment with the order of exercises for a couple weeks until you come up with a sequence that works for you.

- **Change the sequence from time to time.** Changing it up challenges your muscles differently. If you always do the chest fly before the dumbbell chest press, for example, you may never realize your true dumbbell-press potential because your chest muscles are always tired by the time you get to that exercise.

- **Perform 8 to 15 reps.**

Determining your *one-rep max* (the maximum amount of weight you can lift once) is somewhat of an ancient gym tradition with the bench press. Don't try this until you've been lifting weights for a month or two, and don't attempt to *max out* more often than once a week. In fact, some experts believe that maxing out once a month brings better results. When you do attempt a maximum weight, make sure that you have a *spotter* (see Chapter 5 for tips on how to be spotted). If you're going for your one-rep max, do a few warm-up sets, gradually increasing the weight.

Mistakes to Avoid When Pumping Your Pecs

Safety is important when lifting heavy weights. Your form is more important than ever. Because you're working such a large muscle group, you'll have the tendency to want to overcompensate with your arms, shoulders, and other body parts. Isolating the chest muscles can be tricky, so read on to learn a few mistakes to avoid as you work your pecs.

In addition to lifting the proper amount of weight, take the following precautions when working your chest:

- **Don't lock your elbows.** In other words, don't straighten your arms to the point that your elbows snap. This arm extension puts too much pressure on the elbow joints and leads to *tendonitis* (inflammation of the elbow joint itself). When you straighten your arms, keep your elbows slightly relaxed.

- **Don't arch your back.** In an effort to hoist more poundage, some people arch their backs so severely that there's enough room between the back and the bench for a Range Rover to drive through. Sooner or later, this position causes a back injury. Plus, you're doing nothing to strengthen your chest muscles. Instead, you're overstraining your lower back.

- **Don't flatten your back.** In a sincere effort not to cheat, many people do the exact opposite of overarching their backs — they force their lower backs into the bench. This posture is equally bad for your back. When you lie down, make sure that a slight gap exists between your lower back and the bench, reflecting the natural arch of your lower back.

- **Don't lift your shoulder blades off the bench or backrest.** If you do this, your shoulders bear too much weight — without any support from the bench. This error is subtle but one that may be costly for your shoulder joints.

- **Don't stretch too far.** When you lie on your back and perform the bench press, you may be tempted to lower the bar all the way to your chest.

Becoming Skilled at Chest Exercises

If you're following the chest exercises laid out in this chapter, you'll be performing them in order of free weight to machine exercises. Here's a glance at the chest exercises featured in this chapter:

- ✔ Modified push-up
- ✔ Push-up
- ✔ Bench press
- ✔ Dumbbell chest press
- ✔ Vertical chest press
- ✔ Cable crossover
- ✔ Assisted dip

Modified push-up

The modified push-up strengthens your chest muscles, with additional emphasis on your shoulders and triceps.

Be extra careful if you have lower-back, shoulder, elbow, or wrist problems.

Getting set

Lie on your stomach, and bend your knees. Bend your elbows and place your palms on the floor a bit to the side and in front of your shoulders. Straighten your arms and lift your body so that you're balanced on your palms and the part of your thighs just above your knees (see Figure 10-2a). Tuck your chin a few inches toward your chest so that your forehead faces the floor. Tighten your abdominals and use your inner thigh muscles to keep your legs parallel.

The exercise

Bend your elbows and lower your entire body at once (see Figure 10-2b). Push back up to the starting position.

For an easier workout, lower only halfway down, until your arms are parallel to the floor.

Do's and don'ts

- ✔ DO keep your abdominal muscles pulled in tight throughout the exercise so that your back doesn't arch like a swaybacked horse; otherwise, you're begging for a lower-back injury.

✔ DO bring your arms to a full extension.

✔ DON'T lock your elbows at the top of the arm extension.

✔ DON'T do the dreaded head bob. That's when you dip your head toward the floor without moving any other part of your body. Talk about a giant pain in the neck!

Figure 10-2:
Modified
push-up.

Photograph by Nick Horne

Other options

Wall push-up (easier): Stand a few feet away from a wall and place your palms flat on the wall slightly wider than your shoulders. Bend your elbows and lean into the wall. Then press yourself away from the wall by straightening your arms.

Incline push-up: This version is easier than the modified push-up but harder than the wall push-up. Follow the same setup as the basic version of this exercise, but place your hands on top of a step bench that has two or three sets of risers underneath.

Negative push-up (easier): This version is harder than the modified push-up but easier than traditional push-ups (see the following section). Only perform the lowering phase of the military push-up. Slow the movement down and try to lower yourself in five counts. Lower your knees to the ground and follow the modified version when you push yourself up.

Push-up

Push-ups target your chest muscles along with the abdominal muscles and butt to give good core strength and allover toning.

Getting set

Straighten your arms and lift your body in push-up position so that you're balanced equally on your palms (see Figure 10-3a). Tuck your chin a few inches toward your chest so that your forehead faces the floor.

The exercise

Lower your body toward the floor, bending your elbows out to the side (see Figure 10-3b). Straighten your arms pressing against the floor to return to starting position. Complete ten repetitions.

Figure 10-3:
Push-up.

Photograph by Nick Horne

Do's and don'ts

- ✔ DO keep your abdominal muscles tight to help you maintain your balance.

- ✔ DO use proper breathing, inhaling as you lower and exhaling as you press back up.

- ✔ DON'T arch your back. Keep it straight and in line with your head and the rest of your body.

Bench press

The bench press, crowned the king of all chest exercises by bodybuilders, primarily works your chest muscles, with plenty of emphasis on your shoulders and triceps, too.

You may want to try a modified version of this exercise — or avoid it altogether — if you have lower-back, shoulder, or elbow problems.

Getting set

Lie on the bench with your feet flat on the floor or up on the bench if the bench is too tall. Grip the bar so your arms are evenly spaced a few inches wider than shoulder-width apart. Tuck your chin toward your chest and pull your abdominals in tight, but don't force your back into the pad or over-arch it. Lift the bar off the rack and push it directly up over your shoulders, straightening your arms without locking your elbows (see Figure 10-4a).

The exercise

Lower the bar until your elbows are slightly below your shoulders (see Figure 10-4b). The bar may or may not touch your chest — this depends on how long your arms are and how big your chest is. Press the bar back up.

Do's and don'ts

- ✔ DO remember to breathe. Exhale as you press the bar up, and inhale as you lower it.

- ✔ DON'T cheat. In other words, if you have to wiggle around or arch your back in order to hoist the bar, you're not doing much for your chest, but you're asking for lower-back injuries.

- ✔ DON'T press the bar up too high. Keep your elbows relaxed and your shoulder blades on the backrest throughout the exercise.

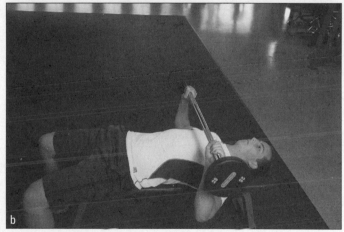

Figure 10-4:
Bench
press.

Photograph by Nick Horne

Other options

Towel chest press (easier): Roll up a large bath towel and place it across your chest. Lower the bar until it touches the towel and then press back up. This variation is good if you have shoulder problems because it reduces the range of motion and lessens the stress on the shoulder joint.

Incline bench press: Incline the bench a few inches and then do the exercise as described earlier. This version emphasizes the upper fibers of your pecs and shoulders.

Decline bench press: Do this exercise on a decline bench, with your head lower than your feet. This requires a special decline version of the bench-press station. (Some bench-press stations can set flat, incline, or decline, whereas others are fixed permanently in the decline position.)

Dumbbell chest press

The dumbbell chest press closely mimics the bench press (see the preceding section). This exercise works your chest muscles, along with your shoulders and triceps.

You may want to modify or avoid this exercise if you have shoulder, elbow, or lower-back problems.

Getting set

Lie on the bench with a dumbbell in each hand and your feet flat on the floor or up on the bench if it's more comfortable (see Figure 10-5a).

Figure 10-5:
Dumbbell chest press.

Photograph by Nick Horne

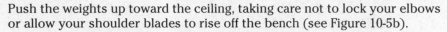

The exercise

Push the weights up toward the ceiling, taking care not to lock your elbows or allow your shoulder blades to rise off the bench (see Figure 10-5b).

Do's and don'ts

- DO allow your lower back to keep its natural arch so you have a slight gap between your lower back and the bench.

- DON'T contort your body in an effort to lift the weight; lift only as much weight as you can handle while maintaining good form.

Other options

Partial dumbbell press (easier): Lower the weights only about three quarters the distance of the basic version of this exercise. Try this version if you have elbow, shoulder, or rotator-cuff problems.

Incline chest press: Perform this exercise on an incline bench, and you use less weight than when you perform a flat bench press. You'll challenge the upper fibers of the pecs more.

Decline chest press: Do this exercise on a decline bench, with your head lower than your feet. The hardest part of this version is picking up and releasing the weights. Grab the weights while you're sitting up, hold them against your chest, and ease yourself into the decline position. When you're done with the exercise, gently ease the dumbbells off to either side to the floor. (Don't just drop them.) Better yet, ask someone to hand the weights to you at the start of the exercise and take them away when you're done.

Vertical chest press

The vertical chest-press machine focuses on your chest muscles, with additional emphasis on your triceps and shoulders. Most vertical chest-press machines have more than one grip so that you can work your chest muscles in different ways.

Use caution if you have shoulder or elbow problems.

Getting set

Sit in the machine so the center of your chest lines up with the set of horizontal handlebars. Let your feet rest on the foot bar for support. Grip the horizontal handles. Keep your abdominals tight so your upper back remains on the pad (see Figure 10-6a).

Figure 10-6:
Vertical
chest-press
machine.

a

b

Photograph by Nick Horne

The exercise

Straighten your arms, pushing the handles forward and press down on the foot bar (see Figure 10-6b). When you've completed your set, let your feet come back up with the foot bar and let your hands return to the starting position before you let go of the handlebars.

Do's and don'ts

- ✔ DO keep your neck against the backrest.
- ✔ DON'T press so quickly that your elbows snap shut and your shoulders come up off the backrest.

Other options

Different angles: You may find chest machines that position you horizontally and at many angles between horizontal and vertical. Other machines work the left and right sides independently of each other; in other words, the left and right levers of the machine aren't connected to one another, so when you raise the weight, both sides of your body have to fend for themselves. Machines with independent action are a good alternative for those with left-right muscle imbalances or those who want to combine the safety of using a machine with the feel of using free weights. Try them all for variety to challenge your chest muscles differently.

Vertical grip (harder): Use the vertical handle of your chest machine. This grip factors out a lot of the help you get from your shoulders when using the horizontal grip.

Cable crossover

The cable crossover strengthens your chest muscles with emphasis on the shoulders as well.

Be careful if you have shoulder, elbow, or lower-back problems.

Getting set

Set the pulleys on both towers of a cable machine to the top position. Clip a horseshoe handle (see Chapter 4 for description of all the different cable pulley handles) to each pulley. Stand between the towers with your legs comfortably apart and with one foot in front of the other. Grasp a handle in each hand, palms facing down and slightly forward (see Figure 10-7a). Tighten your abdominals, lean slightly forward from your hips, and relax your knees.

The exercise

Keeping a slight bend in your elbows, pull the handles down so your hands meet in the center or until one wrist crosses slightly in front of the other (see Figure 10-7b). Then slowly raise your arms up and out to the sides until your hands are level with your shoulders.

Do's and don'ts

- ✔ DO exhale deeply before bringing your hands together.

- ✔ DO initiate the move from your chest; in other words, keep your shoulders, elbows, and wrists in the same position throughout.

- ✔ DON'T forget that slight forward lean: It takes the pressure off your lower back.

Other options

Flat-bench cable fly: Set the cables to the lowest point on the towers, and place a flat bench in the center of the towers. Grasp a handle in each hand and lie on your back. Straighten your arms up directly over your shoulders and then spread your arms down and to the side until your elbows are just below shoulder level. This motion is the same one used in the flat-bench dumbbell chest fly.

One-hand crossover: Do the basic cable crossover one arm at a time. Place the unused hand on your hip or hold onto the cable tower.

Figure 10-7:
Cable
crossover.

Photograph by Nick Horne

Assisted dip

The assisted dip primarily works your chest muscles with a lot of emphasis on your shoulders and triceps, too.

> Use caution if you have elbow, shoulder, or lower-back problems.

Getting set

For this exercise, deciding which plate to put the pin in can be confusing because you follow the exact opposite rule of every other exercise. In this case, you choose *more* plates if you want the exercise to be *easier* and *fewer* plates if you want the exercise to be *harder*. The more plates you select, the more your weight is counterbalanced during the exercise. For example, if you weigh 150 pounds and you place the pin in the plate marked 100, you have to lift only 50 pounds of your body weight. But if you put the pin into the plate marked 50, you have to lift 100 pounds.

After you've set your weight, step onto the platform of the assisted dip machine. Before kneeling on the knee pad or step, grip the lower bars with your palms facing inward and straighten your arms. Kneel on the kneepad or step on the foot bar as required by the machine at your gym. Pull your abdominals in and keep your body tall (see Figure 10-8a).

Figure 10-8:
Assisted
dip.

Photograph by Nick Horne

The exercise

Lower your body until your upper arms are nearly parallel to the floor (see Figure 10-8b) and then push back up.

Do's and don'ts

✔ DO relax your shoulders so they don't hunch up by your ears.

✔ DO keep your abdominals pulled in so your back doesn't arch.

✓ DO keep your neck aligned with the rest of your spine instead of allowing your chin to jut forward.

✓ DON'T explode back to the start and snap your elbows.

✓ DON'T lower your body farther than the point at which your upper arms are parallel to the floor.

Other options

Negative-only dip (easier): If you find a traditional dip too difficult, perform only the *negative* phase: Use your muscle power to lower yourself and then jump up to the start after every repetition. However, when you jump up, take it easy on your elbows.

Traditional dip (harder): Stand facing a dip station, and place your hands on the dip bars. Hop up so your feet are off the floor. Straighten your arms and lift your body upward. Keep your legs straight, or bend your knees slightly and cross one ankle over the other. Remain tall and relaxed with your abdominals pulled inward. Bend your elbows and lower your body only until your upper arms are parallel to the floor. Straighten your arms to lift yourself back up.

Weighted dip (harder): Do the basic version of the exercise with a special waist belt designed to hold a weight plate on the end of it.

Chapter 11

Working Your Shoulders

*W*hen you move your arms in virtually any direction — up, down, backward, forward, sideways, diagonally, or in circles — your shoulders are in charge or at least involved. The ingenious design of your shoulder joint makes the shoulders one of the most mobile, versatile muscle groups in your body.

Unfortunately, their amazing capacity for movement also makes the shoulders, along with a nearby muscle group called the *rotator cuff,* particularly vulnerable to injury. This chapter shows you how to protect your shoulders by performing a variety of exercises.

Understanding the Basics of Shoulder Muscles

Your shoulder muscles (shown in Figure 11-1) are officially called the *deltoids* or *delts.* These muscles rest like a cap on top of the shoulder (the best way to see this is to hold your arm out horizontally). The delts are made up of three sections:

- **Center:** The top or medial deltoid is on top of the shoulder. When this muscle contracts, your arm moves up.

- **Front:** The front or anterior deltoid lies in front. When it contracts, your arm moves inward toward the center front.

- **Back:** When the posterior deltoid in the back contracts, your arm moves back to the midline and can even move slightly farther back.

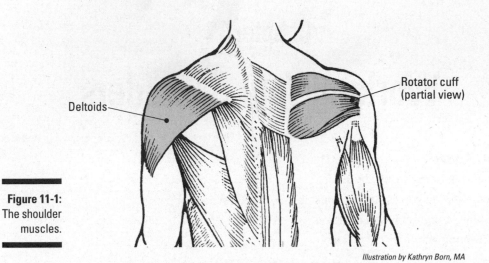

Deltoids

Rotator cuff
(partial view)

Figure 11-1:
The shoulder
muscles.

Illustration by Kathryn Born, MA

Your shoulder is able to move in so many directions because your shoulder joint is a *ball-and-socket joint:* The round head of your arm bone snaps neatly into your shoulder socket. Your hip is another ball-and-socket joint, but even that joint doesn't have the mobility that your shoulder does.

The *rotator cuff* is a group of four muscles that keep your arm from slipping out of its socket. They lie underneath your delts, performing their job in complete anonymity. Unfortunately, the rotator-cuff muscles are so anonymous that many people don't even know that these muscles exist and, therefore, don't bother to train them. The only time they seem to get any recognition is when a professional baseball pitcher is sidelined for the season by a rotator-cuff injury. Your rotator-cuff muscles stabilize your shoulder joint and enable you to twist your arm while your elbow is straight, such as when you turn your palm to face forward and then backward. They also get into the act during throwing and catching motions and when you raise your arms above your head.

Benefiting from Strong Shoulders

Your shoulders do a fair amount of work whenever you perform back and chest exercises, but performing exercises that single out your delts are also important for the following reasons:

✔ **Real-life benefits:** Strong shoulders make most arm movements easier, whether you're throwing a baseball, passing food across the table, or lifting a suitcase that's a little too heavy. Virtually every upper-body exercise involves your shoulder muscles to some extent, so strengthening your shoulders enables you to lift heavier weights for chest and back exercises.

✔ **Injury prevention:** If your shoulders are weak, they're going to take a beating even if you perform chest and back exercises perfectly. Shoulder exercises also can prevent weekend warrior–type injuries, such as a torn rotator cuff from a softball tournament, or slapping a puck into the garbage can that serves as your hockey goal. If your shoulders are weak, you can even injure yourself while opening a dresser drawer.

✔ **Self-confidence factor:** Open up any bodybuilding magazine and you see headlines such as, "Delts to Die For" or "Sexy, Strong Shoulders." Bodybuilders take their shoulder training seriously because they know that these muscles play a big part in their appearance, which, after all, is what bodybuilding is all about. Even if you don't want to build competition-level delts, you can still develop toned, shapely shoulders and reclaim your confidence to wear sleeveless shirts. (You should wear sleeveless shirts any time you please, but a toned shoulder muscle may put a little pep in your sleeveless step.)

Getting a Great Shoulder Workout

You can strengthen your shoulder muscles through four main types of shoulder movements (although dozen of ways exist). Perform the following exercises in the order that they're listed. In general, you lift the heaviest weights while pressing and the lightest weights while doing back-fly movements.

✔ **Press:** Straighten your arms up over your head. Shoulder-press exercises work the entire shoulder muscle.

✔ **Lateral raise:** Raise your arms from your sides out to shoulder level. Lateral raises focus on the top and outside portions of the muscle.

✔ **Front raise:** Raise your arms from your sides directly in front of you. Front raises work the front and top of the deltoid.

✔ **Back fly:** Bend over from the hips as far as your flexibility permits to align your lift against the pull of gravity. Your chest should be as close to parallel to the ground as possible. Raise your arms out to the sides, working the rear and outside portions of the muscle.

From time to time, vary the order of your exercises to target your weaker muscles first and to provide a variety of stimulation for the muscle group to optimize conditioning. You needn't include all four types of exercises in each shoulder workout, but you should aim to perform each type on a regular basis so you develop evenly balanced shoulder muscles.

Perform shoulder exercises with free weights rather than machines. Often, the motion feels unnatural with the machine and places excess strain on the neck. For people of diverse sizes, such as petite women, aligning the machine properly can be hard, especially on a machine that's designed for a larger man's body.

Your rotator cuff muscles are mighty susceptible to injury. Protect these muscles to some degree by

- **Using proper weight lifting form.** Follow the form guidelines within this chapter (and all chapters for that matter) for all upper-body exercises.

- **Performing internal and external rotation exercises.** This chapter includes these two exercises that you can do with dumbbells.

- **Using band exercises.** Rotator cuff exercises that you can do at home or on the road with a rubber exercise band are found in Chapter 23.

Knowing Mistakes to Avoid When Training Your Shoulders

For many avid weight lifters, shoulder injuries don't happen overnight. We know countless people who've lifted for years, sometimes ignoring minor shoulder pain, and then — pop! — they're finished. But what they perceive as a sudden injury is actually the result of years of overuse and poor form. Avoid the common mistakes to keep your shoulders strong and healthy.

Exaggerating the movement

If the instructions say lift the dumbbell "to shoulder height," don't lift the weight up to the ceiling, because lifting your arm to this unnatural angle adds undue stress to the joint with little advantage for increasing muscle tone. In other words, the risk of injury from lifting higher outweighs any minimal benefit of getting slightly stronger by increasing the size of the movement.

Arching your back

When you perform shoulder exercises while sitting on a vertical bench, make sure that you only have a slight gap between the small of your back and the backrest. Yes, arching your back gives you more leverage to lift heavier weights, but arching also cheats the muscles that you're targeting and puts your lower back in a vulnerable position — causing injury.

Rocking back and forth

When you perform shoulder exercises while standing, relax your knees and maintain a tall posture. Many people lock their knees and lean back, a posture that your lower-back muscles don't appreciate. If you're moving any body parts other than your arms, you aren't targeting your shoulder muscles, and you're using too much weight.

Doing behind-the-neck shoulder exercises

You're likely to see lifters press a barbell overhead and then lower it behind the neck rather than in front. Some shoulder machines also involve behind-the-neck movements. Stay away from these exercises! They require a severe backward rotation of your arm, placing your shoulder and rotator cuff muscles in a weakened and precarious position. The movement also compresses the top of your arm bone into your shoulder socket, which tends to grind the bones and place your rotators under a great deal of additional stress. Always keep in mind that the benefit of any exercise should outweigh the risk.

Practicing Shoulder Exercises

Here's a preview of the shoulder exercises coming up:

- Dumbbell shoulder press
- Lateral raise
- Front raise
- Back delt fly
- Internal and external rotation
- Shoulder-press machine

Dumbbell shoulder press

The dumbbell shoulder press targets the top and center of your shoulder muscles. This exercise also works your upper back and triceps.

Use caution if you have lower-back, neck, or elbow problems.

Getting set

Hold a dumbbell in each hand and sit on a bench with back support. Plant your feet firmly on the floor about hip-width apart. Bend your elbows and raise your upper arms to shoulder height so the dumbbells are at ear level. Pull your abdominals in so there's a slight gap between the small of your back and the bench. Place the back of your head against the pad (see Figure 11-2a).

The exercise

Push the dumbbells up and in until the ends of the dumbbells are nearly touching directly over your head (see Figure 11-2b) and then lower the dumbbells back to ear level.

Figure 11-2:
Dumbbell
shoulder
press.

Photograph by Nick Horne

Do's and don'ts

- ✔ DO keep your elbows relaxed at the top instead of locking them.

- ✔ DO stop lowering the dumbbells when your elbows are at or slightly below shoulder level.

- ✔ DON'T let your back arch a great degree off the back support.

- ✔ DON'T wiggle or squirm around in an effort to press the weights up.

Other options

Palms facing in dumbbell press (easier): Do this exercise with your palms facing each other. This position allows your wrists and biceps muscles to help execute the movement.

Lateral raise

The lateral raise works the center of your shoulder muscles. Make sure that you use stellar technique if you have neck or lower-back problems.

Getting set

Hold a dumbbell in each hand and stand up tall with your feet as wide as your hips. Bend your elbows a little, turn your palms toward each other, and bring the dumbbells together in front of the tops of your thighs (see Figure 11-3a). Pull your abdominals in.

The exercise

Lift your arms up and out to the side until the dumbbells are just below shoulder height (see Figure 11-3b). Slowly lower the weights back down.

It may help to imagine that you're pouring two pitchers of lemonade on the floor in front of you.

Do's and don'ts

- ✔ DO lift from the shoulders; in other words, keep your elbows stationary.

- ✔ DON'T arch your back, lean backward, or rock back and forth to lift the weights.

- ✔ DON'T raise the weights above shoulder height.

Figure 11-3:
Lateral
raise.

Other options

Bent-arm lateral raise (easier): Start with your arms bent at a 90-degree angle, palms facing each other, and the dumbbells in front of your body. Keeping your elbows bent at 90 degrees throughout the motion, lift the weights until your elbows are at shoulder height.

The bent-arm lateral raise exercise doesn't give your shoulders quite as good a workout as the basic version, but if you have weak shoulders or a history of shoulder problems, you can do this modified version of the lateral raise exercise.

Seated lateral raise: For a change of pace, perform the lateral raise exercise sitting on a bench, starting with your arms hanging straight down at your sides, elbows slightly bent.

Thumbs-up lateral raise (easier): Do this movement with your palms facing forward and your thumbs pointing upward. This version places the least stress on your rotator cuff muscles and is often used in physical therapy.

Front raise

The front raise isolates the front portion of your shoulder muscles. Use caution if you have a history of lower-back or neck discomfort.

Getting set

Hold a dumbbell in each hand and stand up tall with your feet as wide as your hips. Let your arms hang down at your sides — elbows relaxed and palms facing back. Stand up tall, pull your abdominals in, and relax your knees (see Figure 11-4a).

The exercise

Raise your left arm up to shoulder height (see Figure 11-4b) and then lower it back down. Then do the same with your right arm. Continue alternating until you complete the set. Or, for more of a challenge, do all your reps with one arm and then the other.

Figure 11-4:
Front raise.

a

b

Photograph by Nick Horne

Do's and don'ts

✔ DO keep your elbows slightly bent as you perform the exercise.

✔ DON'T arch, lean back, or wiggle around in an effort to lift the weight.

✔ DON'T lift your arm above shoulder height.

Other options

Palms-up front raise: Turn your palm up and do the exercise exactly as it's described in the basic front raise. Try this version if you're prone to shoulder or rotator cuff injuries.

Diagonal front raise (harder): When the dumbbell is at shoulder height, move your arm a few inches in until the weight is in front of the top of your chest. Skip this version if you have chronic shoulder problems.

Seated front raise (harder): Perform the front raise sitting on a bench with a back support; this position removes *any* possibility of cheating!

Lying front raise (harder): Lie on your stomach on a bench holding a dumbbell in each hand, arms straight in front of you (or slightly out to the side), palms facing in and thumbs up. Raise the dumbbells as high as you comfortably can but no higher than shoulder level. You'll have to use a much lighter weight for this version of the exercise. You can also incline the bench and do the same exercise.

Back delt fly

The back delt fly is an excellent move for strengthening the back of the shoulders and upper back and for improving your posture.

Getting set

Hold a dumbbell in each hand and sit on the edge of a bench. Lean forward from your hips so your upper back is flat and parallel to the floor. Let your arms hang down so your palms are facing each other with the weights behind your calves and directly under your knees (see Figure 11-5a). Pull your chin back and in and draw your abdominals inward.

The exercise

Raise your arms up, bending your elbows a few inches as you bring your arms out to the side until your elbows are level with your shoulders (see Figure 11-5b). Squeeze your shoulder blades together as you lift. Slowly lower your arms back down.

Figure 11-5:
Back delt
fly.

Photograph by Nick Horne

Do's and don'ts

✔ DO keep your chin tilted slightly toward your chest throughout the motion so your head and neck don't drop forward.

✔ DO lean forward from your hips instead of rounding your back.

✔ DON'T allow the rest of your body to move as you do the exercise.

Other options

Back delt row: Use the same starting position except orient your palms backward. As you lift the weights, you need to bend your elbows more than in the basic version.

Standing back delt fly: Do the same exercise while standing with your feet placed as wide as your hips. Lean forward so that your torso forms a 45-degree angle with the floor. Keep your abs pulled in to protect your lower back and resist any rocking movement.

Dumbbell shoulder external rotation

External rotation focuses on your rotator cuff muscles, but these exercises also work your shoulder muscles.

If these movements bother your neck, try resting your head on your outstretched arm.

Getting set

Holding a dumbbell in your right hand, lie on the floor on your left side. Bend your right elbow to a 90-degree angle and tuck it firmly against your side so your palm faces forward. Pull your abdominals in. Bend your left elbow and rest the side of your head in your left hand (see Figure 11-6) or lie on your outstretched left arm.

Figure 11-6:
Dumbbell shoulder external rotation.

Photograph by Nick Horne

The exercise

Keeping your right elbow glued to your side, raise your right hand as far as you comfortably can (the distance depends on your flexibility). Slowly lower the weight back toward the floor. Complete an equal number of repetitions with each arm.

Other options

Band external rotation: See Chapter 23 for a version of this exercise that you can do with exercise bands.

Traffic cop (harder): Hold a weight in both hands and stand with your feet as wide as your hips. Bend your elbows and raise your arms up to shoulder height (in the classic stick-'em-up position). Keeping your elbows still, rotate your forearms down until your palms are facing behind you and then rotate back up to the start.

Dumbbell shoulder internal rotation

Internal rotation also targets your rotator cuff muscles and works your shoulder muscles. This exercise uses a hinging motion where your arm is reaching down to the floor. Your shoulder is the hinge.

Again, if these movements bother your neck, try resting your head on your outstretched arm.

Getting set

Lie on your back with your dumbbell in your right hand and your left arm straight along your side with the palm facing down. Bend your elbow so your forearm is perpendicular to the floor and your palm is facing inward.

The exercise

Maintaining a 90-degree angle in your elbow, lower the dumbbell away from your body until you feel a slight stretch (see Figure 11-7). Lift your dumbbell back up toward your body.

Figure 11-7:
Dumbbell
shoulder
internal
rotation.

Photograph by Nick Horne

Do's and don'ts

- ✔ DO imagine that your shoulder is the hinge of a door that's opening and closing.
- ✔ DO perform the exercise gently and smoothly.
- ✔ DON'T tighten up your neck and face.
- ✔ DON'T throw the weight up.
- ✔ DON'T force the weight farther than your natural flexibility allows.

Other options

Band internal rotation: See Chapter 23 for a version of this exercise that you can do with exercise bands.

Traffic cop (harder): Hold a weight in both hands and stand with your feet as wide as your hips. Bend your elbows and raise your arms up to shoulder height (in the classic stick-em-up position). Keeping your elbows still, rotate your forearms down until your palms are facing behind you and then rotate back up to the start.

Incline shoulder-press machine

The shoulder-press machine is a good overall shoulder exercise because it challenges all your shoulder muscles. It also works your triceps and upper back.

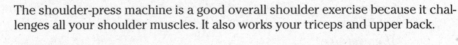

Take extra caution if you're prone to neck, elbow, or lower-back problems.

Getting set

Set your seat height so the machine's pulley is even with the middle of your shoulder. Hold on to each of the front handles (see Figure 11-8a). Pull your abdominals in tight but leave a slight, natural gap between the small of your back and the seat pad.

The exercise

Press the handles up without locking your elbows (see Figure 11-8b). Lower your arms until your elbows are slightly lower than your shoulders.

Do's and don'ts

- ✔ DO relax your shoulders and keep them well below your ears, especially while your arms are straightened fully.
- ✔ DON'T arch your back or wiggle around in an effort to lift the weight.
- ✔ DON'T thrust upward with more force than necessary; this strain puts a lot of stress on your elbows.

Figure 11-8:
Incline
shoulder-
press
machine.

Photograph by Nick Horne

Other options

Many shoulder machines have arms that work "independently" of each other.
That is, the left and right sides aren't connected, so each arm handles its own
share of the load. If your gym has this option, we recommend that you give it
a try. You'll get the structure and support that a machine has to offer but also
develop balance and uniform strength as you would with free weights.

Chapter 12

Working Your Arms

Maintaining muscles in the arms can be difficult because you lose muscle tone as you age. Beautifully sculpted arms are a sure sign that someone has been working hard. Even with all the lifting, pulling, and picking up you do throughout the day, you still need to lift weights to keep your arms toned and strong. This chapter tells you how you can develop strong, firm arms.

Understanding Arm-Muscle Basics

Your *biceps* muscle spans the front of your upper arm. Hang out in any gym and you'll see people flexing these muscles in the mirror, usually when they think that nobody's watching. The main job of your biceps (nicknamed your *bis* or your *guns*) is to bend your arm; in gymspeak, this motion is called *curling* or *flexing*.

Your *triceps,* located directly opposite your biceps, spans the rear of your upper arm. The biceps and triceps, like many muscle groups, work together in pairs. When you squeeze your biceps, your triceps relaxes and your arm bends, and when you squeeze your triceps, your biceps relaxes and your arm straightens. Maintaining a good balance of strength in the relationship between the two muscles is important so that one muscle doesn't dominate the other. That's why you need to train both.

Another group of arm muscles allows your wrists to move in a variety of ways. To spare you some jargon, we're going to refer to these as your *wrist muscles.* These muscles let you bend your wrist up, arch it down, twirl it in a circle, tilt it left and right, and turn your palm up or down. One of the most important jobs of the wrist muscles is to keep the wrist stable and the wrist joint flat or neutral. If your wrists are weak, the wrist muscles can bend at inopportune times (like when you're holding a 100-pound barbell over your chest). Weak wrists also mean that you can't get a grip — on a baseball bat, a stubborn weed, or a can of mushroom soup — and leave you prone to conditions like *carpal tunnel syndrome,* an inflammation of your wrist nerves.

Figure 12-1 helps you locate all your arm muscles.

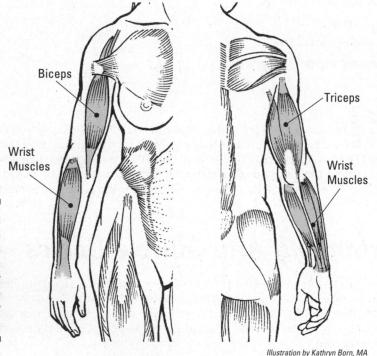

Figure 12-1:
Your arm muscles from the front view (left) and the rear view (right).

Illustration by Kathryn Born, MA

Gaining Strong Arms

Because we use our arms so often in daily life, we tend to take our arm muscles for granted. However, giving these muscles extra attention in the weight room really does pay off.

✔ **Attaining real-life benefits:** Your arms are the link between your upper body and the rest of the world. If your arms are weak, your larger, upper-body muscles can't work to full capacity. You're only as strong as your weakest link. For example, the lat pull-down, a back exercise described in Chapter 9, mainly requires back strength, but weak biceps limit your ability to do this exercise. With stronger triceps, you can more effectively challenge your chest muscles in exercises such as the push-up or the bench press. Strong wrists are crucial for many weight-lifting exercises and for activities outside of the gym: gripping a golf club, shuffling cards, or working at your computer keyboard without pain.

✔ **Preventing injury:** Strong arms help protect your elbows from harm. Carry around a heavy briefcase with a straight arm long enough and eventually your elbow starts to ache. With stronger arm muscles, you can haul that briefcase around longer without pain, and you're less likely to get *tennis elbow,* which is inflammation of the elbow joint. Powerful arms also minimize your chances of soreness or injuries when you perform weight-lifting exercises or when you lift a dumbbell, barbell, or weight plate off of a rack. Strong wrists, in particular, help you avoid carpal tunnel syndrome. Repetitive movements such as typing, scanning items at the grocery checkout, or using the mouse of your computer can cause this painful and sometimes debilitating condition.

✔ **The confidence factor:** The feel-good factor: We tend to equate toned biceps with masculine strength. Popeye's biceps are almost the size of his head. In women, the jury is still out. Popular opinion can't come to a consensus on whether it prefers women with toned arms or weak arms. The bottom line is that strong arms help you to enjoy life better and toned muscles look healthy. Society's judgment about whether men and women should have big or small muscles is likely to change with the winds of fashion, but being healthy and strong and feeling great are always positive.

Getting a Great Arm Workout

Your arm muscles are smaller than your chest, back, and shoulder muscles, so you can spend less time training them and still get great results. If your goal is to increase your arm strength and develop some tone, one to three sets per arm muscle will suffice. You need to do five to eight sets per arm muscle if you want to develop maximum strength and significant size.

Give your biceps and triceps equal time. If one of these muscle groups is disproportionately stronger than the other, you're more prone to elbow injuries. Chances are, you'll enjoy training one of these muscle groups more than the other.

The psychology of weight training can't always be explained, but if you do prefer training one of these muscle groups over the other, work your least favorite group first so you're not tempted to blow it off. If you do some of the split routines described in Chapter 19, you can work these muscle groups on different days.

Always work your arm muscles last in your upper body workouts. Otherwise, they may be too tired to help out when you do the big-money exercises for your much larger chest and back muscles.

Avoiding Mistakes When Training Your Arms

Some people use such herky-jerky form when they perform arm exercises that they look like people dancing under a strobe light. Keep the following tips in mind when training your arms:

- ✔ **Don't cheat.** If you contort your whole body to lift the weight, you work your whole body, not your arms. Rocking back and forth is also a great way to throw out your lower back. Think about how you'll feel explaining to your friends that you wrenched your back while exercising your arms.

- ✔ **Go easy on the elbows.** Exercise captions throughout this chapter tell you to straighten your arms. This, however, doesn't mean snapping your elbows into a fully straightened position.

- ✔ **Keep your elbows still.** When your elbows veer out to the side during many biceps and triceps exercises, you're able to lift more weight. However, this is only because you have more leverage; your arms aren't getting any stronger. When you're doing biceps exercises, you may also have a tendency to pull your arms and elbows forward to lift the weight. You can't avoid this extra movement completely, but keep it to a minimum.

Practicing Arm Exercises

Here's a list of the exercises for strengthening your arms:

- ✔ **Biceps exercises:** Barbell biceps curl, alternating biceps curl, and arm-curl machine

- ✔ **Triceps exercises:** Triceps pushdown, triceps kickback, bench dip, and triceps-dip machine

Barbell biceps curl

The barbell biceps curl targets your biceps.

Be especially careful if you have elbow problems. Whenever you add weight and bend a joint, it increases the stress to that joint. Therefore, if you have a weakened joint, you need to exercise extreme care not to overdo it and cause an injury. If you have lower-back problems, you may want to choose a seated biceps exercise instead.

Getting set

Hold a barbell with an underhand grip and your hands about shoulder-width apart. Stand with your feet as wide as your hips, and let your arms hang down so the bar is in front of your thighs (see Figure 12-2a). Stand up tall with your abdominals pulled in and knees relaxed.

The exercise

Bend your arms to curl the bar almost up to your shoulders (see Figure 12-2b), and then slowly lower the bar *almost* to the starting position.

Figure 12-2:
Barbell
biceps curl.

Photograph by Nick Horne

Do's and don'ts

- ✔ DON'T swing your elbows out wide as you bend your arm to raise the weight. Keep your elbows close to your body *without* supporting them on the sides of your stomach for leverage.

- ✔ DON'T just let the weight fall back to the starting position. Lower it slowly and with control.

Other options

Reverse-grip biceps curl (harder): Do the basic version of the barbell biceps curl holding the bar with an overhand grip. You feel this exercise more in your wrists. (Hint: Use a lighter weight for this version.)

Cable biceps curl: Place the cable on the setting closest to the floor and attach a short or long straight bar. Hold the bar with an underhand grip and stand about a foot away from the cable tower. Curl the weight up and down exactly as in the basic version of the barbell biceps curl.

Double biceps curl: Hold a dumbbell in each hand with your palms facing up, elbows resting lightly against your sides, and arms hanging down. Curl the dumbbells up and down together as if they were a barbell.

Alternating biceps curl

The alternating biceps curl exercise helps balance out the strength in both arms. By pulling the weights up through the midline of your body, you also strengthen your abdominals muscles.

Getting set

Hold your dumbbells with an underhand grip and your hands about shoulder-width apart. Stand with your feet as wide as your hips, and let your arms hang down so the weights are in front of your thighs (see Figure 12-3). Stand up tall with your abdominals pulled in and knees relaxed.

The exercise

Pull in your abdominals as you slowly bring your right weight toward your right shoulder (see Figure 12-3). Hold for a few seconds and then release the weight back down to your right side. Repeat on your left side. Repeat for 2 sets of 10 repetitions.

Do's and don'ts

- ✔ DO contract your abs before lifting them to your shoulder.

- ✔ DO concentrate on your biceps muscle as you do this exercise.

- ✔ DON'T jerk the weights up to your shoulders.

Figure 12-3:
Alternating
biceps curl.

a

b

Photograph by Nick Horne

Other options

Hammer curl: Using dumbbells, start with palms facing in and keep your palms facing in throughout the motion. Imagine that you're pounding nails into a board with two large hammers. This version of the exercise puts more emphasis on your forearm muscles, as well as some of the muscles that reside underneath the biceps.

Zottman curl (harder): Instead of beginning with palms facing back, begin with palms facing front with an underhand grip. As you curl your arm upward, rotate your palm in toward your body and bring it up and across to the opposite shoulder. This version of the dumbbell curl is slightly harder than the basic version.

Seated biceps curl: If you find yourself cheating too much even with light weights, try sitting on a bench or a chair.

Triceps kickback

The triceps kickback works your triceps.

Use caution if you have elbow or lower-back problems.

Getting set

Hold a dumbbell in your right hand, and stand next to the long side of your bench. Lean forward at the hips until your upper body is at a 45-degree angle to the floor, and place your free hand on top of the bench for support. Bend your right elbow so your upper arm is parallel to the floor, your forearm is perpendicular to the floor, and your palm faces in (see Figure 12-4a). Keep your elbow close to your waist. Pull your abdominals in and relax your knees.

The exercise

Keeping your upper arm still, straighten your arm behind you until the end of the dumbbell is pointing down (see Figure 12-4b). Slowly bend your arm to lower the weight. When you've completed the set, repeat the exercise with your left arm.

Do's and don'ts

- ✔ DO keep your abdominals pulled in and your knees relaxed to protect your lower back.

- ✔ DON'T lock your elbow at the top of the movement; do straighten your arm but keep your elbow relaxed.

- ✔ DON'T allow your upper arm to move or your shoulder to drop below waist level.

Figure 12-4:
Triceps
kickback.

a

b

Photograph by Nick Horne

Other options

Cable triceps kickback: Put the pulley on the topmost setting and attach a horseshoe handle. Grasping the handle in one hand, position yourself in the same way described in the basic kickback, and perform the same exercise. You may have to step a foot or two away from the cable tower to prevent the cable from going slack.

Triceps kickback with a twist (harder): As you straighten your arm, twist it so that at the top of the movement, your palm faces up.

Arm-curl machine

The arm-curl machine focuses on your biceps.

Be careful if you've had elbow injuries.

Getting set

Adjust the seat so when you sit down and extend your arms straight out and angled down, your shoulders are above your arms. Sit down and grasp a handle in each hand with an underhand grip (see Figure 12-5a).

The exercise

Bend your elbows and pull the handles up toward your ears and in toward your shoulders (see Figure 12-5b), and then slowly lower the handles back down with control.

Do's and don'ts

- ✔ DO sit up tall and make an effort to pull exclusively with your arms as opposed to hunching up your shoulders or leaning back.

- ✔ DON'T use a chest pad to help lift the weight. If there's a pad, use it for light support only.

Other options

Some gyms have arm-curl machines that do a fair job of mimicking dumbbell work: The two sides aren't connected so each arm has to do the work of lifting the weight. This type of machine is a good substitute or supplement for free weight work.

Figure 12-5:
Arm-curl
machine.

a

b

Photograph by Nick Horne

Triceps pushdown

The triceps pushdown targets your triceps.

Pay special attention to your form if you have elbow problems. Standing up straight with your abdominal muscles pulled in helps you avoid lower-back problems.

Getting set

Set the pulley of the cable at the topmost setting and attach a straight or U-shaped bar. Grasp the bar with your palms facing down and your hands about a thumb's distance from the center of the bar. You can stand either with your feet parallel or with one foot slightly in front of the other. Bend your elbows so your forearms are parallel to the floor and your elbows are alongside your waist (see Figure 12-6a). You can lean *slightly* forward at the hips, but keep your abdominals pulled in and your knees relaxed.

The exercise

Push the bar straight down, keeping your elbows close to your sides (see Figure 12-6b). Then bend your arms to allow the bar to rise slowly back to starting position.

Figure 12-6:
Triceps
pushdown.

a

b

Photograph by Nick Horne

Do's and don'ts

- ✔ DO push down smoothly, exerting the same amount of pressure with both hands so both sides of the bar travel down evenly.

- ✔ DON'T lean too far forward or too heavily on the bar.

- ✔ DON'T allow your elbows to splay out to the sides, especially as you push down.

- ✔ DON'T let your arms fly back up as you return the bar to the starting position. Concentrate on controlling the bar.

Other options

One-hand triceps pushdown: Attach the horseshoe, and grasp it with one hand in an underhand grip. (You can also use an overhand grip, although it's tougher.) Place your other hand on your hip. Straighten your arm, pushing the handle until it's alongside your hip. Then slowly raise the handle back up.

Rope attachment (harder): Use the rope attachment, and move your hands a few inches apart as you press the rope down. You may need to use less weight with the rope than you do with a bar.

Bench dip

The bench dip is one of the few triceps exercises that strengthen other muscles, too — in this case, the shoulders and chest.

Be careful if you have wrist, elbow, or shoulder problems.

Getting set

Sit on the edge of a bench with your legs together and straight in front of you, pointing your toes upward. Keeping your elbows relaxed, straighten your arms, place your hands so you can grip the underside of the bench on either side of your hips, and slide your butt just off the front of the bench so your upper body is pointing straight down (see Figure 12-7a). Keep your abdominals pulled in and your head centered between your shoulders.

The exercise

Bend your elbows and lower your body in a straight line. Hold for a few beats and then push yourself back up (see Figure 12-7b).

Figure 12-7:
Bench dip.

Photograph by Nick Horne

Do's and don'ts

✔ DO try to keep your wrists straight rather than bent backwards.

✔ DO keep hips and back (as you lower) as close to the bench throughout the motion.

✔ DON'T simply thrust your hips up and down, a common mistake among beginners. Make sure that your elbows are moving.

Other options

Bent-leg bench dip (easier): Instead of extending your legs out in front of you, bend your knees at a right angle so you're positioned as if you're sitting in a chair.

Feet-up bench dip (harder): Place your feet on another chair of equal height. Or, for an even tougher version, place a weight plate or dumbbell on your lap.

Triceps-dip machine

The triceps-dip machine targets your triceps and, to some extent, your shoulder and chest muscles.

Take special care if you have shoulder, elbow, or neck problems.

Getting set

Set the seat height so that when your arms are fully bent, your elbows are at or below chest level. Sit in the seat with your feet on the bar foot rest or flat on the floor. Grasp a handle in each hand so your elbows are bent and your palms are facing in. Pull your abdominals in and sit with your back, buttocks, and shoulder blades against the back support (see Figure 12-8a).

The exercise

Press the handles down until your arms are straight (see Figure 12-8b). Slowly bend your arms until your elbows return to the starting position.

Do's and don'ts

✔ DO keep your shoulders relaxed instead of hunching them up near your ears.

✔ DO keep your wrists in line with your forearm instead of bending them outward.

✔ DON'T slam your arms or lock your elbows.

Figure 12-8:
Triceps-dip
machine.

Photograph by Nick Horne

Other options

Different grips: Most triceps-dip machines have the option of a narrow or a wide grip. Start with the wide grip because you're more likely to use correct form. However, when you become more proficient with this machine, the inside grip does an excellent job of isolating the triceps muscles.

Modified triceps-dip machine: You can raise the seat higher to restrict the distance your arms travel. This variation is an excellent option for those with neck and shoulder problems because the raised seat keeps you from raising your arms too high and ensures that the neck and shoulders won't be hunched and tight.

Triceps-extension machine: Some gyms have a triceps-extension machine rather than a triceps-dip machine. The extension machine works the muscles the same way except that you start with your arms at shoulder height with your elbows resting on a pad; then you press the handles, straightening your arms out in front of you instead of downward.

Chapter 13

Working Your Abdominals

Sitting, driving, and slouching lead to weak abdominal muscles. And with weak abdominals comes a weak lower back. Strengthening the abs or abdominals works wonders for your entire body. Better posture, better balance, and feeling more stable with all your movements are the results you can expect from building strong abdominals.

In this chapter, we give you some fantastic abdominal crunches that you can do while lying on your back or on your side. They will help you build strength in your abdominals where you need it most and will help support all your movements.

Introducing Abdominal-Muscle Basics

At this point, every household in America probably knows that the abdominal muscles are collectively referred to as the abs. Keep in mind that your abs aren't just in front of your body but wrap around your body. This fact is important in training because many people only seem to be concerned with training what they see — the front and center — but your abs cover much more of your body.

You have four abdominal muscles:

✔ *Rectus abdominis:* This is the largest abdominal muscle and runs from your breastbone to your pubic bone, a few inches below your belly button. The rectus abdominis

  • Curls your spine forward when performing crunches.

  • Keeps your spine still when you move other parts of your body, such as when you lift a heavy box off the floor.

✔ ***Obliques, internal and external:*** These muscles run diagonally up and down your sides. Your obliques

- Help your rectus abdominis curl your spine forward.

- Enable you to twist and bend to the side.

- Provide lower back support.

✔ ***Transversus abdominis:*** The transversus abdominis sits directly beneath the rectus abdominis and is the deepest of all your abdominal muscles. This muscle

- Is continuously working when you're sitting and standing.

- Helps support your lower back and keep good posture.

This chapter features exercises that emphasize the rectus abdominis and the obliques. To tone the transversus abdominis while doing these exercises, breathe deeply and pull your abdominals inward as you exhale. Figure 13-1 gives you a view of your abdominal muscles. To understand more about the importance of the transversus abdominis muscle, check out Chapter 15.

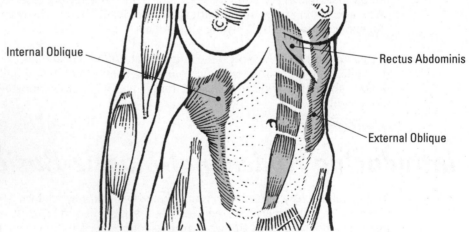

Internal Oblique — Rectus Abdominis

External Oblique

Figure 13-1: The main abdominal muscles.

Illustration by Kathryn Born, MA

Enjoying Strong Abdominals

Abdominal exercises won't eliminate fat around your midsection, but abdominal exercises serve you in many other important ways.

✔ **Real-life benefits:** Your abs play a crucial behind-the-scenes role in your daily life, supporting your spine in all your movements. For instance, as you're sitting here reading this book, you probably think your abs have very little to do. In fact, they're the reason you sit up reasonably straight in your chair, as opposed to oozing off the edge like a blob of Jell-O. Your abs are even more important when you perform more complicated movements. Strong abs enable you to stand in line or shovel dirt in your garden for a lot longer without getting a backache.

✔ **Injury prevention:** Most back pain can be reduced — perhaps even eliminated — by strengthening the abdominal muscles along with the lower back muscles and the buttocks. All your abdominals work together to support and move your spine. The most common way people injure their back is when they combine bending with rotation, especially during lifting. Strong muscles and proper movement habits prevent this and other injuries.

The "Feel Good" factor: The notion of washboard abs creates a great deal of anxiety and insecurity among many individuals. Unless you have the genetics to not store fat above your rectus abdominus muscle, the tone of your abdominals, no matter how fit you are, will show directly under your skin. Models and celebrities often have this fat vacuumed out through liposuction to reveal the muscularity underneath or they have airbrush contour tans sprayed on to give the appearance of "cut" abs. Feel good about yourself from simply knowing that you have strong abdominal muscles, regardless of whether the world can see them or not.

Preventing Mistakes When Training Your Abdominals

Mistakes are so common with abdominal exercises that the crunch has the dubious honor of qualifying for the number-one spot.

Here's a close look at abdominal training no-no's:

✔ **Avoid pulling your neck.** In other words, lift from your abs, not your neck; otherwise, you're asking for neck pain. Your head and neck shouldn't be involved in abdominal exercises at all — they're just along for the ride. Place your hands behind your head without lacing your fingers together, slide your shoulders down, and tilt your chin slightly so there's about a fist's worth of space between your chin and your chest. Your head and neck need to stay in this position throughout the exercise.

✔ **Don't move your elbows.** Your elbows have nothing to do with abdominal exercises. After you position your elbows out and slightly rounded inward, leave them there. If you pull your elbows up and in, you'll end up pulling on your neck.

✔ **Don't arch or flatten your back.** We frequently remind you to pull your abs in, but always keep a slight gap, the width of a finger or two, between the small of your back and the floor. Avoid squeezing your buttocks and jamming your lower back into the floor.

✔ **After the lift, don't forget the curl.** The crunch involves more than simply lifting your head, neck, and shoulder blades off the floor; you also need to curl forward, as if you're doubling over. Imagine how you'd move if you were lying on the floor and someone dropped a weight on your stomach. That's the movement you're aiming for here.

Discovering Exercises in This Chapter

Here's a list of the abdominal exercises in this chapter:

✔ Basic abdominal crunch

✔ Reverse crunch

✔ Oblique crunch

✔ Bent-knee side crunch

✔ Roll-down negative curl

Basic abdominal crunch

The basic abdominal crunch is the fundamental abdominal exercise that works all your abdominal muscles.

Pay special attention to your form if you have lower-back or neck problems.

Getting set

Lie on your back with your knees bent and feet flat on the floor hip-width apart. Place your hands behind your head for support. Keep your head upright and don't press it into your chest. Gently pull your abdominals inward (see Figure 13-2a).

Figure 13-2:
Basic
abdominal
crunch.

Photograph by Nick Horne

The exercise

Curl up and forward so your head, neck, and shoulder blades lift off the floor
(see Figure 13-2b). Hold for a moment at the top of the movement and then
lower slowly back down.

Do's and don'ts

- ✔ DO keep your abdominals pulled in so you feel more tension in your abs
  and so you don't overarch your lower back.

- ✔ DO curl as well as lift. For an explanation of curling, refer to the introduction to this chapter and to Chapter 8, in which you ascertain common
  crunch mistakes.

- ✔ DON'T pull on your legs with your hands.

Other options

Cross-arm crunch (easier): Fold your arms across your chest, palms down,
and tuck your chin so it rests on your hands. This position saves you the
effort of having to lift the weight of your arms.

Legs-up crunch: Keeping your knees bent, pick your legs off the floor, and cross your ankles.

Weighted crunch (harder): Hold a *lightweight* plate on your chest, or for an even greater challenge, hold a weight on top of or behind your head. Just don't press the plate down too hard.

Reverse crunch

The reverse crunch emphasizes the lower portion of your main abdominal muscles (the rectus abdominis).

Use caution if you're prone to lower-back discomfort.

Getting set

Lie on your back with your legs up, knees slightly bent, and feet in air. Rest your arms on the floor and place your fingertips behind your head. Rest your head on your hands, relax your shoulders, and pull in your abdominals (see Figure 13-3a).

The exercise

Lift your butt 1 or 2 inches off the floor so your legs lift up and a few inches backward (see Figure 13-3b). Hold the position for a moment, and then lower slowly.

Do's and don'ts

- ✔ DO keep your shoulders relaxed and down.
- ✔ DO keep the crunch movement small and precise; you don't have to lift very high to feel this exercise working.
- ✔ DO use a minimum of leg movement.
- ✔ DON'T thrust or jerk your hips.
- ✔ DON'T involve your upper body at all.
- ✔ DON'T cross your feet at the ankles.
- ✔ DON'T roll your hips so your buttocks and back come way off the floor. This type of movement involves your front hip muscles more than your abdominals.

Other options

Modified reverse crunch (easier): Hold onto the back edges of an exercise mat or stable object such as the underside of a couch or stuffed chair to help stabilize your upper body. Perform the reverse crunch.

Photograph by Nick Horne

Figure 13-3: Reverse crunch.

One-leg reverse crunch (easier): Lift one leg at a time. Bend your other knee so your foot is flat on the floor. Avoid pushing on your foot. Use your abs to lift your hips.

Incline reverse crunch (harder): Place three risers underneath one end of a step bench and one riser underneath the other end. Lie on the step with your head at the higher end of it. Stretch your arms out behind you and hold on to the undercling of the step directly behind your head. Perform a reverse crunch by lifting your hips up. This version of the reverse crunch is more difficult because you're working against gravity.

Oblique crunch

The oblique crunch works all your abdominal muscles with an emphasis on your obliques.

WARNING!

Pay special attention to form if you have a history of lower-back or neck discomfort.

Getting set

Lie on your back with your knees bent and your feet hip-width apart and flat on the floor. Place your left hand behind your head so your thumb is behind your left ear. Place your right arm along the floor beside you. Bring your elbow out to the side and round it slightly inward. Tilt your chin so your chin and your chest are a few inches apart. Pull your abdominals in (see Figure 13-4a).

a

Figure 13-4:
Oblique
crunch.

b

Photograph by Nick Horne

The exercise

As you curl your head, neck, and shoulder blades off the floor, twist your torso to the right, bringing your left shoulder toward your right knee (see Figure 13-4b). (Your elbow won't actually touch your knee.) Lower back down. Do all the repetitions on one side and then switch to the other side.

Do's and don'ts

- ✔ DO concentrate on rotating from your middle instead of simply moving your elbows toward your knees.

- ✔ DO keep both hips squarely on the ground as you twist to protect your lower back.

- ✔ DON'T pull on your neck. Support your head with your hands behind your neck.

Other options

Legs-up crunch with a twist (harder): Lift your bent knees off the floor and cross one ankle over the other.

Straight-arm crunch with a twist (harder): Reach for your opposite knee with your arm straight rather than your elbow bent. Reach past the outside edge of your knee.

Bent-knee side crunch

The bent-knee side crunch challenges your obliques to work together with all of your abdominal muscles.

Getting set

Lie on your back with your knees bent and your feet hip-width apart and flat on the floor. Drop both of your knees to one side and keep your legs stacked together. Place one hand behind your head without lacing your fingers. Your other arm will be resting on the floor with your forearm wrapped around your waist (see Figure 13-5a).

The exercise

Lift your torso off the floor using your waist muscles or obliques. Draw your ribs to your hips as you keep your knees pressed together (see Figure 13-5b). Lower back down. Do all the repetitions on one side and then switch to the other side.

Figure 13-5:
Bent-knee side crunch.

Photograph by Nick Horne

Do's and don'ts

✔ DO keep your torso rotated at the waist and your legs together.

✔ DO keep your head, neck, and shoulders relaxed.

✔ DO move slowly and take the time to feel your abs working.

✔ DON'T pull on your neck or touch your elbow to your knee.

Other options

Weighted bent-knee side crunch (harder): Hold a *lightweight* plate or dumbbell on your chest, or for an even greater challenge, hold a weight on top of or behind your head. Just don't press the plate down too hard.

Roll-down negative curl

The roll-down negative curl focuses on the hardest part of the crunch — the lowering phase.

Pay special attention to your form if you have lower-back or neck problems.

Getting set

Sit with your knees bent and feet flat on the floor hip-width apart. Reach forward and place your hands on the outside of your thighs. Slide your shoulders down and tilt your chin slightly so there's a few inches of space between your chin and your chest. Gently pull your abdominals inward (see Figure 13-6a).

The exercise

Tuck your pelvis and slowly lower back as far as you can go and keep your feet on the ground (see Figure 13-6b). Hold for a moment and then curl slowly back up.

Figure 13-6: Roll-down negative curl.

Photograph by Nick Horne

Do's and don'ts

- ✔ DO keep your abdominals pulled in so that you feel more tension in your abs.

- ✔ DO curl as well as lift. For an explanation of curling, refer to the introduction to this chapter.

- ✔ DON'T hunch or collapse your shoulders.

Other options

Hands on chest negative curl (harder): Fold your arms across your chest, palms down and tuck your chin in slightly. This position increases the weight of your upper body.

Hands behind head negative curl (harder): Place your hands behind your head without lacing your fingers. This version further increases the weight of your upper body.

Spray tanning and etching those perfect abs

If you've seen the popular TV show *Dancing with the Stars,* you're familiar with the trick of spray tanning. Each week, the dancers get darker and darker and they look more and more sleek, don't they? Yes, a lot of it has to do with their dance training, which does work their abs for weeks on end, but the finishing touch is the spray tan!

Much better than going out in the sun these days, visiting a tanning salon that offers spray tanning is the hottest trend. Although you have to stand without a bathing suit in a booth while someone of the same sex sprays you with something that looks like a blow-dryer (you can wear a bathing suit but it does leave a stain),

spray tanning is painless and super quick! Costing anywhere from $40 to $50 a session, your new spray tan will last around ten days, depending on how often you shower or swim. You'll want to shower first and exfoliate after or wash with a loofah before you get a spray tan so it goes on evenly and lasts longer.

For best results, we suggest doing the workout in this chapter two to three times a week for the next month and then go for your new spray tan. You'll see a bigger difference in your tummy after you shore up your core a bit and — believe it or not — they can actually etch a line down the middle of your rectus abdominus or midsection to make it look like you have a six-pack.

Chapter 14

Working Your Butt and Legs

Your butt and legs are the largest muscle groups in your body, and these muscles carry you everywhere you go. Having strong lower-body muscles is key to living independently into old age. Being able to stand up from chairs, pick yourself up off the floor, climb stairs, step out of cars, and even get off the toilet are key factors to enjoying life on your own. Your lower body muscles, therefore, deserve plenty of attention. If you give them their proper due in your strength training routine, they'll carry you even farther and faster. This chapter introduces you to terms such as *glutes* and *quads,* and explains how best to strengthen and tone these and other lower-body muscles.

Understanding Butt- and Leg-Muscle Basics

You have several muscles that make up the lower portion of your body. Each muscle serves a purpose and works with the other muscles in your lower body to help you move around. Take a look at the breakdown of the muscles below your waist:

✓ **Gluteus maximus (glutes):** The glutes is the granddaddy of all muscles in your body and covers your entire butt — both cheeks. The gluteus maximus straightens your legs from your hips when you stand up and propels you forward when you walk or run.

- ✔ **Hip flexors:** The muscles opposite your gluteus maximus, located at the front of your hips. Your hip flexor muscles help you lift your leg up high so you can march in a parade or step up onto a ladder. You don't need to spend much time working your hip flexors; they tend to be relatively stronger than the glutes in most people.

  When the hip flexors become disproportionately strong and tight compared to other muscles, they pull your pelvis forward and throw your hip and lower spine into an excessively arched position. This strength imbalance may contribute to poor posture and lower-back pain. Keep in mind that balanced muscle development is as important as strong muscles.

- ✔ **Abductors:** The sides, or meat, of your hips: your outer thighs. Your outer hips move your leg away from your body, like when you push off while ice-skating. The main outer hip muscle is called the *gluteus medius*.

- ✔ **Adductors:** The muscles that span the inside of your upper leg or inner thighs. They pull your leg in toward the center of your body or, when they're feeling ambitious, they sweep one leg in front of and past the other, like when you kick a soccer ball off to the side.

- ✔ **Quadriceps (quads):** The quads are located at the front of your thighs. Together these four muscles have one purpose: to straighten your leg from the knee.

- ✔ **Hamstrings (hams):** These muscles reside directly behind your thigh bone. They bend your knee, bringing your heel toward your buttocks, and help the glutes do their thing.

- ✔ **Gastrocnemius (gastroc):** The gastroc is shaped like a diamond. The gastroc allows you to rise up on your tiptoes to see over your neighbor's fence. Check out the calves of any competitive bicyclist, and you'll see precisely what this muscle looks like.

- ✔ **Soleus:** Your soleus lies directly underneath the gastroc and helps out the gastroc when your knee is bent and you need to raise your heels up, like when you're sitting at the movies and you realize that you just stepped in gum.

- ✔ **Tibialis anterior:** The partner to your calf muscles is your shin muscle, covering the front of your lower leg. Whenever you're listening to music that makes you feel like tapping your toes, you can thank this muscle for allowing you to literally make this movement happen.

Check out Figures 14-1 and 14-2 for a look at all the muscles you'll be working on when you do the exercises in this chapter.

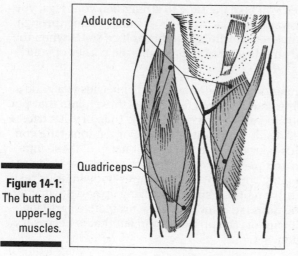
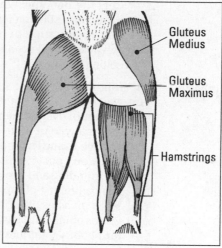

Adductors

Quadriceps

Gluteus Medius

Gluteus Maximus

Hamstrings

Figure 14-1: The butt and upper-leg muscles.

Illustration by Kathryn Born, MA

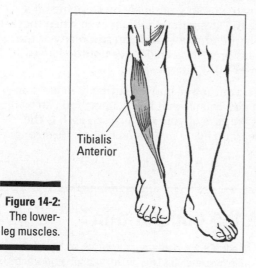
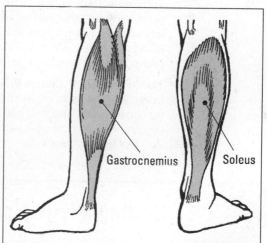

Tibialis Anterior

Gastrocnemius

Soleus

Figure 14-2: The lower-leg muscles.

Illustration by Kathryn Born, MA

Reaping the Benefits of a Strong Lower Body

According to research, the key predictor of whether you'll need to live in an assisted living facility when you're elderly is your leg strength. Here's why you need to work on those glutes, quads, hams, and calves:

✔ **Real-life benefits:** When you take the time to strengthen your legs, you have more stamina for waiting in line at the post office, racing through the grocery store to catch a small child, climbing office stairs when the elevator is broken, and standing on tiptoe to paint the corner of your ceiling.

✔ **Injury prevention:** Strengthening your lower-body muscles is a good way to preserve your hip, knee, and ankle joints — three joints that put in a lot of overtime and are particularly susceptible to injury. It's true that many joint injuries result from torn ligaments or tendons (the connective tissue that holds your bones in place), but many of these injuries won't occur in the first place if you have a strong army of muscles surrounding and protecting your joints. Often, lower-body injuries result from a lifetime of repetitive motions such as walking up and down stairs. Weak muscles allow the bones to grind down the protective cartilage more rapidly and can't support the proper alignment that is necessary for healthy joint function.

By strengthening the muscles that surround the joints, you give them the support they need to do their job day after day. With strong lower-body muscles you're less likely to sprain your ankle by stepping off a curb because your joints have the strength to hold up even when they're wrenched into positions they'd prefer to avoid. If you're already at the point where you have bad knees or a "trick ankle," it's not too late to pump some iron with your lower-body muscles.

✔ **The "Feel Good" factor:** When your lower body is strong, you feel confident because you know that you can lift that heavy item, you can walk up those stairs, and you can take care of yourself. Leg strength is the leading indicator of who will end up living in nursing homes. Be strong and feel good about you.

Getting a leg up on the competition

If you're on an aerobic mission like training for a 10K or a bike-a-thon, strong legs are even more essential. Many runners and cyclists are afraid to lift weights, figuring that they'll develop bulky legs that'll slow them down. But the reality, according to mounds of research, is that leg and butt exercises help you go farther and faster. The key is in maintaining a good balance between strength and endurance training.

One guy we know couldn't break the four-hour barrier in the marathon until he started doing lower-body weight-training exercises. His hips used to tire out at around mile 16, so he wasn't able to stretch his legs out to their full stride, and he'd shuffle through the last 10 miles. At age 49, thanks to a regular leg routine, he was finally able to cruise through the finish line in 3 hours and 50 minutes. Even if your athletic goals aren't as ambitious as running 26.2 miles, leg workouts are important. Say you simply want to ride your stationary bike for 30 minutes three times a week. Stronger legs help you pedal faster and harder so that you can burn more calories during that half-hour.

Getting a Great Lower-Body Workout

In general, work your large muscles before moving on to your small ones. So perform your lower body workouts in the following order:

1. Glutes

2. Quads

3. Hamstrings

4. Inner and outer thighs

5. Calves

6. Shins

The only exception to this rule is if you specifically want to target a smaller muscle that's lagging far behind in its strength and is creating a too notice-able weak link. If that's the case, it's a good idea to switch your exercise order around so you target the weakest muscle when it's fresh.

Do at least four or five lower-body exercises on a regular basis for balanced muscle development and visible training results. Your workouts need to include two types of exercises:

✔ *Compound exercises,* which involve several muscle groups at once

✔ *Isolation exercises,* which hone in on a single muscle group

If you're starting out with bad knees or hips, you may want to take a few weeks to simply focus on the muscles surrounding those joints. If your knees are the problem, for example, start with exercises that isolate your quads (the thigh squeeze and the leg-extension machine) and your hams (the leg-curl machine) and wait a few weeks before graduating to compound exercises (the squat and the lunge; shown in Figure 14-3 and Figure 14-4).

Here are some tips for working specific lower-body muscle groups:

✔ **Glutes:** It's tough to isolate your butt muscles because nearly every butt exercise also involves the front and/or rear thigh muscles. However, you can maximize the emphasis on your maximus with a few simple technique tricks. For instance, when you're doing the leg press or the squat, keep your toes pointed straight ahead as much as possible and your weight shifted slightly back onto your heels, especially as you press back up into the straight-leg position. The more weight you shift onto your toes, the more your quadriceps become involved. Also, when you stand up, squeeze your cheeks to make sure your glutes are really working and aren't just going along for the ride.

- ✔ **Quadriceps:** The leg extension — an exercise in which you straighten your legs from a bent position — may give you a twinge of pain in your kneecap as you near the fully extended position. In this case, stop just before your legs are straight. Many leg-extension machines have a device that stops the lever of the machine from going past the point you set. The machine may also let you start from a higher position than normal if you feel pain when you're initiating the movement.

- ✔ **Hamstrings:** The most popular way to work the hamstrings is with a leg-curl machine; you start with your legs straight and curl your heels toward your butt. You typically find this machine in three varieties: lying, seated, and standing. In this chapter, we show you how to use the lying-leg curl because it's the one you see most often and the one we generally like best (although our opinions vary from brand to brand). With some leg-curl machines, you lie flat on your stomach; others have a severe bend in the support pad. Our favorite variety has you lying at an angle with your hips above your head. Try all the hamstring machines available to you, and use any of the machines that feel comfortable.

- ✔ **Calves:** When you perform the standing calf raise, experiment with the angle of your toes to find the position that's most comfortable. But don't angle your toes too much outward or inward or you'll place too much stress on your knees and ankles. And perform calf exercises slowly. Bouncing your heels up and down causes your calf muscles to tighten and uses momentum to power the movement instead of maximally challenging your muscles.

Expect to feel sore and walk a little stiffly for a day or two after your first few lower-body workouts. Of course, any muscle that's new to weight training is likely to be sore after the first few sessions, but leg muscles seem particularly prone to this phenomenon. Start out with just your own body weight or light weights; otherwise, you may find yourself wincing in agony when you get up from the breakfast table.

Avoiding Mistakes When Working Your Lower Body

Here are the most common pitfalls to watch out for when training your butt and legs:

- ✔ **Don't play favorites.** In other words, don't work your butt muscles and neglect your thighs just because you want to fill out the back of your jeans. Strive for balance. If one lower-body muscle group is monstrously strong compared to the others, it pulls your posture out of alignment and you may end up with an injury.

✔ **Don't put your knees in jeopardy.** Avoid locking your knees when you're lifting a weight, and don't allow your knees to shoot out past your toes in the squat, lunge, or leg press. If you feel knee pain during an exercise, stop immediately. Try another exercise and return to the one that gave you trouble after you've been training for a few weeks. Or perform a simpler version of the exercise, restricting the distance you move the weight.

✔ **Don't perform more than 15 repetitions for any leg exercise for strength training.** Some people, afraid of developing bulky legs, use extremely light weights and perform 40 repetitions. You're not going to build much strength this way, and you'll probably fall asleep in the middle of a set. You also increase your chance of injury from placing too much repetitive stress on your joints.

Practicing Lower-Body Exercises

Here's a preview of the exercises we show you in this chapter:

✔ **Butt and leg exercises:** Squat, lunge, kneeling butt blaster, leg press

✔ **Quadriceps (front-thigh) exercises:** Leg-extension machine, inner- and outer-thigh machine

✔ **Hamstring (rear-thigh) exercises:** Leg-curl machine

✔ **Inner- and outer-thigh exercises:** Side lying leg lift, inner-thigh lift, inner- and outer-thigh machine

Performing Lower-Body Exercises without Machines

The following exercises do not require machines and can be done without weights.

Squat

In addition to strengthening your butt muscles, the squat also does a good job of working your quadriceps and hamstrings.

If you have hip, knee, or lower-back problems, you may want to try the modified version.

Getting set

Hold your arms straight out in front of you or hold a dumbbell in each hand for more of a challenge. Stand with your feet as wide as your hips and with your weight slightly back on your heels. Pull your abdominals in and stand up tall with square shoulders (see Figure 14-3a).

Figure 14-3: Squat.

Photograph by Nick Horne

The exercise

Sit back and down, as if you're sitting into a chair (see Figure 14-3b). Lower as far as you can without leaning your upper body more than a few inches forward. Don't lower any farther than the point at which your thighs are parallel to the floor, and don't allow your knees to shoot out in front of your toes. When you feel your upper body fold forward over your thighs, straighten your legs and stand back up. Take care not to lock your knees at the top of the movement.

Do's and don'ts

- ✔ DON'T allow your knees to travel beyond your toes. We know we said this before, but it bears repeating.

- ✔ DON'T look down. Your body tends to follow your eyes. So if you're staring at the ground, you're more likely to fall forward. Instead, keep your head up and your eyes focused on an object directly in front of you.

✔ DON'T shift your body weight forward so your heels lift up off the floor. When you push back up to the standing position, concentrate on pushing through your heels.

✔ DON'T arch your back as you stand back up.

Other options

Bench squat (easier): Place the end of a bench behind you and allow your buttocks to lightly touch the top of it as you sit downward. This placement helps you guide your movement and perfect your form.

Plié squat: To add emphasis to the inner and outer thighs, place your feet out a little wider apart and angle your toes outward. Most people lower farther in this position because they feel more stable. Still, don't travel any lower than the point at which your thighs are parallel to the floor, and don't let your knees shoot out past your toes.

Barbell squat (harder): When you've mastered the squat, progress to the barbell squat for even greater challenges. Place a weighted bar in a power cage so when you stand underneath it, the bar rests gently across the top of your shoulders. Stand with your feet as wide as your hips, weight shifted slightly back on your heels, and hold on to either side of the bar with your hands wider than shoulder-width apart. Pull your abdominals in and stand up tall with square shoulders.

Sit back and down, as if you're sitting into a chair. Lower as far as you can without leaning your upper body more than a few inches forward. Don't lower any farther than the point at which your thighs are parallel to the floor, and don't allow your knees to shoot out in front of your toes. When you feel your upper body fold forward over your thighs, straighten your legs and stand back up.

Lunge

The lunge is a great overall lower-body exercise: It strengthens your butt, quadriceps, hamstrings, and calves.

If you feel pain in your hips, knees, or lower back when you do this exercise, try using a chair to touch your butt to — it'll keep you from sitting too far down toward the floor.

Getting set

Stand with your feet as wide as your hips and your weight back a little on your heels, and place your hands on your hips. Pull your abdominals in and stand up tall with square shoulders.

The exercise

Lift your right toe slightly and, leading with your heel, step your right foot forward an elongated stride's length, as if you're trying to step over a crack on the sidewalk. As your foot touches the floor, bend both knees until your right thigh is parallel to the floor and your left knee is perpendicular to the floor. Your left heel will lift off the floor (see Figure 14-4). Press off the ball of your foot and step back to the standing position.

Figure 14-4:
Lunge.

Photograph by Nick Horne

Do's and don'ts

- ✔ DO keep your eyes focused ahead; when you look down, you have a tendency to fall forward.

- ✔ DON'T step too far forward or you'll have trouble balancing.

- ✔ DON'T lean forward or allow your front knee to travel past your toes.

Other options

Lunge with weights (harder): Hold a dumbbell in each hand with your arms down at your sides, or place a barbell behind your neck and across your shoulders. You also can do the lunge while holding a dumbbell in each hand or by using the Smith Machine.

Backward lunge (harder): Step your right leg back about a stride's length behind you, and bend both knees until your left thigh is parallel to the floor and your right thigh is perpendicular to it. You'll feel this version a bit more in your hamstrings.

Traveling lunge (harder): Perform the basic lunge, alternating legs so you travel forward with each repetition. You need a good 10 yards of space to do this. Bend your arms to 90 degrees and swing them purposefully. This variation is great for skiers, hikers, and climbers as it mimics the moves that are used in those activities.

Kneeling butt blaster

The kneeling butt blaster works your butt with some emphasis on your hamstrings, too.

Make sure that you keep your abdominals pulled in on this exercise, especially if you're prone to lower-back discomfort.

Getting set

Kneel on your elbows and knees on a mat or towel, with your knees directly under your hips and your elbows under your shoulders. Your palms will be flat on the floor. Flex your right foot so it's perpendicular to the floor. Tilt your chin slightly toward your chest, and pull your abdominals in so your back doesn't sag toward the floor (see Figure 14-5a).

The exercise

Keeping your knee bent, lift your right leg and raise your knee to hip level (see Figure 14-5b). Then slowly lower your leg back down. Between repetitions, your knee almost, but not quite, touches the floor. Complete all the repetitions with one leg before switching sides.

Do's and don'ts

- ✔ DO keep your neck still and your shoulders relaxed.
- ✔ DO move slowly.
- ✔ DON'T throw your leg up in the air.
- ✔ DON'T raise your knee above hip height.
- ✔ DON'T arch your back as you lift your leg.

Figure 14-5:
Kneeling
butt blaster.

Photograph by Nick Horne

Other options

Kneeling butt blaster with weight (harder): Add an ankle weight to this exercise or squeeze a small dumbbell in the well of your knee. We love this last option because your muscles have to work even harder to hold the weight in place.

Butt-blaster machine: This machine mimics the kneeling butt blaster. You kneel with one knee on a platform, place your other foot onto a foot plate, and then press back and up. This machine is fine as long as you remember to keep your abdominals pulled in and resist arching your lower back.

Side lying leg lift

The side lying leg lift strengthens your outer-thigh muscles.

Pay attention to the instructions marked by the Posture Patrol icon, particularly if you have a history of lower-back pain.

Getting set

Lie on the floor on your left side with your legs a few inches in front of you, knees bent slightly, and head resting on your outstretched arm. Bend your right arm and place your palm on the floor in front of your chest for support. Align your right hip directly over your left hip and pull your abdominals in so your back isn't arched (see Figure 14-6a).

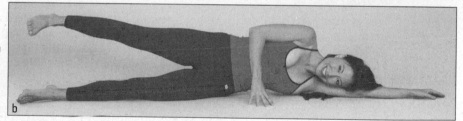

Figure 14-6: Side lying leg lift.

Photograph by Zoran Popovic

The exercise

Keeping your leg straight, raise your right leg until your foot reaches shoulder height (see Figure 14-6b). Then slowly lower your leg back down. Switch sides and do the same number of repetitions with your left leg.

Do's and don'ts

- ✔ DO keep your top hip stacked directly over your bottom hip; don't roll backward.
- ✔ DO keep your head down and your neck and shoulders relaxed.

   ✔ DO keep your abdominals pulled in to help your body remain still so you work only your outer thigh.

   ✔ DON'T raise your foot any higher than shoulder height.

Other options

Modified leg lift (easier): Bend your top knee even more when performing the side lying leg lift.

Leg lift with rotation (harder): When you reach the top of the movement, rotate your thigh outward by turning your knee up to the ceiling; then rotate back to the original position and lower your leg back down.

Leg lift with a weight (harder): Place an ankle weight on your ankle or, if you have knee problems, on top of your thigh.

Inner-thigh lift

The inner-thigh lift strengthens your inner thigh muscles.

Use caution if you have lower-back problems.

Getting set

Lie on your right side with your head resting on your outstretched arm. Bend your left leg so that your knee is level with your hip and your top hip is directly over your bottom hip. Place your left hand on the floor in front of your chest for support (see Figure 14-7a). Pull your abdominals in.

The exercise

Lift your bottom (right) leg a few inches off the floor (see Figure 14-7b). Pause briefly at the top of the movement, and slowly lower your leg back down. Switch sides and do the same number of repetitions with your left leg.

Do's and don'ts

   ✔ DON'T lift your leg more than a few inches. Stop when you feel tension in your inner thigh. How high you need to lift depends on your flexibility, your strength, and your build.

   ✔ DON'T arch your back as you lift your leg.

Other options

Inner-thigh lift with a weight (harder): Wear an ankle weight while performing the inner-thigh lift. If you have bad knees, drape the weight on top of your inner thigh.

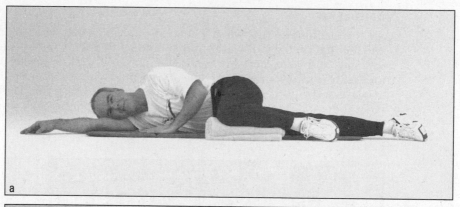

Figure 14-7:
Inner-thigh
lift.

Photograph by Daniel Kron

Performing Lower-Body Exercises with Machines

The following lower-body exercises are done on machines.

Leg-press machine

The leg-press machine covers a lot of ground, strengthening your butt, quadriceps, and hamstrings. It's a good alternative if the squat or lunge bothers your lower back.

You may want to try the modified version if you experience pain in your hips or knees.

Getting set

Set the machine so that when you lie on your back with your knees bent and feet flat on the foot plate, your shoulders fit snugly under the shoulder pads and your knees are bent to an inch or so below parallel to the foot plate. Place your feet as wide as your hips with your toes pointing forward and your heels directly behind your toes. Grasp the handles. Pull your abdominals in and keep your head and neck on the back pad (see Figure 14-8a).

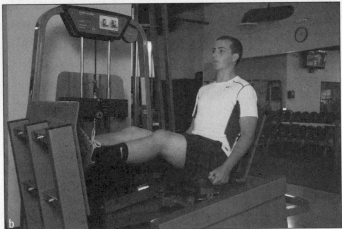

Figure 14-8: Leg-press machine.

Photograph by Nick Horne

The exercise

Pressing through your heels, push against the platform until your legs are straight (see Figure 14-8b). Then bend your knees until your thighs are parallel with the platform and the weight plates you're lifting are hovering just above the weight stack.

Do's and don'ts

- ✔ DO press your heels into the foot plate instead of allowing them to lift up.

- ✔ DON'T lower your thighs past parallel with the foot plate or allow your knees to shoot in front of your toes.

- ✔ DON'T arch your back off the pad to help move the weight.

- ✔ DON'T lock your knees when your legs are straight.

Other options

Different types of machines: You may run across several types of leg-press machines. One has you sitting in an upright position, pressing your legs out straight. Another is called a 45-degree leg press: You lie in a reclining position and press up and out diagonally. Yet another version has you lie on your back and press your legs straight up. All these variations are acceptable. Just remember: Don't bend your legs so far that your thighs are smooshed against your chest and your knees are hanging out there in Never-Never Land. Keep in mind that your foot position changes the emphasis of the exercise. The higher you place your feet on the foot platform, the more you emphasize your butt muscles.

Modified leg press (easier): If you have chronic knee problems, you can still do this exercise. Set the seat height so your thighs are a few inches above parallel — this position limits the distance you can bend your knees. However, this version focuses more on your front thigh muscles and less on your butt.

One-leg leg press (harder): Use the same form as with the basic version of this exercise with one foot lifted up and off the foot plate. After you complete your reps, switch legs.

Leg-extension machine

The leg extension machine zeroes in on your quadriceps muscles.

If this exercise bothers your knees, try the modified version or choose a different exercise.

Getting set

Set the machine so your back sits comfortably against the backrest, the center of your knee is lined up with the machine's pulley, and your shins are flush against the ankle pads. (On most machines you can move the backrest forward and back and the ankle pads up and down.) Sit down and swing your legs around so your knees are bent and the tops of your shins are resting against the underside of the ankle pads. Hold on to the handles. Sit up tall and pull your abdominals in (see Figure 14-9a).

Figure 14-9:
Leg-extension machine.

Photograph by Nick Horne

The exercise

Straighten your legs to lift the ankle bar until your knees are straight (see Figure 14-9b). Hold for a second at the top position, and then slowly bend your knees.

Do's and don'ts

➔ DO make sure that you take the time to set the machine properly.

➔ DO move slowly.

➔ DON'T ram your knees at the top of the movement.

➔ DON'T arch your back in an effort to help you lift the weight.

Other options

Single-leg extension: Many leg-extension machines have a mechanism you set to limit the distance that you bend and straighten your legs. Use this device if your knees give you trouble at any point of the exercise.

Ball-squeeze modified leg extension (harder): Place a soccer ball, weighted ball, or rolled towel between your knees. As you extend your leg, concentrate on squeezing the ball so it doesn't slip out of place. This version of the exercise forces your quads to work harder in order to hold onto the ball.

Leg-curl machine

The leg curl machine does a great job of strengthening your hamstring muscles.

Use caution if you have a history of lower-back discomfort.

Getting set

Set the ankle pads of the machine so that when you lie on your stomach, the underside of the pads are flush with the tops of your heels. Lie down, rest the side of your face on the support pad, and grasp the handles. Gently flex your feet. Pull your abdominals in and tuck your hips down so your hipbones press into the pad (see Figure 14-10a).

The exercise

Bend your knees to lift the ankle bar until your calves are perpendicular to the floor (see Figure 14-10b). Then slowly straighten your legs.

Do's and don'ts

- ✔ DO keep your hipbones pressed against the machine and your abdominals pulled in. You may want to lift your thighs just a hair upward before you bend your knees.

- ✔ DO lower your legs back down slowly so the weights you're lifting don't slam down against the rest of the stack.

- ✔ DON'T — and this is a *big* don't — allow your butt to pop off the pad. This puts stress on your lower back and minimizes the work being done by your hamstrings.

- ✔ DON'T kick your heels all the way to your butt.

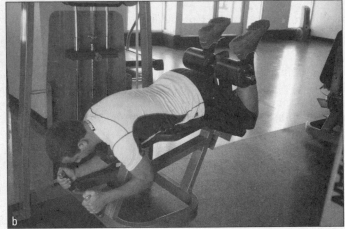

Figure 14-10:
Leg-curl
machine.

Photograph by Nick Horne

Other options

Other curl machines: Some machines work your hamstrings from a standing or seated position. Others have independent left and right sides so that each leg has to carry its own share of the weight. Still others have a "range limiting" device that allows you to cut off the movement at the top or bottom — a good variation if you're experiencing any pain while doing this exercise.

Single-leg curl: Lift with both legs, straighten one out of the way, and lower the weight down with one leg only.

Inner- and outer-thigh machine

The inner/outer thigh machine sets to strengthen either your inner thigh muscles or your outer thigh muscles. Skaters, skiers, and basketball players — anyone involved in side-to-side movements — can help prevent injury by using this machine.

Getting set

Set the machine so the leg mechanisms are together and the knee and ankle pads are rotated to the outside. Sit up tall in the seat, and bend your knees so they rest against the thigh pads and the outside of your ankles rest against the ankle pads. If there's a seat belt, wear it to help keep you from popping out of the machine. Pull your abdominals in and sit up tall (see Figure 14-11a).

Figure 14-11:
Inner- and outer-thigh machine.

Photograph by Nick Horne

The exercise

Press your knees outward until you feel tension in your outer thighs (see Figure 14-11b). Hold the position for a moment, and then slowly allow your legs to move back together. This is the outer thigh, or *abduction*, exercise.

To set the machine for the inner thigh, or *adduction,* exercise, shift the leg mechanisms so they're comfortably spread apart, and turn the knee and ankle pads toward the inside. Position your legs so that the inside of your knees rest against the thigh pads, and the inside of your ankles rest against the ankle pads. Pull your legs together, and then slowly move them back out to a point at which you feel a comfortable stretch through your inner thighs.

Do's and don'ts

✔ DO control the movement in both directions. If you hear the weight stack come crashing down, slow down.

✔ DO change the weight between exercises if you need to. Most people use approximately the same weight for both inner and outer thigh exercises, but don't take that for granted.

✔ DON'T arch your back or wiggle around in the seat in an effort to assist your legs.

Other options

Vary seat position: Some machines allow you to decline the seat back a few degrees or even all the way down so you can lie flat. Experiment with different back positions to see what's most comfortable for you and to give the exercise a different feel.

Chapter 15

Weights for Core Strength

- -

In This Chapter

▶ Knowing why you need to use weights to strengthen your core

▶ Seeing how to lift weights for your core

▶ Finding out the right number and sets to use with weights

▶ Choosing the right amount of weight for you

- -

*I*n this chapter, we cover weight training to help strengthen your core. Which means, you're going to learn how to use free weights or dumbbells to combine exercises to work your core — like a squat to overhead press or a reverse lunge using weights with a lateral shoulder raise. By combining two different movements, you're forced to transition the exercise through your core, so your core muscles become stronger and in turn, you're able to maintain good posture and alignment throughout the exercise. The end result is a stronger core that helps mimic the movements you use in everyday life while creating better posture and increasing stability and balance.

The best way to build strength in any part of your body is with resistance training — and using weights is the preferred form of resistance to use.

Transitioning any movement you're doing with weights through your core is what builds core strength. It also helps build functional strength, which is what you use throughout each day to reach, bend, grab, pull, and so on.

Weight training can also help reshape your body in addition to adding muscle and tone to areas that perhaps are too flat (your butt), and add definition to muscles that are just too round (your arms). If any of these body types or scenarios sound familiar to you — not to worry! Using weights works — and it works fast! Within a few short weeks, you'll begin to see tighter, toned muscles peeking through and legs like a racehorse appearing . . . well, maybe not to that extreme, but you get the point. You'll see changes by adding a bit of muscle all over and reducing your body fat with weight training. So, let's get started!

Weight Guidelines

Whether it's 5, 10, or 15 pounds, with free weights, that's all you get. Dumbbells and barbells on the other hand (no pun intended) have metal bars that you can add weight to, called *changeable plates*. Because they have changeable plates, they're good for quickly adding weight to your workout on one device rather than having five different pairs of free weights lying around. Well, now that you've had a crash course in weights, how much weight should you actually be using? Read on to find out more about the perfect weight for you!

Picking the right amount of weight for you

How much weight you use makes a big difference in the effectiveness and the success of your workout. It's always smart to choose an amount of weight that you can complete 10 to 12 repetitions with and making the last two difficult to complete.

For example, if you were doing 12 repetitions, at number 10, you should feel close to failure or have a really difficult time finishing the last two. If you can do 15 repetitions, you're using too light of weights and should try increasing your weight in 3- to 5-pound increments. The more weight you use, the more you challenge your body and will see the changes you're looking for faster.

Increasing repetitions and sets

Instead of increasing the amount of weight you use, to challenge your body and create change, you can simply increase the amount of repetitions you do or add another set. We usually suggest starting off with one set of ten repetitions using the recommended amount of weight. That allows you to practice using good form and see where you're at in terms of evaluating your level of difficulty. After a few weeks, you should be adding at least one more set or increasing the amount of weight you use. The body adapts quickly to any amount of weight you exercise with so you have to keep up!

Dumbbell Workout for a Flat Tummy and Tiny Waist

The following exercises are challenging and fun to do. Many of them involve doing *compound movements,* which means they combine two exercises and use two major muscle groups at one time.

Be sure to work up slowly and only do as much and as many of the exercises that you can do while using proper form.

The wood chop

The wood chop is called just that because it's similar to the move you use when you're chopping wood. It is the king of all core with weight strengthening exercises because it works your back, butt, abs, and chest all at the same time.

To do this exercise, follow these steps:

1. **Stand up tall with your feet hip-width apart and hold a weight in your right hand. Bending at your waist, hold the weight to the right side of your body (as shown in Figure 15-1a).**

2. **Sweep your arm upward and across your body so you end up with your right arm over your left shoulder (see Figure 15-1b).**

   Lift from your core and hold for a breath at the top of the movement.

3. **Come back to starting position, and continue the wood chop for five repetitions before switching sides.**

Figure 15-1: The wood chop.

a

b

Photograph by Nick Horne

To protect your back and spine, your hips should move with you and not remain forward throughout the moves.

A few do's and don'ts for this exercise:

✔ DO inhale as you reach up and exhale as you bring your arm back down.

✔ DO hold your abdominals tight to protect your back.

✔ DON'T arch or compress your lower back.

✔ DON'T swing or create too much momentum; keep the movement fluid and under control.

Dumbbell bent-over row

This exercise transitions the movement through your core to help strengthen your back. You'll want to be sure to tighten your abdominals before performing this movement with your weight to protect your lower back.

To do this exercise, follow these steps:

1. **Holding your weight in your right hand, place your left foot in front of your right, bend at the waist, and place your opposite hand on your knee for support (see Figure 15-2a).**

2. **Pull the dumbbell toward your chest until your elbow is past your body and the muscles in your upper back are contracted (as shown in Figure 15-2b).**

3. **Lower the weight back down to starting position before continuing the next repetition.**

   Repeat for five repetitions before switching sides.

A few do's and don'ts for this exercise:

✔ DO contract your abs throughout the exercise to engage your core and protect your back.

✔ DO make sure your knees are bent slightly and not locked.

Crunches with weights

This is your standard abdominal crunch but with added weight for additional strengthening of the core muscles. This exercise can be challenging, so start out slowly, using only your body weight as resistance before adding the additional weight of dumbbells.

Beating stress

Exercise can cut your stress level in half and lower your blood pressure, which isn't a bad combination. Here are a few tips you can use to help you get back on track or just to encourage you to slow down a little:

✔ **Do yoga or Pilates, or take the time to stretch to ease your body of aches and rid you of tension.** It may even help you take a few much-needed breaths.

✔ **Do something you love every day.** Whether it's biking, walking, or playing with the kids, being active while doing something you love is the best stress reducer of all.

✔ **Realize that stress is cumulative.** Reevaluating where you are in your life and making small changes along the way can really make a difference that shows up on a daily basis.

✔ **Think about working from home.** Many people can control their schedules and work from home nowadays. Taking on less of a work load, delegating chores to a relative or family member, or even moving to a smaller, tight-knit community may help you get back the simplicity you need in life to maintain a good, long, healthy life.

✔ **Don't stress about stressing!** Everybody is pretty much in the same boat when it comes to worrying about the everyday mundane things like work and paying bills. Be thankful for the things you do have and try not to worry about the things you don't!

Figure 15-2: Dumbbell bent-over rows.

a

b

Photograph by Nick Horne

1. **Sit on the floor with your knees bent and your feet on the floor in front of you. Hold weights in both your hands in front of your chest. Lean back slightly (see Figure 15-3a).**

2. **Contract your stomach muscles before bringing your shoulders and upper body farther off the floor and toward your knees (as shown in Figure 15-3b).**

3. **Slowly return your back down to the floor before starting the next repetition.**

Repeat for five to ten repetitions.

A few do's and don'ts for this exercise:

- ✔ DO hold the position for a moment before returning back down to the floor.
- ✔ DO squeeze the weights into your chest to help keep them steady throughout the crunch.
- ✔ DON'T let the bottom of your feet come off the floor.

Figure 15-3: Crunches with weights.

Photograph by Nick Horne

Dead lifts

This exercises strengthens the lower back and entire core. You'll also feel this exercise in your lower body from the additional weight you'll be using as you lift up through your core.

To do this exercise, follow these steps:

1. **Taking a shoulder-wide stance, start with weights on the floor in front of you.**

2. **Pull your shoulders back by squeezing your shoulder blades together as you bend forward from the waist. Keep a straight back as you bend forward (see Figure 15-4a).**

3. **Push through your heels and contract your glutes and hamstrings as you return to the upright position (see Figure 15-4b).**

   Repeat for five to ten repetitions.

Figure 15-4:
Dead lifts.

a

b

Photograph by Nick Horne

A few do's and don'ts for this exercise:

- ✔ DO grip the weights using palms facing down or using an overhand grip.
- ✔ DO keep your arms straight throughout this exercise.
- ✔ DON'T forget to contract your glutes and tighten your abdominal muscles before lowering down toward the floor.

T-raises

This exercise requires you to lift your arms while holding weights straight up directly through the core of your body. It's great for arms, shoulders, and upper back as well.

To do this exercise, follow these steps:

1. **Standing tall and holding weights down at your sides, slowly raise your weights until they're straight out in front of you at chest level (as shown in Figure 15-5a).**

2. **Then like an airplane or a "T," move arms out to either side of your body (see Figure 15-5b).**

3. **Return to starting position by bringing your arms back in to your chest using your "T" shape, before lowering your weights back down to your sides.**

   Repeat for five to ten repetitions.

Use an exercise ball or an Xerdisc (a dome-shaped ball) to give you extra strengthening in your core by challenging your stability.

A few do's and don'ts for this exercise:

- ✔ DO keep your back straight during this exercise.
- ✔ DO inhale as you lift the weights through your core to chest level and exhale as you lower back down to starting position.
- ✔ DON'T move your arms out past your shoulders when you make your "T" shape during this exercise.

Squat to overhead press

Combining two powerful movements or compound exercises is the way to go to strengthen your core with weights. This is a good overall upper- and lower-body exercise combining the squat and the overhead press.

Figure 15-5:
T-raises.

a   b

Photograph by Nick Horne

To do this exercise, follow these steps:

1. **Starting with feet hip-width apart, bend your knees and squat down as if you were going to sit in a chair (see Figure 15-6a).**

2. **Holding your weights in your hands at head level and even with your shoulders, press your weights upward as you press through your heels to a standing position (see Figure 15-6b).**

3. **Release your arms back down to shoulder level as you stand back up straight to starting position.**

4. **Repeat the movement five to ten more times.**

Try to do the squat press movement slow and controlled to increase the tightening of your core muscles.

A few do's and don'ts for this exercise:

- ✔ DO press your weights straight up during this exercise.
- ✔ DO keep your palms facing forward.
- ✔ DON'T lean forward. Keep your back straight and stand tall.

Figure 15-6:
Squat to
overhead
press.

a

b

Photograph by Nick Horne

Reverse lunges with weights

This reverse lunge with an added leg lift is done while you're holding weights. It's a great butt and back strengthener, and it also gives you killer abs from the extra knee lift.

To do this exercise, follow these steps:

1. **Holding your weights at waist level with palms facing each other, stand with your feet shoulder width apart. Step or lunge back with your right leg, bending your left knee behind you (as shown in Figure 15-7a).**

2. **Holding your weights with palms facing in and elbows to your sides, push through your left heel as you pull your right knee up to your waist (see Figure 15-7b).**

3. **Hold the knee raise for a few seconds before returning your leg behind you to starting position.**

Photograph by Nick Horne

Figure 15-7:
Reverse lunges with weights.

a

b

A few do's and don'ts for this exercise:

✔ DO keep a straight back and not an arched one.

✔ DO make sure you hold for a few seconds as you raise your knee.

✔ DON'T forget to pull your abs in tight and contract your butt muscles before doing this exercise.

Ab Central Machines

Ever go into the gym and see lots of ways to do a crunch except the old fashioned way — on the floor? Different ways of training your core are popular and are mostly made to stave off boredom because — let's face it — doing crunches can get a little boring! Read on to find other ways to work your core that may add a little spice to your regular routine.

Bosu ball

A Bosu ball looks like something that should be part of a jungle gym or, at the very least, something kids may enjoy playing with. The Bosu ball is the half-dome piece of equipment that you place on your back as you put your feet flat on the floor. As you rock forward, the ball helps you lift your shoulders off the ground and guides your spine through the natural curved movement as you lift your shoulders. The Bosu ball is definitely for beginners — it helps you take baby steps to getting an actual core workout or completing an abdominal crunch!

Foam roller

With a foam roller, you're lying on your back with your legs straight out as you place the roller perpendicular to your lower back. Great for sit-ups, crunches, and all abdominal exercises, the foam roller provides you with a killer core workout and is a good piece of equipment to use if you already have a lot of core strength.

Ab board

An ab board looks like a weight bench sloped downward. You lie on the board on your back. Because you aren't just lying on your back on a flat surface but you're at a 45-degree angle, you're increasing the range of motion that you use to perform sit-ups, which increases the intensity of the exercise.

Ab wheel

Inexpensive? Yes. Convenient? Oh yes. Easy to use? Forget it! The ab wheel requires a ton of core strength along with balance and control. Picture this: Starting with the wheel at your feet and your legs straight but hips up in the air (think downward dog in yoga), roll the wheel out until you're in push-up position. It may sound easy, but you have to control the movement or the wheel will take right off from under you and you'll need a new nose when it hits the floor. Again, the key word here is *control* — and not many people have what it takes to train with an ab wheel. Definitely something to work up to slowly.

Why build muscle to burn fat?

Using different forms of resistance, such as hand weights and dumbbells, to reduce overall body fat by building muscle is the hottest and latest trend. Usually weights are incorporated as part of a circuit-training program or added to some form of cardio training to be most effective. Using weights can help tone, add definition, and reshape your body faster than any other form of exercise alone.

Here are a few of the many benefits you get from building muscle with resistance training:

✔ You burn 30 to 50 calories more per day for each pound of muscle you put on.

✔ Building bigger muscles boosts your *metabolic rate* (the rate at which you burn calories) and reduces overall body fat.

✔ Lean body mass burns more calories than fat does. So, if you have more muscle, you can burn more calories while you sleep.

✔ It improves your posture as a result of strengthening and enhancing your back muscles, which help develop a strong spine.

✔ It increases your strength and muscle mass, which reduces the risk of osteoporosis.

✔ It protects your joints and muscles from deterioration.

✔ It strengthens the connective tissue within your body.

To burn the most amount of calories in the shortest amount of time, you need to work the larger muscle groups in your body. Next time you're doing a workout, try a few compound exercises (like squats, lat pulls, and chest presses) rather than exercises that target individual muscles. These exercises are great examples of ways to burn the most calories in the shortest amount of time.

Chapter 16

Stretching: The Truth

Stretching seems like such a straightforward topic that you may expect us to explain it in a sentence or two and then show you a stretching routine. Well, as it turns out, a lot of confusion surrounds the subject of stretching. The American College of Sports Medicine (ACSM), one of the most respected sports and fitness organizations in the world, provides guidelines on how to stretch, but the organization still admits that more research is needed to determine exactly what stretching can and can't do for you. This chapter explains that stretching maintains freedom of movement and enhances muscular performance. It's true, stretching isn't just about isolated muscle fibers. This chapter outlines the ACSM guidelines for stretching and covers other promising stretching methods.

The stretches in this chapter target the quads, hamstrings, and chest to help improve your range of motion. The combination of these stretches helps create strength and flexibility.

Discovering Why and When to Stretch

Stretching lengthens your muscles and loosens up the joints that your muscles connect to so you can move more freely but still keep your joints stable. Too much flexibility leads to unstable joints; too little flexibility leads to restricted movement. When your muscles are at their ideal length, you can walk without stiffness, reach down to tousle a toddler's hair, or turn around when someone calls your name — everyday movements that you take for granted until you have trouble doing them. This is known as *functional fitness,* movements you use in everyday life. When your muscles and joints lack flexibility, you feel *tight.*

Two stretching methods we describe in this chapter — active isolated and proprioceptive neuromuscular facilitation (PNF) — actively stimulate the nervous system to increase the release of muscular tightness. With these methods, you hold stretches for a shorter period of time than you do with traditional stretching, and you contract the muscle ultimately to encourage more relaxation.

Elongating your muscles

This muscular tension isn't simply a result of tight muscle tissues. For example, if you were under anesthesia, your body would be much more flexible. The neuromuscular system regulates muscular tension. So, when you stretch, you aren't simply pulling on muscle fibers. Instead, you're stimulating your nervous system to signal the muscle to rest in a longer position.

Several studies show that the optimal amount of time to hold a stretch is between 20 and 30 seconds. Holding a stretch for 60 seconds doesn't seem to make you more flexible. In fact, it's better to do two stretches of 30 seconds each or three stretches of 20 seconds each than to do a one-minute stretch. Theory states that stimulating your nervous system multiple times to encourage your muscle to be longer leads to a greater likelihood of "re-setting" the resting muscle tension length in a longer position. Studies show that the greatest increases in flexibility come from the first four repetitions.

Alleviating stressed and tense muscles

Another important concept to understand is muscular balance affects the resting length of your muscles. In other words, the back of your leg doesn't exist in isolation from the rest of your body. For example, the tightness you feel in your calves relates to the strength of your shins. If your calves are relatively stronger than your shins, the calf muscle dominates the pair and your calf feels tight. To decrease this muscular tension, you need to strengthen your shin.

Stretching alone can't eliminate muscular tension. To address tight muscles, your weight lifting program must consist of both strengthening exercises for the opposing muscle group and stretching exercises for the tight muscles.

Avoiding injuries

Stretching has been widely recommended to prevent injury and ease muscle soreness, but many recent studies find that traditional methods of stretching may not accomplish either goal and may, in fact, *cause* injuries (like muscle tears from overstretching). A University of Hawaii study of more than 100 runners found that the nonstretchers performed better, reported fewer injuries, and experienced less muscle soreness after their running workouts than those runners who stretched regularly. Why? Perhaps tighter muscles better stabilize the joints, thereby protecting knees and hips from the trauma of running.

However, having tighter muscles for stability may be true only to a point. If muscles are too tight, the risk of injury appears to increase. For instance, runners who sit a lot during the day — and therefore have tight hamstrings — are prone to herniated disks because their hamstrings pull on the pelvis, rotating it backward. Over time, tension from tight hamstrings creates a flat-back posture; the disc fluid moves toward the back of the disc, creating pressure and a bulge. Inflexible runners aren't the only ones who can be troubled by inflexibility. A recent study found that, two and three days after moderately heavy weight lifting, less flexible exercisers feel more muscle tenderness than more flexible subjects.

Keep in mind that these studies are just a few among many, and that little research exists to prove or disprove previous studies. So, we're left with a hodgepodge of studies that seem to compare apples to oranges.

The official word on stretching

How do you achieve and maintain your muscles at their ideal length so that you can move easily and freely? According to the ACSM, stretching is important to achieve this goal.

The ACSM's position stand on exercise for health, last published in 1998, states that growing evidence supports stretching for the purpose of improving range of motion and joint function and enhancing muscle performance, as well as substantial "real-life" reports to support its role in preventing injuries. The ACSM issues the following guidelines on how to stretch:

- Hold each stretch for 10 to 30 seconds and repeat up to four repetitions.
- Perform at least one stretch for each major muscle group.
- Stretch at least two to three times a week, preferably every day.
- Stretch to the point of discomfort but not beyond.
- Don't hold your breath while stretching.

An important concept to understand when it comes to stretching is the *stretch reflex mechanism*. This mechanism defends against overstretching and tearing and signals the muscle to shorten and tighten when stimulated. An example of the stretch reflex: when your doctor taps your knee with a little hammer and your leg kicks up. To avoid stimulating the stretch reflex, never stretch to an extreme length or stretch quickly as in a bouncing movement.

To date, most stretching studies have looked at traditional stretching. Other varieties of stretching, which we describe later, show some promise in the areas of preventing injuries and easing muscle soreness. But no major studies that we know of have compared the various stretching methods head to head. In fact, more and more studies show that there isn't necessarily one best way for all people because we each have different body types, experiences, and goals. Experiment with a variety of stretching methods, and find out which stretches feel most comfortable to you. You may even want to combine a number of stretching methods. You may find, for example, that you enjoy doing active isolated stretches (covered later in the chapter) for your *hamstrings* (rear thigh muscles) but traditional stretching for your shoulders.

Static Stretching: Stretching the Traditional Way

In traditional stretching, also called *static stretching,* your body stays still. You hold each stretch for 10 to 30 seconds without bouncing. As you hold the position, you feel a pull that spreads up and down the length of the muscle. Traditional stretching is the method performed at the end of many exercise classes and in exercise videos. While it may not achieve as much increase in flexibility as some of the other methods, it's very safe, easy to understand, and has a low risk of injury.

Traditional stretching has some definite advantages:

- ✔ Almost anyone can perform some static stretches; you can easily modify the position to suit your level of flexibility.

- ✔ Many people find this method of stretching a good way to relax and to cool down after a workout.

- ✔ If you perform traditional stretches at least three days a week, you'll probably notice an increase in flexibility after a few weeks.

On the other hand, some cons coincide with traditional stretching:

- ✔ If you're inflexible, this type of stretching may be far from relaxing. In fact, it may be so uncomfortable that you end up skipping your stretches altogether.

- ✔ Separating one muscle group from another with traditional stretches is difficult; you often are forced to stretch several different muscle groups at once. This situation is a problem if one of the muscles being stretched is tighter than the others.

Stretching guidelines

Follow these simple guidelines, which apply to all methods of stretching:

✔ **Aim to stretch daily, but make sure that you stretch at least three times per week.** You improve your flexibility the same way you get to Carnegie Hall: practice, practice, practice. Your muscles will "remember" to stay loose and flexible if they're reminded often enough.

✔ **Stretch after your workout, not before.** Follow this rule whether you're doing aerobic exercise, weight training, or both. On days when you do only weight training, you need to do at least five minutes of rhythmic, low-intensity aerobic exercise such as walking, jogging, cycling, or stepping. Warming up gets your blood flowing and raises your body temperature so your muscles are more receptive to the stretch. Never stretch a cold muscle. (This rule doesn't apply to active isolated stretching (covered at the end of this chapter), which can safely be included as part of a warm-up.)

✔ **Never force a stretch.** Stretch to the point at which you're right on the edge of discomfort, never to the point of "Ouch!" There's no optimal amount of flexibility, so stretch within the limits of each individual joint.

✔ **Don't forget to breathe.** Deep, natural breathing increases your flexibility by helping you to relax and by sending oxygen-rich blood into your muscles. Inhale deeply just before you go into a stretching position, and exhale through your mouth as you move into the stretch. Breathe deeply several times as you hold the stretch.

✔ **Don't just go through the motions and declare, "There, I've stretched."** Concentrate. Focus. Do you feel the stretch where you're supposed to? Are you using correct form? Do you need to back off or push a little further? You don't need to quiz yourself with the intensity of a prosecutor; stretching is supposed to be relaxing, after all.

✔ **Give priority to the muscles you use the most in your workouts and in everyday life, but don't neglect any major muscle group.** For instance, cyclists should perform a few extra sets of stretches on their thighs, calves, and lower back, but they shouldn't skip upper-body stretches altogether. You want your entire body to be flexible so that you can reach across the bed to snag the remote control from a spouse who inexplicably watches reruns of *The Iron Chef* on Food Network.

Contrary to popular belief, you should never perform traditional stretching before you warm up. Stretching in and of itself doesn't constitute a warm-up. See the sidebar, "Stretching guidelines," to find out what constitutes a proper warm-up.

If you're a stretching neophyte, start with 10 seconds of stretching and gradually work your way up to a full 30 seconds. Don't bounce. Jerky movements may actually make you tighter. Get in the proper stretching position slowly and smoothly and then stay there. After you've held the stretch for a few seconds, slowly stretch a bit farther.

Hold each of the following positions for 10 to 30 seconds.

Quadriceps (front thigh): Lie on your left side with your legs bent and your head resting on your outstretched arm. Bend your right knee so your heel is close to your butt, and grab your ankle or toes with your right hand. Pull your heel back and toward your butt, taking care to keep your hips stacked directly on top of one another. Try to keep your knees together, not separated. Don't arch your back (see Figure 16-1) or allow your butt to stick out. Use the image of trying to press your pocket forward and flat. After you stretch your right quadriceps, turn over (to lie on your right side) and stretch your left.

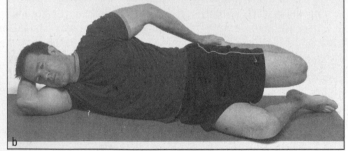

Figure 16-1:
Side lying quad stretch.

Photograph by Tilden Patterson

Hamstrings (rear thigh): Lie on your back with your left knee bent and your left foot flat on the floor. Straighten your right leg out in front of you along the floor, and flex your toes toward yourself. Slowly raise your right leg off the floor as high as you can without allowing your back or butt to lift up. As you hold this position, you feel a stretch through the back of your thigh. Clasp your hands around your thigh above your knee (see Figure 16-2) or use a stretching strap with loops to help raise your leg. (Using your hands or a stretching strap to help is an especially good idea if you're not very flexible.) Lower your leg slowly and repeat the stretch with your left leg. Before you hold the stretch, you can use the strap to lower and lift your leg and explore your active range of motion. Be sure to relax your thighs and use the strap for support to maximize your stretch (see Figure 16-3).

Figure 16-2:
Lying
hamstring
stretch.

Photograph by Tilden Patterson

Figure 16-3:
Hamstring
stretch with
strap.

Photograph by Tilden Patterson

The pretzel stretch (butt, lower back, and outer thigh): Lie on your back and bend your knees. Lift your legs up so that your knees are directly over your hips and your calves are parallel to the floor. Cross your left ankle over the front of your right thigh. Clasp both hands around the back of your right thigh and pull back with gentle, steady pressure (see Figure 16-4). Keep your butt in contact with the floor. Don't round hips up and off the floor. As you hold this position, you should feel the stretch spread through your left buttock and outer hip and through the center of your lower back. Repeat this stretch with your right ankle over the front of your left thigh.

Reach up (entire upper body and lower back): Sit up tall either cross-legged on the floor or in a chair. Raise your arms directly above your shoulders. Lengthen your right arm upward as you lightly hold your left wrist and slightly lean to the right side. Hold this position for two to four slow counts. Without relaxing your right arm, stretch your left arm upward holding your right wrist and stretch lightly to the left side. Sit up tall and keep your shoulders relaxed (see Figure 16-5) as you alternate stretching each arm upward and to the side for five times. Try to reach a little higher each time — without hunching your shoulders up to your ears. You should feel this stretch throughout the length of your spine, in the "wings" of your upper back, along the sides of your body, and in your shoulders and arms.

Figure 16-4:
The pretzel
stretch.

Photograph by Tilden Patterson

Figure 16-5:
Shoulder
and arm
stretch.

Photograph by Nick Horne

Hand clasp (chest, shoulders, and arms): Stand up tall and bend at the waist (see Figure 16-6) as you clasp your hands behind your back. Drop your shoulders and shoulder blades downward as you lengthen your arms out behind you. You should feel the stretch across the top of your chest, in your shoulders, and along the length of your arms. If you don't have enough flexibility to clasp your hands together, hold an end of a towel in each hand.

Figure 16-6: Chest stretch.

a   b

Photograph by Tilden Patterson

Assisted Stretching: Lean on Me

Assisted stretching is a traditional-type stretch that requires a partner. Your partner helps you into position and then gently helps you stretch farther than you can by yourself. As with traditional, or static, stretching, you hold the position for 10 to 30 seconds without bouncing. The best way to figure out how to perform assisted stretches is from an experienced fitness trainer. While the ACSM's guidelines don't offer strategies for this type of stretching, the organization does reference it as promising and possibly effective.

The pros of assisted stretching are as follows:

✔ Having someone else do a lot of the work for you is relaxing. This technique is particularly valuable for a tight muscle that you have trouble stretching yourself.

✔ If have trouble mastering some of the common stretching positions, assisted stretching helps you understand the techniques while you develop enough flexibility to do them more comfortably on your own.

✔ A partner tends to push you a bit further than you can push yourself.

Assisted stretching also comes with its cons:

✔ If you don't have a partner, you're out of luck (although some assisted stretches can be mimicked by using a towel or stretching strap).

✔ If your partner overstretches you, you may end up injured.

✔ Assisted stretching requires less muscle awareness than the other techniques, so you may not gain much from doing it. (We discuss muscle awareness in "Proprioceptive Neuromuscular Facilitation," later in the chapter.)

Sample assisted stretch (see Figure 16-7): This stretch focuses on your lower back and butt. Lie on the floor with your partner standing in front of your feet; relax your arms at your sides, and keep your head on the floor. Lift your legs, and bend your knees into your chest. Have your partner place her palms just below your knees and gently press down and in so your knees move even closer to your chest. As you hold this position, you should feel the stretch spread from your butt into your lower back.

Figure 16-7:
An assisted lower-back and butt stretch.

Photograph by Nick Horne

Proprioceptive Neuromuscular Facilitation

The term *proprioceptive neuromuscular facilitation* (PNF) sounds like some high-tech, life-saving medical procedure, but really, it's a simple method of stretching. You get into a stretch position, tighten a muscle for about 6 seconds, allow it to relax, and then hold a static stretch for 10 to 30 seconds. In theory, when the muscle is stimulated by contracting, more of the muscle fibers are triggered to relax. Some PNF stretches work best with the assistance of another person; others you can perform yourself. The best way to be taught PNF stretches is from a trainer who is familiar with the technique.

Check out these pros to PNF stretching:

✔ Many studies, including some referenced by the ACSM, show that PNF stretching is a good way to increase your flexibility.

✔ The tightening part helps strengthen the muscle being stretched. This is especially true if the muscle is injured and you can't do the bending and straightening necessary to perform strength-training exercises.

✔ Some studies have found that PNF stretching increases blood flow into joints and muscles, especially if they've experienced a recent injury.

✔ PNF teaches you about your muscles. If you're doing a PNF hamstring stretch, you need to know where your hamstring is and how it feels to tighten this muscle. This knowledge also comes in handy when you perform weight-training exercises.

The cons of this type of stretching are

✔ Many people find PNF stretching uncomfortable or even painful.

✔ You need extra motivation to tighten a muscle as hard as you can for six seconds. Not everyone has the strength or the patience for this.

✔ If you do PNF stretches with a partner, your buddy may be overenthusiastic and try to force the stretch beyond your abilities, and then *snap!* Pay attention so that this doesn't happen.

✔ Avoid PNF stretches if you have high blood pressure, because the stretches may result in sharp, sudden increases in blood pressure.

Sample PNF stretch (see Figure 16-8): This PNF stretch loosens up your hamstrings. Lie on your back with your left knee bent and left foot flat on the floor. Have your partner kneel on one knee in front of your feet. Raise your right leg, and place the back of your heel on top of your partner's shoulder.

Have your partner place one hand on your thigh, just above your knee, and the other hand on top of your shin. Forcefully press your heel down into your partner's shoulder, and concentrate on tightening your hamstring as much as possible for six seconds. Relax the muscle, and have your partner gently push your leg up and back without allowing the knee to bend. Hold the stretch for 10 to 30 seconds and repeat the stretch four times. Switch legs.

To do the previous stretch without a partner, wrap a towel or stretching strap around your ankle or the back of your calf, and then pull your leg toward you as you tighten your hamstring and press it downward.

Figure 16-8:
A PNF hamstring stretch.

Photograph by Nick Horne

Active Isolated Stretching

Active isolated (AI) stretching involves tightening the muscle opposite to the one that you're planning to stretch and then stretching the target muscle for two seconds. You repeat this process 8 to 12 times before going on to the next stretch. By stretching for such a brief period of time, you don't give the muscle enough time to trigger its stretch reflex. (We define the stretch reflex earlier in this chapter, in "Discovering Why and When to Stretch.") What's the purpose of tightening the muscle opposite the one you're stretching? When a muscle tightens, the opposing muscle has no choice but to relax.

Although active isolated stretching has been around since the 1950s, it's been gaining in popularity in the past decade or so — largely through the efforts of father-and-son physiologist team Phil and Jim Wharton, authors of *The Whartons' Book of Stretching* (Times Books). Many sports teams and elite athletes favor the AI method.

AI stretching has its advantages:

- ✔ Many AI stretching exercises do a good job of isolating one muscle group at a time. For example, with an AI stretch, you can stretch the hamstrings without involving the lower back and hip muscles.

- ✔ If you're particularly weak in one area or are rehabilitating a muscle from injury, the tightening may help strengthen that muscle.

- ✔ Many people find AI stretches less painful than traditional stretches.

This method of stretching also has disadvantages:

- ✔ The technique is harder to master than traditional stretching, and some of the positions are difficult to get into.

- ✔ AI stretching is time consuming. You need about 20 minutes to stretch your entire body, whereas you can do an adequate traditional stretch routine in 5 to 10 minutes.

Sample AI stretch (see Figure 16-9): This move stretches your calf muscles. Hold one end of a belt or towel in each hand. Sit on the floor, and lift your left leg a few inches off the floor, positioning your right leg in the most comfortable position. Loop the center of the belt around the instep of your left foot. Point your toes away from you to tighten your calf muscles and then pull your toes back to stretch your calf muscles. Hold the position for two seconds. Repeat 8 to 12 times and then stretch your right calf.

Figure 16-9:
An AI calf muscle stretch.

Photograph by Nick Horne

Back and Spine Stretch Series

We recommend the following stretches to help keep you loose and flexible after your workout. These stretches work your back and help build flexibility in your spine.

Lying spinal rotation

The lying spinal rotation is a good stretch to do when you want to stretch several muscles at once. In this stretch, you feel your back, oblique, neck, and chest muscles all stretch at the same time.

This stretch may be a bit uncomfortable at first, so always begin the stretch in your comfort zone for the first 10 to 15 seconds of the stretch, and then gradually increase the resistance of the stretch for the remainder. Never stretch beyond your pain threshold. Beginning slowly gives your muscles a chance to release and loosen up before you try to deepen the stretch.

This stretch involves the following steps:

1. **Lie on your back with your knees bent and your feet lifted off the floor. Extend both arms out along your sides (see Figure 16-10a).**

2. **Inhale and slowly cross your knees over your body to the left (see Figure 16-10b).**

3. **Turn your head to the right as you relax into the stretch.**

   Make sure to keep both arms and shoulder blades on the floor during this stretch.

4. **Hold the stretch for 30 seconds; release the stretch, and repeat on the other side.**

A few do's and don'ts for this stretch:

- ✔ DO breathe regularly as you hold the stretch.
- ✔ DO progress through the stretch gradually.
- ✔ DON'T arch your back.
- ✔ DON'T force your knees to the floor; it's better to keep your shoulder blades on the floor than to get your knees to touch the floor.

Figure 16-10: Lying spinal rotation.

Photograph by Tilden Patterson

Spinal rotation for back and buttocks

A traditional stretch exists to stretch your buttocks, but by adding a spinal rotation to this buttocks stretch, you can stretch your back and buttocks at the same time. The two-in-one stretch can save you time and stretch your muscles the way you use them in daily life, also know as *functional moves*.

To do this stretch, follow these steps:

1. **Lie on your back with both legs extended and both arms extended out from your sides, palms down.**

2. **Inhale and draw your left knee toward your chest; slowly cross your knee over your body to the right.**

3. **Turn your head to the left as you relax into the stretch (see Figure 16-11).**

4. **Hold the stretch for 30 seconds and then release.**

5. **Repeat on the other side.**

Figure 16-11:
Spinal rotation for the back and buttocks.

Photograph by Tilden Patterson

A few do's and don'ts for this stretch:

✔ DO breathe regularly throughout the stretch.

✔ DO progress through the stretch gradually.

✔ DON'T arch your back.

✔ DON'T force your knee to the floor; it's better to keep your shoulder blades on the floor than to force your knee to touch the floor.

Why am I so sore after working out?

For decades, it was thought that the achy feeling you get after an intense workout was the result of a lactic acid buildup in the tissues of your muscles. Lactic acid is a normal by-product of the process of turning oxygen into energy, also known as *glycolysis*. When you work extra hard, your blood doesn't carry enough oxygen to wash your muscles clean of lactic acid, and a residue builds up. Although in the past, many trainers would tell you that your soreness was due to a lactic acid buildup in your muscles, that soreness now has been attributed to tiny tears in the muscle fibers caused by the requirements of unfamiliar training and overtraining. By helping to ensure that your muscles stay elastic and have a full range of motion in your joints, stretching can help protect you from being the beneficiary of those microscopic tears caused by newly intense levels of exercise.

Part IV
Setting Up Your Workout Programs

Photograph by Nick Horne

In this part . . .

- ✔ Discover a variety of training routines, from beginner to advanced.

- ✔ Give your workouts extra oomph.

- ✔ Find strategies for preventing back pain and injury and improving your balance.

- ✔ Modify your training the meet the needs of the stages of your life — from kids to older adults.

- ✔ Understand how yoga and Pilates can contribute to your workout program.

Chapter 17

Basic Workouts to Get Started

. . . .

In This Chapter

▶ Designing your own routines

▶ Reviewing the essential elements of every routine

▶ Understanding circuit training

▶ Trying sample routines that strengthen your whole body

. . . .

*I*n this book, you find over 150 exercises. Good news: You're not expected to do all these exercises in one workout — if you did, your workouts would last longer than the Academy Awards! So, how do you choose?

In this chapter, we explain how to create a routine based on your own goals, preferences, time schedule, and available equipment. We walk you through your program variables — the ingredients essential to all weight-training routines (covered in Chapter 2). Then we show you how to select the right weight for each exercise so you're ready to begin lifting!

We include a number of sample beginner routines to get you started. All the workouts in this chapter strengthen the entire body. In Chapters 17, 19, 20, 21, and 22, we include a variety of routines that suit every time situation and provide more challenging workouts and a variety of demographics.

Designing a Routine

You've probably read magazine articles that reveal an athlete or actor's weight-training routine. Often, the stories imply that if you follow the routine, you, too, can become a sculpted celebrity — or at least look like one. Don't buy into this notion. Everyone has a unique genetic makeup — and a unique set of preferences and priorities. In other words, you may not be able to dedicate three hours daily to training, hire a personal trainer to work with you daily, and hire a chef to cook all your meals. You certainly can pick up good ideas from reading about other people's workouts, but you're better off designing your own routines by considering the following factors.

Why you should want to train

Too many people blindly go through the motions of a weight-training program without stopping to ask themselves, "What am I trying to accomplish?" So, give this question some serious thought. Are you planning to scale a mountain, or do you just want to strengthen your back to add oomph to your golf swing? (See *Golf All-in-One For Dummies* for tips on fairway fitness with LaReine Chabut.) Remember the principle of specificity.

Here's a rundown of some common goals and how you can reach each of them. You may want to consult a trainer or doctor for advice that's even more specific to your needs.

✔ **Improve your health.** If you aspire to increase your strength, keep your bones strong, and avoid common injuries, you don't need to spend half of your waking hours with heavy weights in your hands. You can get by with one exercise for every major muscle group in your body. Simply perform one set of 8 to 15 repetitions for each of the following muscle groups:

- Glutes (butt)
- Quadriceps (front thighs)
- Hamstrings (rear thighs)
- Calves
- Pectorals (chest)
- Back
- Abdominals
- Deltoids (shoulders)
- Biceps (front of upper arm)
- Triceps (rear of upper arm)

The American College of Sports Medicine (ACSM) recommends doing two or three workouts a week.

✔ **Alter your looks.** Weight training can be a powerful tool for changing your appearance by toning up your muscles, adding definition to your body's shape, and adding size (if desired and if your genetics permit). If you're large boned and muscular, however, weight training can't make you lean and flexible — and vice versa. You need to work within your body's parameters.

Significantly overhauling your body's appearance requires more of a time commitment than simply improving your health. (And keep in mind that your diet, lifestyle, and cardiovascular workouts play a large role, too.) Instead of training your entire body in 25 minutes, you may need to spend 20 minutes simply on your upper body. In Chapter 18, we offer several 20-minute workouts for the time challenged. The 20-minute circuit workout in Chapter 18 can be found online at www.dummies.com/extras/weighttraining. To develop a noticeably firmer body, we suggest performing at least three sets per muscle group. To build some serious bulk, you may need to perform even more sets and use some of the advanced techniques described in Chapter 19.

✔ **Train for an athletic event.** Preparing for an athletic challenge at any level takes time and dedication (and weight training, of course, is just one aspect of your training). For best results, you need to tailor your weight routine precisely to the event. For example, if you're working toward a hilly 10K walk or run, you need to give extra attention to your leg and butt muscles. And your workout will be completely different if you want to simply complete a 10K run rather than win it. Serious competitors should expect to spend a lot of serious time in the weight room at certain times of the year (primarily the off-season). And, you should consult a trainer or coach who specializes in working with athletes for a comprehensive, periodized program.

When you've identified the reason why you want to train, use the S.M.A.R.T. goal system explained in Chapter 3 to set short-term goals that ensure your long-term success. Your short-term goals should focus on the behaviors, in other words, the things that you need to do or not do, to achieve your long-term objective. Your training program should reflect your specific training objectives.

Plastic versus real results

Take a reality check: Don't expect to look like the sculpted, fat-free people who sell weight-training products on TV infomercials or in magazine ads. Many of these models have unusual genetics, have taken drugs, and/or have undergone liposuction and added implants to achieve their looks (in addition to being digitally enhanced by professional film producers). In fact, among men, chest or pec and calf implants are popular, while more and more women are getting butt implants. We're *not* mentioning this phenomenon to advocate plastic surgery. We just want you to know that most people who have bodies that look a little too perfect are likely to have achieved that look through unnatural means. So don't set yourself up for failure before you begin by trying to look like a model by using natural methods. It's impossible. Simply aim to be your best *you!*

Your equipment

Naturally, the exercises you choose are limited to the equipment that's available to you. If you belong to a health club the size of Walmart, you may be able to try every exercise in this book — and probably a few thousand more. One four-story club in New York City devotes an entire *floor* to leg machines.

If you work out at a smaller club or at home, your choices are more limited, but even with minimal equipment, you can get your body into great shape! In Part III, for example, we describe dozens of exercises that you can do at home with nothing more than dumbbells and a bench. If you're short on equipment, you may want to consult a trainer to find out how to make the most of the gizmos you have access to or to help you decide which key pieces of equipment you should own to achieve your particular goals.

Your exercise preferences

When you first take up weight training, you may be overwhelmed by the challenge of knowing the basics of each exercise — how to stand, where to grab the weight, how to adjust the machines, when to inhale and exhale. But you soon develop strong preferences for certain exercises and equipment. Before you know it, you'll be saying things like, "I love the incline chest fly, but I'd much rather do the dumbbell chest press on a flat bench."

Pay attention to which exercises feel good to you and which equipment you enjoy using, and design your workout accordingly. Keep in mind, however, that it's natural to prefer the exercises that you're better at doing. Sometimes, you may need to push yourself to do exercises that you don't love to balance out your conditioning. Keep an open mind. You may even surprise yourself when you grow to love the push-ups that you used to hate.

Your lifestyle

Ask yourself (and answer honestly): "How many times can I work out each week? How many hours can I spend at the gym, including time in the shower and the locker room?" If you're a busy parent who also works full time, chances are, you have less time to work out than a college student or retired person.

Be realistic. Don't vow to do six sets per muscle group if the only time you're able to lift weights is during your 30-minute lunch break on Tuesdays and Thursdays. Otherwise, you fall into that "Why bother?" trap. You're better off doing a 20-minute routine (as shown in Chapter 18) than skipping that two-hour workout you planned but somehow never got around to.

Your current level of fitness

If you haven't lifted weights since high school 20 years ago, don't start with the routine your old football coach gave you. Otherwise, you can expect a lot of muscle soreness — and maybe an injury or two — in your immediate future. Don't let your enthusiasm, your flexible schedule, or your access to fancy equipment cloud your judgment as you design your routine.

The best goals are those that are achievable, and to be achievable, your plans need to be realistic.

Reviewing Your Program Variables

There are six basic program variables that you need to keep in mind when designing your training programs:

- Exercise selection
- Training frequency
- Exercise order
- Amount of weight and number of reps
- Number of sets
- Rest periods

Performing exercises in the right order

In general, follow the rule of doing your upper- and lower-body exercises starting with your larger muscles first and ending with your smaller muscles. Finally, exercise your middle body, lower back, and abdominals — they serve to stabilize your body as you do all the prior exercises.

Here's what this might look like:

Upper body

1. Chest and back (It doesn't matter which comes first.)

2. Shoulders

3. Biceps and triceps (It doesn't matter which comes first.)

4. Wrists

Lower body

1. Butt

2. Thighs

3. Calves and shins (It doesn't matter which comes first, although we prefer to work our calves before our shins.)

Middle body

Perform your abdominal and lower-back muscle exercises in any order you want. Mix up your core stabilization exercises with those that target the mover muscles; or do your mover exercises first, followed by your stabilizer exercises, or vice versa. Researchers haven't yet determined whether an ideal order exists for training the muscles of this part of the body.

Picking the right amount of weight

The right weight level depends on what you want to achieve from your training, because it relates to the number of reps that you perform. To develop strength, you want to do one to six reps. To increase muscle size, do 6 to 12 reps. And, to improve endurance, do 12 to 20 reps.

A one-rep max is the total amount of weight you can lift with one repetition and means you're giving a 100 percent effort. More reps represent what are referred to as *submaximal loads.* See the following table for reference:

Number of Reps	Percentage of Your One-Rep Max You Can Lift
1	100 percent
2–3	95 percent
4–5	90 percent
6–7	85 percent
8–9	80 percent
10–11	75 percent
12–13	70 percent
14–15	65 percent
16–20	60 percent

As you can see, a moderate-intensity workout of lifting 70 percent to 80 percent of your one-rep max is in the 8-to-13-rep range. Performing fewer reps — and using ultra-heavy weights — carries a greater risk of injury. And doing more than 12 reps is generally not effective for building strength, but doing up to 20 to 25 reps does improve muscular endurance.

To keep yourself motivated and your muscles challenged, you may want to vary the number of reps you perform. You can use a periodized program (as explained in Chapter 3) that first emphasizes muscular strength and then later emphasizes muscular endurance. For example, you can do 6 to 8 repetitions one month and then 12 to 15 reps the next month. Finding the right weight for each exercise requires some trial and error.

Don't be afraid to add or subtract weight after you start a set. We've seen people contort their bodies to finish a set just because they overestimated what they could lift but were too embarrassed, too stubborn, or simply not aware of the huge risk of injury to drop down a plate.

Using the rest period

How long you rest between sets is also a part of your routine. If you want to increase maximal strength, you need a long rest period of up to four minutes. If you're looking to improve muscular endurance, 30 seconds or even less rest is fine. If you want to increase size, your rest period should be about 30 to 90 seconds. If you're a beginner, take as long as you need. You're considered a beginner until you've completed three consecutive months of consistent training at least two to three days a week.

Trying Sample Beginner Routines

You can combine exercises in countless ways to create an effective weight routine. All the routines in this section include one or two exercises per muscle group.

Doing circuits at the gym

Many gyms have a dozen or so machines arranged in a circle or row called a *circuit.* They're placed in a logical order (from larger to smaller muscles) so you can move from machine to machine without having to use any brainpower to decide which exercise to do next. For reasons we explain in Chapter 13, we suggest skipping the abdominal machines and doing the basic abdominal crunch (or other ab floor exercises) at the end of your circuit instead.

Some fitness facilities, such as Curves, revolve entirely around circuit training. Many facilities also offer cardio-resistance circuits where, between strength-training stations, they have cardio stations. For example, you may jog or march in place, do jumping jacks, or jump on a trampoline in between lifting weights. The concept behind these workouts is keeping your heart rate at the low end of an aerobic training zone so you also receive some aerobic conditioning benefits as well. Because this workout represents a compromise, you're not getting an optimum cardio or strength workout. Instead, you're trying to hit two goals at once, which is of course, better than hitting only one or no goals, especially if you're time crunched.

After reviewing weight-training principles, you may understand why circuits are a good place for beginners to start training. Typically, you'll do one set at each machine and have about a 30-second rest interval between stations. This is the lower-intensity side of the spectrum and has a reduced risk of injury. See Table 17-1 for a sample weight-machine circuit.

Table 17-1	Sample Weight-Machine Circuit
Part of the Body	*Exercise*
Butt and legs	Leg-press machine, leg-extension machine, leg-curl machine
Back	Lat pull-down
Chest	Vertical chest-press machine
Shoulders	Shoulder-press machine
Biceps	Arm-curl machine
Triceps	Triceps-dip machine
Abdominals	Basic abdominal crunch

Doing circuits at home

If you like the idea of doing circuits, design your own home circuit. You may choose to stick with one circuit for a few weeks and then switch to another circuit. Or you may integrate circuit training on a rotating schedule for a lower-intensity workout that you incorporate into a plan that also includes a high-intensity strength workout component and a bulk-building segment. See Table 17-2 for a sample at-home circuit.

Table 17-2	Sample At-Home Dumbbell/Band Circuit
Part of the Body	*Exercise*
Butt and legs	Squat, lunge
Back	Band lat pull-down, one-arm dumbbell row
Chest	Push-up
Shoulders	Dumbbell shoulder press, lateral raise
Biceps	Dumbbell reverse curl
Triceps	Triceps kickback
Abdominals	Basic abdominal crunch, bicycle, plank

Dumbbells-and-a-bench routine for the gym or home

For this routine (see Table 17-3), you need several sets of dumbbells and a bench with an adjustable backrest. This workout is typical for someone who works out at home, but many gym-goers like it, too.

Table 17-3	Sample Dumbbells-and-a-Bench Routine
Part of the Body	*Exercise*
Butt and legs	Squat, lunge, standing calf raise
Back	One-arm row, back extension, chest, incline chest fly
Shoulders	Lateral raise
Arms	Dumbbell biceps curl, triceps kickback
Abdominals	Abdominal crunch with a twist

The mix-and-match routine at the gym

Most experienced weight lifters use a combination of machines and free weights. Over time, you develop certain preferences — some exercises feel better with free weights; others are more fun with machines. Using your body weight for resistance is a great workout — you don't need any equipment, except yourself! So, if you weigh 150 pounds, that's how much you'll be lifting as you perform a push-up, bench dip, and pull-up. We encourage you to try all the equipment at your disposal at least a few times. See Tables 17-4 and 17-5 for sample mix-and-match routines.

Table 17-4	Machine and Body-Weight Routine
Part of the Body	*Exercise*
Butt and legs	Lunge, leg press, inner- and outer-thigh machines, standing calf raise
Back	Cable row
Chest	Push-up
Shoulders	Cable lateral raise
Arms	Dumbbell biceps curl, triceps pushdown, wrist curl
Abdominals	Abdominal crunch

Table 17-5	Dumbbell Routine
Part of the Body	*Exercise*
Butt and legs	Squat, lunge, inner- and outer-thigh lifts
Back	Dumbbell pullover, dumbbell row
Chest	Incline chest fly, push-up
Shoulders	Dumbbell lateral raise, shoulder press
Arms	Dumbbell reverse curl, triceps kickback
Abdominals	Reverse crunch, bent-knee side crunch, bicycle

Chapter 18

20-Minute Workouts for the Time Challenged

. . . .

In This Chapter

▶ Trying a 20-minute workout available at Dummies.com

▶ Squeezing in 20-minute routines

▶ Setting up your home gym for quickies

. . . .

*I*n this chapter, you get a variety of quickie workouts to use for those busy periods when you can't follow an ideal training schedule. The quickies are organized in 20-minute segments and are appropriate for either the gym or at home. Try to find at least 20 minutes each day in your schedule for a workout so that exercising becomes part of your daily routine — like brushing your teeth. These routines give you plenty of choices for what to do in those 20-minute increments.

If you go to www.dummies.com/extras/weighttraining, you can try a 20-minute workout video. LaReine did the video as she was writing the book to help you do an actual dumbbell workout that you can follow along with.

For best results, you want to train your entire body at least two to three times a week. Three times a week gives you faster results but takes more of your personal time. Studies show that if you train two days a week, you get 75 percent of the results you get from training three days a week.

Shorter workouts are better than no workouts, but don't get the impression that it's the best or only way to train. The exercises in this chapter are supposed to be the exception rather than the rule. Some marketers make the claim that this is "all" you need to do, and yes, these quickies can contribute to improved health, but you can't get very fit exercising this way. That's not realistic or truthful.

Making the Most of Quickie Training

Organize these quickies in whatever way works best for you. The following suggestions give you several ideas on how to fit quickie workouts into your lifestyle.

- ✔ **Squeeze in one total-body conditioning workout in a week.** Normally, you do three 30-minute weight-training workouts. But what happens when your schedule is overloaded and you can't possibly follow your normal workout routine? Instead of doing nothing, do one of the total-body workouts to keep your muscles stimulated.

- ✔ **Add on to your cardio workout.** Say you weight-train two days a week and hit the gym for three days a week. When you can't make it for your dedicated weight-training sessions, add a 20-minute quickie workout on the weight machines, after you finish your cardio-training.

- ✔ **Divide your workout throughout the day.** Sometimes it's simply impossible to find more than a few spare minutes. Instead of giving up on strength training entirely, fit in a quickie workout in the morning and in the afternoon. You may even want to add on another session at night. Three 10-minute workouts easily add up to 30 minutes of training.

- ✔ **Do a daily quickie.** Maybe all you ever have time for during the week is a quickie workout. Until your life settles down and you find more time, schedule a daily quickie workout. Each day, target either the upper or lower body and the core. Take Friday off. On Saturday, fit in one total-body workout and rest on Sunday.

Putting Together Your 20-Minute Routine

Even when you're doing 20-minute programs, you need to keep in mind the basic weight-training principles explained in Chapter 2. Observe the following points each time that you train:

- ✔ **Always warm up.** Even for a quick workout, you need to prepare your body for more rigorous work. Walk briskly for five minutes before you exercise. This warm-up can include walking quickly around the house, in the yard, or in the parking lot at the office.

- ✔ **Work all major muscle groups.** Be sure to do exercises for your upper body, your lower body, and your core at least twice a week.

- ✔ **Apply program variables.** Even for short workouts, training frequency, exercise selection, order, amount of weight, number of reps, number of sets, and rest periods are all still important components. Just because you're doing a quickie workout doesn't mean that you can throw all the weight-training principles out the window. All the rules still apply.

✓ **Train in one-minute sets.** In general, one set of a particular exercise takes approximately one minute. If each rep requires two seconds up, a brief pause, and two seconds down, plan on five to six seconds per rep. So, a set of 12 reps takes roughly one minute.

✓ **Alternate upper- and lower-body exercises.** When you want to reduce the waiting time during rest periods, switch between upper- and lower-body exercises so that one part of your body rests while the other works. Save your core exercises for last.

✓ **Mix in stretching exercises.** To be even more efficient, use your rest periods for stretches that target the muscle that you just worked. You can stretch your body all throughout the workout, and you won't need extra time for a stretching segment at the end.

Doing 20-Minute Workouts

Perform these 20-minute workouts in any of the suggested manners. We suggest starting by going to www.dummies.com/extras/weighttraining to try the 20-minute routine in Table 18-1. You may even think of more ways to use these quickie suggestions. The important thing is to do exactly that — use these workouts to get fit and stay toned and firm.

Table 18-1	20-Minute Video Circuit
Segment of Routine	*Exercises*
Warm-up	Squat side-to-side, skater jump, alternating back lunge, rope-a-dope
Shoulders	Shoulder press, plié with shoulder press, front raise, lateral raise
Arms	Biceps curl, triceps kickback, plié biceps curl
Legs	Side leg raise, inner-thigh raise, kneeling butt blaster, kneeling crossover
Abdominals and core	Hip lift with weights, bicycle crunch, bicycle with straight legs, oblique crunch
Shoulders	Shoulder press, plié press, front raise, lateral raise
Arms	Biceps curl, triceps kickback, plié biceps curl
Legs	Side leg raise, inner-thigh raise, kneeling butt blaster, kneeling crossover
Abdominals and core	Hip lift with weights, bicycle crunch, bicycle with straight legs, oblique crunch
Cool-down stretch	Pretzel quad stretch, sitting side reach, sitting triceps stretch, standing breath

Total-body workouts in the gym

The workouts shown in Tables 18-2 through 18-4 are the absolute bare minimum and are for super time-crunch situations — they're by no means complete routines. But these workouts tide you over for a few sessions until you can get back on track for a more thorough total-body workout.

Table 18-2	20-Minute Machine Routine
Part of the Body	*Exercise*
Butt and legs	Leg-press machine
Back	Machine row
Chest	Vertical chest-press machine
Shoulders	Shoulder-press machine
Abdominals	Basic abdominal crunch, bicycle, oblique crunch

Table 18-3	20-Minute Mix-and-Match Routine
Part of the Body	*Exercise*
Butt and legs	Squat
Back	Machine row
Chest	Push-up, plank
Shoulders	Shoulder-press machine
Abdominals	Basic abdominal crunch, bicycle

Table 18-4	20-Minute Mix-and-Match Routine
Part of the Body	*Exercise*
Butt and legs	Leg-press machine, kneeling butt blaster
Back	One-arm dumbbell row
Chest	Vertical chest-press machine
Shoulders	Dumbbell shoulder press
Abdominals	Basic abdominal crunch, bicycle

Take five minutes to warm up before you start lifting by doing some form of aerobic movement: walking, marching, jumping rope, cycling, rowing, and so on.

Total-body workouts at home

When you're really pressed for time, sometimes the best thing to do is plan your workout for home — either first or last on your day's schedule. This way, you'll always be sure to complete your workout, no matter what happens. Use Tables 18-5 through 18-7 as your guides.

Table 18-5	20-Minute Band Routine
Part of the Body	*Exercise*
Butt and legs	Band squat
Back	Band lat pull-down
Chest	Band push-up
Shoulders	Band one-arm shoulder press
Abdominals	Basic abdominal crunch, bicycle

Table 18-6	20-Minute Ball Routine
Part of the Body	*Exercise*
Butt and legs	Ball bridge, ball march
Back	Ball explosion
Chest and shoulders	Ball push-up
Abdominals	Ball crunch, ball oblique crunch, ball plank

Table 18-7	20-Minute Body Weight Routine
Part of the Body	*Exercise*
Butt and legs	Squat, lunge, kneeling butt blaster
Back	Pelvic tilt, back explosion
Chest	Push-up
Arms	Bench dip
Abdominals	Basic abdominal crunch, bicycle
Core	Side plank, reverse plank, plank

Upper- and lower-body workouts

If you decide to organize your 20-minute workouts into split routines, focusing on either the upper or the lower body, use the following suggestions, or create your own workouts modeled after the ideas in Tables 18-8 through 18-11.

Table 18-8	20-Minute Upper-Body Dumbbell Routine
Part of the Body	*Exercise*
Chest	Push-up, dumbbell chest press
Back	One-arm dumbbell row
Shoulders	Dumbbell shoulder press
Front upper arms	Concentration curl
Rear upper arms	Triceps kickback
Abdominals	Basic abdominal crunch
Core	Plank

Table 18-9	20-Minute Upper-Body Band Routine
Part of the Body	*Exercise*
Back	Band lat pull-down
Chest	Band push-up
Shoulders	Band one-arm shoulder press
Front upper arms	Band biceps curl
Rear upper arms	Band triceps press
Abdominals	Basic abdominal crunch
Core	All-fours spinal stabilization

Table 18-10	20-Minute Lower-Body Dumbbell Routine
Part of the Body	*Exercise*
Butt	Squat
Front thighs	Lunge
Rear thighs	Kneeling leg curl
Inner thighs	Inner-thigh lift
Outer thighs	Side lying leg lift
Calves	Standing calf raise

Table 18-11	20-Minute Lower Plank Core Body Band Routine
Part of the Body	*Exercise*
Butt	Band butt blaster
Rear thighs	Band squat
Inner thighs	Band inner-thigh lift
Outer thighs	Band outer-thigh lift
Calves	Band calf press
Core	Hands-and-knees spinal stabilization

Exercising with the 20-Minute Routines

On some days, you may not even have 20 minutes to lift weights. Instead of skipping your workout altogether, try Plan B: the absolute bare minimum. The workouts listed in Tables 18-12 and 18-13 are for emergency situations only — they're by no means complete routines. But a 20-minute workout tides you over for a few sessions until you get back on track.

Table 18-12	20-Minute Machine Routine
Part of the Body	*Exercise*
Butt and legs	Leg-press machine
Back	Machine row
Chest	Vertical chest-press machine

Table 18-13	20-Minute Dumbbell Routine
Part of the Body	*Exercise*
Butt and legs	Squat
Back	One-arm dumbbell row
Chest	Dumbbell chest press

Home gym mix-and-match routines

You can do a quickie mix-and-match routine with whatever type of equipment you've chosen for home use. Tables 18-14 through 18-16 show some fun combination workouts.

Table 18-14	Dumbbells and Band Mix-and-Match Routine
Part of the Body	*Exercise*
Butt and legs	Band butt blaster
Back	Band lat pull-down
Chest	Dumbbell chest press
Shoulders	Band one-arm shoulder press
Abdominals	Abdominal crunch

Table 18-15	Dumbbells and Ball Mix-and-Match Routine
Part of the Body	*Exercise*
Butt and legs	Squat
Back	Ball extension
Chest	Ball push-up
Shoulders	Dumbbell shoulder press
Abdominals	Ball crunch

Table 18-16	Band and Ball Mix-and-Match Routine
Part of the Body	*Exercise*
Butt and legs	Band squat
Back	Band lat pull-down
Chest	Ball push-up
Shoulders	Band one-arm shoulder press
Abdominals	Ball plank

Upper- and lower-body workouts

Tables 18-17 through 18-20 list 20-minute workouts organized as split routines focusing on either the upper or the lower body. Use the following suggestions, or get creative and design your own quickie split workouts.

Table 18-17	20-Minute Upper-Body Dumbbell Routine
Part of the Body	*Exercise*
Back	One-arm dumbbell row
Chest	Dumbbell chest press
Shoulders	Dumbbell shoulder press
Abdominals	Basic abdominal crunch, plank

Table 18-18	20-Minute Upper-Body Band Routine
Part of the Body	*Exercise*
Back	Band lat pull-down
Chest	Band push-up
Shoulders	Band one-arm shoulder press
Abdominals	Bicycle, abdominal crunch

Table 18-19	20-Minute Lower-Body Dumbbell Routine
Part of the Body	*Exercise*
Butt and legs	Squat, kneeling butt blaster
Inner thighs	Inner-thigh lift
Outer thighs	Side lying leg lift
Calves	Standing calf raise

Table 18-20	20-Minute Lower-Body Band Routine
Part of the Body	*Exercise*
Butt and legs	Band squat
Inner thighs	Band inner-thigh lift
Outer thighs	Band outer-thigh lift
Calves	Band calf press

Stretching workout

Stretching feels great at the end of a workout. It restores length to muscles that may feel tighter after being contracted during exercise. Stretching also releases muscular tension from your body, leaving you feeling more relaxed in general. You can also do the stretch sequence in Table 18-21 as an early-morning wake-up routine or as an end-of-day relaxation session. Breathe deeply and hold each stretch three breath cycles. One breath cycle equals one inhalation and one exhalation. As time permits, repeat each stretch three to five times.

Table 18-21	20-Minute Stretch Routine
Part of the Body	*Exercise*
Butt and legs	Pretzel stretch, hamstrings stretch, quadriceps stretch
Back	Cat stretch, reach-up stretch
Chest and shoulders	Hand-clasp stretch

Chapter 19

Tackling More-Advanced Programs

• •

In This Chapter

▶ Understanding progression with weight training

▶ Practicing split routines

▶ Varying your weight training with the latest methods

▶ Trying advanced training techniques

• •

*Y*ou may come to a point in your weight-training career when moving through the same 12 weight machines or performing the same old dumbbell exercises isn't enough — not enough to keep you interested and not enough to keep giving you results. Out of boredom or disappointment, you may start skipping your workouts. This is a warning sign that it's time to start progressing your program.

In this chapter, we show you how to go beyond the basics to create a more advanced and stimulating weight-training program. The strategies we present fall into three basic categories:

✔ Designing your weekly schedule

✔ Arranging your exercises during a particular workout

✔ Structuring an individual set

You can experiment with one of the strategies we discuss in this chapter, or you can use every one. Just don't try them all at once. You're less likely to feel overwhelmed if you incorporate change gradually. Plus, you can pinpoint more precisely which strategies work for you and which don't.

Beginners certainly can benefit from the techniques we discuss here and should read this chapter. But you'll find the strategies here more valuable if you've been lifting weights for at least a month.

Understanding Progression

Progressing your program or increasing intensity over time requires skill and patience. You don't want to progress too quickly or you risk injury, but if you don't progress your program, it'll become stale. After you've mastered 15 reps to fatigue at a particular weight, you're ready to progress to two sets. After you've mastered two sets of 15 reps to fatigue, you can add an additional set or you can progress to a heavier weight level in the 8- to 12-rep range. Increase your weight by up to 5 percent. For example, let's say you've been lifting 40 pounds for 15 reps for two sets. To progress, you would increase by 2 pounds and lift 42 pounds for 8 to 12 reps for one set.

The challenge with lower weight ranges is that it's difficult to find small weights to add the incremental poundage. If you're working on machines, look for the small 5-pound bars that you can rest on top of the stack. If you're working with dumbbells with narrow handles, you can hold more than one in your hand.

Another way to progress your program is to add variety by performing more exercises for each muscle group. This continues to stimulate the muscle by working the muscles through different movement patterns and by requiring more muscle fibers to work.

Practicing Split Routines

Regardless of your goals, you need to hit each muscle group at least twice a week. The simplest way to accomplish this is to perform two *total-body* workouts per week; in other words, twice a week perform a routine that works every major muscle group.

Total-body workouts are great if you're doing only one or two exercises per muscle group. But when you get serious about weight training — adding exercises and sets — a total-body workout can become tedious. If your schedule permits you to lift weights at least four days a week (the sessions can be as short as 15 minutes), consider doing a *split routine*. You split a total-body routine into two or three shorter routines. For example, you can train your upper body on one day and your lower body the next. You can even split your upper-body muscles into three different workouts. (We discuss these options in detail later in this section.)

Split routines are ideal for people who have the time to work out several days a week but may not have much time for each workout session. Split routines also work well for people who have a short attention span for weight training or who want to give each muscle group an extra-hard workout. Brief, focused workouts help you stay motivated. If you walk into the gym knowing that all you have to do today is work your back and biceps, you're more likely to give those exercises an all-out effort.

When designing a split routine, follow two basic rules:

- ✔ Hit each muscle group at least twice a week.
- ✔ Don't work the same muscle group on consecutive days.

This second rule is a bit more complicated than it sounds. For example, you may think that it's okay to work your triceps and thighs on Monday and then your chest and butt on Tuesday. Actually, it's not, because most chest exercises *also* work the triceps and most butt exercises *also* work the thighs. So, if you work your triceps on Monday, they won't have recovered sufficiently by Tuesday to help out on your chest exercises.

These rules may sound confusing, but within a few weeks, they'll become second nature. Until then, here's a list of muscle pairs that you *shouldn't* work on back-to-back days:

- ✔ Chest and triceps
- ✔ Back and biceps
- ✔ Butt and thighs

The split routines that we describe in the following sections heed the preceding two basic rules.

The upper-body/lower-body split

The upper-body/lower-body split is perhaps the simplest split, a good one for beginners to try. You don't have much to remember: It's pretty obvious which exercises work the muscles above the belt and which work the muscles down south. When you work your upper body one day and your lower body the next, each zone of your body gets more of a complete rest than for any other way you do your split.

People who do the upper-body/lower-body split generally train their abdominals with their lower body, but this isn't a hard-and-fast rule. Don't make the mistake of working your abs every workout.

The abs are like any other muscle group: They need time to recover. Two or three abdominal workouts a week will suffice.

Table 19-1 shows two sample weekly schedules based on the upper-body/lower-body split.

Table 19-1	Sample Weekly Schedules for Split Routines
Day of the Week	*Body Area or Rest Period*
Sample Split #1	
Monday	Upper body
Tuesday	Lower body and abdominals
Wednesday	Rest
Thursday	Upper body
Friday	Lower body and abdominals
Saturday	Rest
Sunday	Rest
Sample Split #2	
Monday	Upper body and abdominals
Tuesday	Rest
Wednesday	Lower body and abdominals
Thursday	Rest
Friday	Upper body and abdominals
Saturday	Rest
Sunday	Lower body

Tables 19-2 and 19-3 are two examples of the exercises you can include in your upper-body/lower-body split routine — one routine is for beginners, and the other is for more experienced lifters.

Table 19-2	Sample Exercises for a Basic Upper-Body/ Lower-Body Split Routine
Body Part	*Exercises*
Upper Body	
Back	Lat pull-down, machine row, pelvic tilt
Chest	Dumbbell chest press, incline chest fly
Shoulders	Dumbbell shoulder press, lateral raise
Biceps	Hammer curl, concentration curl
Triceps	Triceps push-down, triceps kickback

Body Part	Exercises
Lower Body	
Butt and legs	Squat, lunge, leg-extension machine, leg-curl machine, inner- and outer-thigh machines, standing calf-raise machine
Abdominals	Slide, basic abdominal crunch

Table 19-3	Sample Exercises for an Advanced Upper-Body/ Lower-Body Split Routine
Body Part	**Exercises**
Upper Body	
Back	Chin-up, lat pull-down with triangle grip, seated cable row, back extension, machine pullover
Chest	Bench press, incline dumbbell press, assisted dip, decline fly
Shoulders	Military press, lateral raise, back delt fly, internal and external rotation
Biceps	Barbell biceps curl, preacher curl, alternating dumbbell biceps curl
Triceps	Triceps push-down, French press, bench dip
Lower Body	
Legs	Barbell squat, backward lunge, stiff-legged dead lift, leg-extension machine, leg-curl machine, inner- and outer-thigh machines, single-leg calf raise
Abdominals	Hanging abs, reverse crunch, abdominal crunch with a twist

Push/pull split routine

This type of split separates your upper-body *pushing* muscles (the chest and triceps) from the upper-body *pulling* muscles (your back and biceps). You can do your lower-body and abdominal exercises on either day or on a separate day altogether. Or you can include your legs with your pushing muscles and your abdominals with your pulling muscles.

You may have noticed that we haven't mentioned where your shoulders fit into the push/pull split. There's no simple answer because shoulders don't fit neatly into either the push or the pull category; the shoulders are partially involved in both movements. Where you work in your shoulders is a matter of personal preference. Some people like to work their shoulders right after their chest muscles. Others like to do shoulder exercises after their back exercises. Still others prefer to divide their body into three workouts: back and biceps; chest and triceps; shoulders, leg, and abs.

Push/pull split routines are popular among experienced exercisers who want to go to town with each muscle group. You may see people spend two hours just working their back and biceps. However, other people feel unbalanced after one of these routines because they worked only one side of the torso. Table 19-4 shows sample push/pull split routine schedules.

Table 19-4	Sample Push/Pull Split Routine Schedules
Day of the Week	*Body Area or Rest Period*
Sample Four-Day Week	
Monday	Chest, triceps, and shoulders
Tuesday	Back, biceps, abdominals, and lower body
Wednesday	Rest
Thursday	Chest, triceps, and shoulders
Friday	Rest
Saturday	Back, biceps, abdominals, and lower body
Sunday	Rest
Sample Five-Day Week	
Monday	Chest and triceps
Tuesday	Back and biceps
Wednesday	Shoulders, lower body, and abdominals
Thursday	Rest
Friday	Chest, triceps, and shoulders
Saturday	Back, biceps, lower body, and abdominals
Sunday	Rest

Table 19-5 suggests exercises to include for each of the four main push/pull split combinations. You can mix and match these combinations to fit the workouts that we describe for the weekly schedules in Table 19-4.

Table 19-5	Sample Exercises for Push/Pull Split Routines
Body Parts	*Exercises*
Back and Biceps	
Back	Assisted pull-up, lat pull-down, seated cable row, dumbbell pullover, one-arm row, back extension
Biceps	Barbell biceps curl, concentration curl, arm-curl machine
Chest and Triceps	
Chest	Bench press, incline chest fly, vertical chest-press machine, cable crossover, push-up
Triceps	Triceps push-down, triceps kickback, triceps-dip machine
Shoulders	
Shoulders	Dumbbell shoulder press, cable lateral raise, front raise, back delt fly, internal/external rotation
Lower body and Abdominals	
Legs	Lunge, leg-press machine, leg-extension machine, leg-curl machine, inner- and outer-thigh machines, standing calf raise
Abdominals	Rolling like a ball, reverse crunch, abdominal crunch with a twist

Practicing Sequencing in Your Workouts

Now we're going to narrow the focus even further. After you decide that you're going to work, say, your chest, triceps, and shoulders on Monday, you need to decide the order in which to do the exercises. In Chapter 2, we explain that you should work your large muscles before your smaller ones within each zone of your body. However, you still have plenty of options. Certain exercise sequences can save you time by reducing the amount of rest you need between sets; other sequences take longer but give your muscles a tougher challenge. Use the suggestions in the following sections to vary the order of your exercises.

Super sets

Doing a *super set* simply means performing two different exercises without resting between the sets. There are two types of super sets, each with a different purpose.

Same-muscle super sets

You do consecutive sets of different exercises that work the same muscle group. For example, go immediately from the dumbbell chest press to the chest fly, rest for a minute, and then do the press plus fly sequence again. This type of super set challenges the muscle in question. Just when your pecs think that they've completed a job well done — *bam!* — you blindside them with another exercise right away.

You can do super sets with just about any two exercises. Keep in mind that you'll probably use less weight than usual on the second exercise because your muscles are already fairly tired. You may want to enlist a spotter if you're doing super sets that involve lifting a weight directly over your face or head.

Table 19-6 shows some super-set combinations. You can string them all together to form a whole super-set workout, or you can insert any number of these combinations into your workout.

Table 19-6	Sample Same-Muscle Super-Set Routine
Body Parts	*Exercise Combinations*
Butt and legs	Squat + lunge
Back	Lat pull-down + machine row
Chest	Bench press + push-up
Shoulders	Dumbbell shoulder press + lateral raise
Biceps	Barbell biceps curl + dumbbell biceps curl
Triceps	French press + bench dip
Abdominals	Basic abdominal crunch + abdominal crunch with a twist

Different-muscle super sets

With this type of super set, you do back-to-back exercises that work different muscles. For example, go from a front-thigh exercise directly to a rear-thigh exercise. This type of super set is a great way to speed up your routine because it cuts back on the rest you need to take during a routine. Your front thighs rest while you perform the rear-thigh exercise, and vice versa. Table 19-7 shows a sample different-muscle super-set routine.

Table 19-7	Sample Different-Muscle Super-Set Routine
Body Parts	*Exercise Combinations*
Butt and legs + chest	Leg press + vertical chest-press machine
Back + quadriceps	Dumbbell pullover + leg-extension machine
Shoulders + hamstrings	Shoulder press + leg-curl machine
Biceps + legs	Barbell biceps curl + calf raise
Triceps + abdominals	Triceps push-down + basic abdominal crunch
Wrists + lower back	Wrist curl + back extension

Giant sets

Giant sets take the super-set idea one step further: Instead of doing two consecutive sets of different exercises without rest, you string *three* exercises together. For example, for a killer abdominal workout, you could link together three different abdominal exercises, rest, and then repeat the sequence. Or, to save time in your workout, you could move from a back exercise to a chest exercise to a butt exercise.

Table 19-8 shows some of our favorite giant sets that you can work into your routines.

Table 19-8	Suggested Giant Exercise Sets
Body Parts	*Exercise Combinations*
Abdominals	Basic abdominal crunch + reverse crunch + abdominal crunch with a twist
Butt and legs	Leg-press machine + leg-extension machine + leg-curl machine
Back	Lat pull-down + cable row + seated back machine
Chest	Dumbbell chest press + chest fly + cable crossover
Shoulders	Shoulder press + front raise + lateral raise

Advanced Training Techniques

After you choose which exercises to do and what order to do them in, you still have a few decisions to make. Suppose you're going to perform three sets on the leg-extension machine. Will you perform the same number of repetitions for each set? Or do you want to decrease the number of repetitions from one set to the next so that you can lift more weight?

Pyramids

If you have the time or inclination to perform at least five sets of an exercise, consider a pyramid. You start with a light weight and then gradually work your way up to the heaviest weight you can lift for one or two repetitions. Or you can do a modified pyramid: Instead of piling on the weight until you can do only one repetition, stop at the point where five or six reps is tough. This approach is better for beginners and for people who don't have a buddy to spot them while lifting heavy weights.

You can also do a descending pyramid, starting with the heaviest weight you think you can lift once, and working down until you're lifting a weight that allows you to perform 12 to 15 reps. However, don't do your heaviest set without first doing at least one warm-up set.

A third option is to combine a regular pyramid with a descending pyramid. In other words, you could start with ten reps and a light weight, work your way up to a heavy weight and one to three reps, and then work your way back down to a light weight and ten reps again. This technique brings new meaning to the word *fatigue.* Expect to lift a lot less weight on the way down than you do on the way up. For example, if you can bench-press 80 pounds ten times on the way up, you may be able to bench press 80 pounds only six times on the way down. For the ten-rep set, you may be lifting only 50 pounds.

Breakdowns

Breakdown training is just another way of tiring out the muscle. You do multiple sets of an exercise without resting between sets; meanwhile, you decrease the weight for each set. Suppose that you're doing the lateral raise. First, line up four to six sets of dumbbells near you, from heaviest to lightest. After a light warm-up set, do ten repetitions with the heavy set, put the weights down, do eight reps with the next-lightest dumbbells, put those down, and so on (until you either run out of gas or run out of dumbbells). Breakdowns also are fun to do with machines because, instead of putting down and picking up weights, all you have to do is move the pin.

Another option is to do modified breakdowns by using just two different weights. For example, choose a weight that enables you to do ten repetitions, and then immediately put it down and pick up a lighter weight, squeezing out as many repetitions as possible until failure, usually about four or five.

Negatives

Negatives is an advanced technique that can cause extreme muscle soreness, so beginners shouldn't try it. Someone helps you lift a weight, and then you're on your own for the lowering, or *negative,* phase of the lift. The negative phase is also referred to as the *eccentric phase* (pronounced EE-sen-tric, as opposed to eck-SEN-tric). The lifting, or *positive,* phase is called the *concentric phase.*

Your muscles generally can handle more weight when you lower a weight than when you lift it, so this technique gives you a chance to max out on the negative phase. This technique is a good one to try on the bench press and many lower-body machines such as the leg extension and leg curl because it's easy for your buddy to help you lift up a handle or a machine's lever. Negative sets done with machines are safer than free-weight negative sets because you're not in danger of dropping a dumbbell on your head if your arms or shoulders suddenly give out.

Varying Your Workout with the Latest Trends

To stave off boredom, there are some really popular and exciting ways to work out. Reaching a plateau when you're exercising is hard to overcome, but by trying out a few of the suggestions in this section, you can find new motivation and a new routine.

Circuits

A *circuit* is a routine in which you do one set each of several exercises, taking little or no rest between sets. Then you repeat the whole circuit as many times as you want. The typical circuit uses weight machines because they save you time. In Chapter 18, we provide a weight-machine circuit.

However, you can create your own circuit by using free weights or a free-weight/machine combination. Here are some basic rules to keep in mind when designing your circuit workout:

✔ **Try to alternate upper-, lower-, and middle-body (abdominal and lower-back) muscles so that no single muscle group gets tired too quickly.** You also can do opposing muscle groups in the same region of the body, such as chest and back or quadriceps and hamstrings.

- ✔ **Switch between lying, standing, and seated exercises very carefully.** Moving from one posture to another too quickly can cause sudden changes in blood pressure, which can cause you to feel dizzy or pass out.

- ✔ **Even though you're moving quickly between exercises, don't speed up the repetitions within a set.** Good form still applies.

- ✔ **Expect to use about 20 percent less weight than usual for each exercise because you're moving so fast.** Sure, your front thighs are resting while you work your rear thighs, but your whole body (including your heart and lungs) is still working at a pretty quick pace.

- ✔ **Keep your concentration and focus on each exercise.** It's easy to adapt to doing a circuit that you become familiar with and give less effort. Remind yourself each time to approach your circuit with energy.

- ✔ **Try not to do circuits more than once a week.** Circuit training is a good way to pull yourself out of a rut, but you won't gain as much strength from working out this way.

High-intensity interval training

High-intensity interval training (HIIT) has become a very popular way of training to burn more fat, improve endurance, and build strength. The basic idea is that moderate levels of intensity are alternated with high levels of intensity. By working at a higher level of intensity, you're able to work both aerobically and anaerobically, burning more fat as a result. Good news, right? Plus, it boosts your metabolism so you can burn more calories throughout the day.

The people who benefit the most from HIIT are those who want to burn a great amount of fat and increase their anaerobic endurance. Similar to soccer and basketball, HIIT varies high-intensity running with low periods of activity. As an example, a basic HIIT workout would be a 30-second jog, followed by 30 seconds of sprinting, and then repeating this pattern seven more times for a total of eight minutes. Compared to regular cardio training like running, HIIT burns more fat because when you run for a period of time at the same pace, your body kicks into a steady state (meaning your body adjusts itself to that speed and, in turn, works hard to conserve energy/calories for that pace). HIIT definitely gives you more bang for your buck — if you want to burn fat.

Kettlebells

Burn calories and fat without dumbbells by using kettlebells instead. A 20-minute workout with a kettlebell burns over 300 calories and really works your arms, shoulders, and back as it challenges your core. Because the weight isn't evenly distributed (see Chapter 4), you have to work harder and incorporate your butt and thighs to balance it out. Bent rows, dead lifts, and front squats all can be done with kettlebells. However don't be fooled by the plural in *kettlebells* — you use just one for a kettlebell workout.

Check out *Kettlebells For Dummies,* by Sarah Lurie (Wiley), for more information.

Sandbags

Sandbags have evolved into neoprene-filled versions called Sandbells. They're perfect for getting a functional workout — a workout that mimics the moves you make in everyday life. So, instead of needing dumbbells and an exercise ball and a kettlebell, all you need is one Sandbell to stabilize core muscles as you work everything else. Squats, presses, throws, swings, and slams are some of the movements that make up this new form of working out.

The weight varies anywhere from 2 pounds to 50 pounds, but most classes at the gym use 8, 10, 12, 15, and 20 pounds. The color around the outer rim of the neoprene Sandbells indicates the weight; the weights are clearly marked on the outside, too. Arms, core, abs, glutes, and thighs all can be "sandblasted" with a sandbag workout. Try a class at your gym or local YMCA to beat the boredom of your regular workout routine!

Chapter 20

Workouts for the Family: New Moms, Moms-to-Be, Kids, and Teens

In This Chapter

▶ Weight-training tips for kids and teens

▶ Training before and after baby comes

▶ Enjoying fitness for the whole family

▶ Building and maintaining strong bones for life

Today's conveniences of modern living eliminate almost all the natural activity that would normally challenge us physically as we go through the day. That's why weight training and physical activity are more important than ever.

In this chapter, you discover how to modify basic training for different stages in life. As you probably know all too well, life is filled with ups and downs and twists and turns. Here, you see how to keep on training or start a training program regardless of your current age or circumstance. Whether you're designing a program for yourself, supervising your kids while they exercise, or giving suggestions to your family for some family exercise, the information in this chapter offers valuable insight into important considerations to keep weight training safe, effective, and fun. For specific medical conditions, always be sure to check first with your healthcare provider.

Training Tips for Kids and Teens

LaReine's kids (shown with LaReine in Figure 20-1) are training at age 8 and 11 and are very much interested in sports and getting stronger. LaReine speaks with parents and in schools about how to encourage kids' interest in training. The main goal, of course, is to make sure that they don't hurt themselves or affect the natural progress of their growth — because of this, kids need to be guided when they start. And because kids will be kids and monkey around, you have to be sure to do everything safely and properly from the outset.

Figure 20-1:
Author
LaReine
Chabut and
her kids
love to train
together!

Photograph by Nick Horne

Benefiting from youth resistance training

Today's youth definitely benefit from training their muscles. Kids are subject to the same conditions as adults — a life filled with computers, cars, and inactive forms of recreation and entertainment. Leading researchers who specialize in youth fitness have found that children as young as 6 years old benefit from training. The key factor is the maturity of the child and whether he pays attention and follows directions.

Youth training has its risks of injury, but the benefits outweigh the risks as long as the activities are supervised and kept safe. The following list shows some of the benefits kids gain from strength training:

✔ Strong muscles

✔ Strong bones

✔ Muscle endurance

- Confidence and self-esteem

- Coordination and balance

- More lean muscle mass and less body fat

- Energy to participate in other physical activities

- Reduced risk of injury from youth sports

- Better sports performance

- Social skills (gained from interaction and cooperation by finding out how to work with others while training)

Plus, when kids train, they're starting a good habit of regular exercise for a healthy lifestyle — one that can last a lifetime.

Knowing what's age appropriate

Children aren't mini-adults. They're growing. Inappropriate training damages growth cartilage with serious consequences. Kids don't need to use a lot of fancy equipment. Body weight provides the challenge for many child-appropriate exercises. You need to show children that weights aren't toys.

Workout safety guidelines for kids

Here are a few of the important safety guidelines for you and your kids to follow:

- Get approval from your child's healthcare provider before starting.

- Make sure your child always trains under the supervision of a qualified professional.

- Don't allow your child to train more than two days a week.

- Keep training sessions short and include a warm-up and stretching.

- Have your child do eight to ten strength exercises per session, one set per exercise, with 13 to 15 reps per set.

- Don't add weight until your child can do 15 reps easily. When you do add weight, add it in small 1- to 3-pound increments.

- Never allow your child to lift a maximum or near-maximum weight load.

- Keep training fun and noncompetitive.

- Always take a conservative approach. You don't want to push your kids (or allow them to push themselves) too hard — that could lead to an injury.

- Balance weight training with aerobic activities.

- Make sure your child eats properly and gets plenty of sleep.

- Don't allow your child to overtrain.

Safety guidelines for teens

Children and adolescents shouldn't do power lifting, bodybuilding, or repetitive use of maximal weight loads in strength-training programs until they've reached a level of developmental maturity. This level is described as "Tanner stage 5" in medical circles and means that they've passed the period of maximal speed in the growth of their height. The reason for concern about the dangers of serious weight training is that when teens are growing, the *epiphyses,* a part of bone, is especially vulnerable to injury. As an average, both boys and girls reach this stage of development by age 15. However, individuals differ widely. This is why any more rigorous training should never be undertaken without consulting your child's healthcare provider and a sports medicine physician.

All the kids' guidelines (see the preceding section) apply to teens, with the added caveat that more rigorous training shouldn't be undertaken until the teen has reached physical maturity. At that point, a teen can start training as an adult at a moderate level.

Keep in mind that kids are subject to tremendous amounts of body image pressure both from the media and from their peers. Listen carefully to how your child describes how she feels about training. Pay attention to personal comments about appearance. If your child shows any sign of exercise or eating disordered behavior, consult a professional right away.

Trying sample kid and teen routines

The following routines are samples of total-body conditioning routines that uses body weight for resistance. The risk of injury is very low and the potential conditioning benefits are great. The readiness of a child to begin training using his own body weight as resistance is defined by the American Council on Exercise (ACE) as when a child is old enough to be involved in sports and able to follow directions.

For kids ages 6 to 11

The following workout includes a warm-up and upper-body/lower-body exercises that are fun and easy to do. Kids do these exercises at school to meet the physical education requirements.

Warm-up

Jumping jacks are a great way to warm up your body and strengthen your core. By raising your arms above your head and lowering them back down toward your body, you get a nice workout for your back, waist, and abdominals.

Getting set: Hold your arms straight to your sides with your feet together. Pull your abdominals in and stand up tall with square shoulders (see Figure 20-2a).

The exercise: Jump with your legs apart as you bring your arms overhead to cross your wrists (see Figure 20-2b). Repeat for 10 to 15 repetitions.

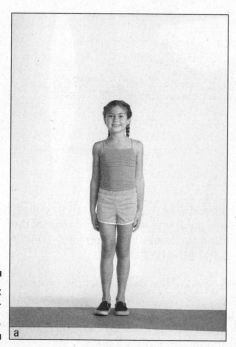 

Figure 20-2:
Warm-up for kids.

a

b

Photograph by Nick Horne

Back stretch

Kids like to run, jump, and kick with ease, but stretching is really important, too. Building flexibility, as you do in this back stretch, helps improve balance in sports and prevent injuries.

Getting set: Lie on the floor on your stomach. Place your palms on the floor next to your shoulders, the same as in push-up position.

The exercise: Inhale and arch your back, as you straighten your arms and bring your feet in to try and touch the back of your head (see Figure 20-3). Keep your hips on the floor and look toward the ceiling. Hold the stretch for a few seconds and then release the position back down to the floor. Repeat this exercise two to four times.

Figure 20-3:
Back stretch
for kids.

Photograph by Nick Horne

Push-up on knees

Push-ups on your knees are a good way to gain strength in your belly and core area. Kids, can progress to push-ups with straight legs as they get stronger, but always keep in mind that the back should remain straight and not buckle in or dip from the weight of the body.

Using a mat or towel will help cushion the knees from the ground.

Getting set: Kneel on your knees and place your hands shoulder-width apart on the floor in front of you (as shown in Figure 20-4a). Make sure that your hands are directly below your shoulders on the floor.

The exercise: Look straight down and lower toward the ground as far as you can go (see Figure 20-4b). Push back up to starting position. Repeat for four to six repetitions.

Bicycle crunches

Bicycle crunches are the best exercise for working your abs. The twisting and pulling motion you do with your knees and upper body is perfect for getting any kid in shape fast and is a lot of fun for kids and adults to do.

Getting set: Lie on your back with your knees bent and your feet on the floor. Place your fingers just behind your ears.

The exercise: Lift your shoulders off the floor and bring the right knee in toward your left elbow (see Figure 20-5a). Without relaxing the torso or returning your shoulders to the floor, repeat on the other side by bringing the left knee in toward your right elbow (see Figure 20-5b). Alternate the legs in a slow bicycling movement, ten times on each side.

Figure 20-4:
Push-ups for
kids.

Photograph by Nick Horne

For kids ages 12 to 15

On average, kids have reached puberty by age 15. During this time, resistance training using the weight of your own body is preferred over strength training with weights. The following workout should be done in 20 to 30 minutes, two to three times a week, to help build endurance and increase energy. Do this in addition to a sport like soccer, baseball, basketball, or something that involves running!

Warm-up

The goal of this warm-up is to get the heart rate up.

Getting set: Hold your arms straight to your sides with your feet together. Pull your abdominals in and stand up tall with your shoulders square (see Figure 20-6a).

Figure 20-5: Bicycle crunches for kids.

Photograph by Nick Horne

The exercise: Jump your legs apart as you bring your arms overhead to cross your wrists (see Figure 20-6b). Increase your speed to complete 25 repetitions in one minute. Repeat four times.

Back stretch

Not only does this move help make your back feel better, but it also improves the range of motion in the spine and enhances strength and coordination of the muscles around the spine, which is important as teens are growing.

Getting set: Get on the floor on your hands and knees with your hands directly under your shoulders and your knees directly under your hips.

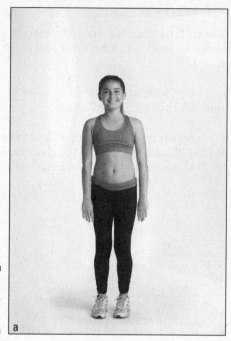 

Figure 20-6:
Warm-up for
teens.

Photograph by Nick Horne

The exercise: Inhale and arch your back, lifting your tailbone and eyes
toward the ceiling (see Figure 20-7). Hold the stretch for a few seconds then
release the position back to neutral spine, and inhale again. Repeat this exercise four to six times.

Figure 20-7:
Back stretch
for teens.

Photograph by Nick Horne

Push-up

The teen version of a push-up is with the legs out straight instead of knees bent. A teen should be old enough to hold his or her own body weight without having to be on the knees.

Getting set: Get into push-up position with arms extended straight on the floor and hands beneath the shoulders (see Figure 20-8a).

The exercise: Lower your body toward the floor, trying to keep your back straight but also keeping your hips lifted so you don't sag in the middle of your back (see Figure 20-8b). Pull in your abdominals to help keep your back in line with your spine.

Figure 20-8: Push-ups for teens.

Photograph by Nick Horne

Squats

For the lower body and building a strong foundation, squats are great for teens. In addition to strengthening the butt muscles, the squat also does a good job of working the quadriceps and hamstrings.

Getting set: Hold your arms straight out in front of you and stand with your feet as wide as your hips, with your body weight slightly back on your heels. Pull your abdominals in and stand up tall with square shoulders.

The exercise: Sit back and down, as if you're sitting into a chair (see Figure 20-9). Lower as far as you can without leaning your upper body more than a few inches forward. Don't lower any farther than the point at which your thighs are parallel to the floor, and don't allow your knees to shoot out in front of your toes. When you feel your upper body fold forward over your thighs, straighten your legs and stand back up. Be careful not to lock your knees at the top of the movement.

Figure 20-9:
Squats for teens.

Photograph by Nick Horne

Bicycles

See the earlier "Bicycles" section for kids. The modification for teens is to straighten the leg as you bring the opposite elbow to your knee each time instead of bringing bent knees in to meet the opposite elbow (see Figure 20-10).

Figure 20-10:
Bicycle
crunches for
teens.

Photograph by Nick Horne

Lifting Weights Before and After Baby

Being physically fit helps you through your pregnancy and speeds your recovery after you have a baby. However, pregnancy isn't the time to *increase* your training program. What you should strive for is to maintain a healthy, moderate level of activity.

Always check with your healthcare provider before you start an exercise program when you're pregnant. Continue to evaluate the safety and appropriateness of your training with your doctor as your pregnancy progresses and after you give birth.

Benefiting from prenatal and postpartum resistance training

Every woman's pregnancy is unique. All pregnancies follow the same general pattern, but each mother carves her own experience. Weight training is beneficial because it helps relieve the stress of pregnancy, targets supportive muscles while the body is undergoing significant change, and helps prepare the body for birth.

Tackling the new Presidential Youth Fitness Program

You may remember taking the Presidential Fitness Test when you were in school — students climbed rope, ran through a required number of sit-ups and pull-ups, and did timed runs and endurance runs. Facing the tough requirements of 40 push-ups, 10 pull-ups, and a 6.3-mile run was daunting for a lot of kids.

Today, the requirement for push-ups is just over 7. As of the 2012–2013 school year, a new initiative was passed making this kind of testing a thing of the past. It has now been replaced with the Presidential Youth Fitness Program, described as a "health-related, criterion-based assessment" resulting from a partnership between the President's Council on Fitness using the Cooper Institute's fitness program. These standards are called the Healthy Fitness Zones Standards, and they represent the minimum level of fitness required for a health-based program according to a student's age and gender.

Each student is measured in the following areas to identify his or her health and fitness level:

- **Aerobic capacity:** Measures the body's endurance and ability to perform physical activities such as walking and running.

- **Muscle strength, endurance, and flexibility:** Measures strength and endurance of the upper body and joint flexibility. Strength and flexibility are important for good posture and lower-back health.

- **Body composition:** Provides an indication of a student's weight relative to his or her height. Increased weight may lead to a number of health problems for children and adults, including high blood pressure, diabetes, respiratory disease, and more.

The new physical fitness test is used to help identify where a child is doing well and to plan activities to help kids improve in their weaker areas. You can find out more at www.pyfp.org.

Here are some of the benefits that pregnant and postpartum women gain from strength training:

- Muscle strength and endurance
- Improved circulation and relief from swelling
- Feelings of well-being and good self-esteem
- Coordination and balance (especially important when your center of gravity is changing frequently)
- Relief from back pain
- Prevention or relief from urinary incontinence
- Energy for daily activities

✔ Improved digestion (keeping your body regular)

✔ Improved quality of sleep

✔ Relief from muscle cramps

✔ Heightened body awareness during a time of rapid change

Several studies show that women who exercise throughout their pregnancies have less problematic deliveries and more rapid recoveries after giving birth than women who don't exercise during their pregnancies.

Modifying exercise routines for safety

The American College of Obstetrics and Gynecology provides guidelines for exercise during pregnancy. Multiple studies have been conducted that show that exercise during pregnancy doesn't increase risk of miscarriage or birth abnormalities. However, any type of extreme training is *not* recommended. And sports that involve a high risk of falling — such as downhill skiing or adventure racing — aren't recommended either.

Here are a few of the important safety guidelines for prenatal and postpartum women:

✔ Get approval from your healthcare provider first.

✔ Follow a balanced program of weight training, aerobic activity, and stretching.

✔ Don't overstretch.

✔ Avoid holding your breath. Always remember to breathe.

✔ Avoid exercising to the point of exhaustion.

✔ Avoid standing for long periods of time.

✔ After the first trimester, avoid lying on your back for more than a minute or at all, depending on whether you feel faint.

✔ Eat appropriately and drink plenty of fluids (6 to 8 ounces of water for every 15 minutes of activity).

✔ Wear loose, comfortable clothing; a supportive bra; and a maternal support belt as needed.

✔ Exercise at a moderate intensity, without excess fatigue.

✔ Never lift a maximum or near-maximum weight load.

✔ Avoid quick changes in body position.

> ✔ Always opt for a conservative approach.
>
> ✔ Include aerobic activities in your overall training program.
>
> ✔ Don't overtrain.
>
> ✔ Don't start training after delivery until at least six weeks have passed and your healthcare provider has approved you for exercise.

Trying a pregnancy sample routine

Body positioning becomes more of a challenge as pregnancy progresses, but you can make some simple modifications to traditional exercises in order to keep your body fit during pregnancy. In this section, we walk you through a sample pregnancy weight-lifting routine.

Cat/cow

Not only does this move help make your back feel better, but it improves the range of motion in your spine, enhances strength and coordination of the muscles around your spine, and improves core muscle awareness in your entire back — all factors that make your lower back feel better and stay healthy.

Getting set: Get on the floor on your hands and knees with your hands directly under your shoulders and your knees directly under your hips.

The exercise: Inhale and arch your back, lifting your tailbone and eyes toward the ceiling (see Figure 20-11a). Hold the stretch for a few seconds and then release the position back to neutral spine, and inhale again. Exhale and contract your abdominals, rounding your back like an angry cat (see Figure 20-11b). Repeat this exercise four to six times.

Side lunges

The side lunge strengthens your pelvic floor and works your abdominals during pregnancy.

Getting set: Standing with your feet about shoulder-width apart, keep your legs straight but not locked (see Figure 20-12a).

The exercise: Take one large step sideways with your right leg and you're your knee, making sure your knee doesn't extend past your toes (see Figure 20-12b). Slowly push back up to standing position, using your right leg and core muscles. Repeat on the other side.

Figure 20-11: Cat/cow.

Photograph by Nick Horne

Modified side plank

The side plank (with a slight modification for pregnancy) works the core and includes the obliques. It's one of the few exercises you can do to directly help strengthen your abs during pregnancy.

Getting set: Start by lying on your right side, with your right arm bent, legs straight or knees slightly bent, whatever is most comfortable (see Figure 20-13a). Aim for keeping your right elbow directly below your right shoulder. Place your left hand on the floor in front of you or on your hip.

The exercise: Use your abs to lift your hips off the ground, keeping your body as straight as possible (see Figure 20-13b). Hold for 10 seconds. Repeat one to three times and then switch sides.

Figure 20-12: Pregnancy side lunge.

a

b

Photograph by Nick Horne

a

Figure 20-13: Pregnancy side plank.

b

Photograph by Nick Horne

Trying a sample mommy-and-me routine

The following mommy-and-me exercises are so much fun to do with your baby — it's hard to find time to work out after giving birth, but now you have no excuse not to! Just grab a front baby carrier like a Bjorn or a sling and get to work with your little one.

Plank with baby

The plank, with your baby lying underneath you, really makes you work your core because you won't want to fall on your little one! Be sure to stay strong and lifted and maintain a long, straight back during this exercise.

Getting set: Kneeling over your baby with your knees and forearms on the floor, keep your elbows directly below your shoulders.

The exercise: Lift your body up on your forearms and toes, keeping your body as straight as possible (see Figure 20-14). Maintain this position for as long as possible. Hold the position for 10 to 15 seconds in the beginning, and then work your way up until you can hold the position longer.

Figure 20-14:
Mom and
baby plank.

Photograph by Nick Horne

Lunges with baby

This exercise uses a front baby carrier or sling. You can hold onto a wall or chair for additional balance if you need to. Lunges work to strengthen your abdominals, butt, and hips as you press back up to a standing position. Adding the weight of your baby makes for great resistance and a more intense workout.

Getting set: Standing tall with your abs engaged to support you and your baby, step your right leg forward and left leg back so there is a wide distance between your feet (see Figure 20-15a).

The exercise: Lower down toward the floor by bending both knees. Your front knee should be bent at a 90-degree angle, with the ankle directly below it. Your back knee should lower straight down toward the floor (see Figure 20-15b). Push back up to the starting position to complete one rep. Complete 10 to 15 repetitions on each side.

Figure 20-15:
Mom and
baby lunge.

a

b

Photograph by Nick Horne

Crunches with baby

Ah yes, the abs crunch — a great exercise to do with baby. You can play peek-a-boo as you lift your shoulders up and down off the floor in this exercise, and your baby will crave more — maybe before you do!

Getting set: Lie down on the floor or a mat with your knees bent and feet flat on the floor. Sit your baby on your hips, resting her back against your thighs. Gently hold your baby in that position. Place your hands behind your head, elbows out to the side (see Figure 20-16a). Engage your abs by pulling your belly button toward your spine.

The exercise: Raise your chest until your shoulder blades lift off the floor (see Figure 20-16b). Slowly lower back to floor. Complete 10 to 15 repetitions.

TIP

If you prefer, you can hold on to your baby as you do your crunches instead of keeping your hands behind your head. Do whatever feels most comfortable for you and your baby.

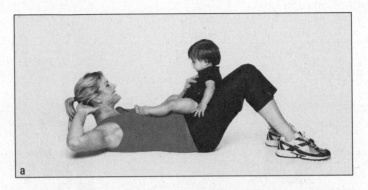

Figure 20-16:
Mom
and baby
crunch.

Photograph by Nick Horne

Family Style: Teaming Up for Exercise

Seeing kids really enjoying a physical activity that benefits them in so many different ways is truly a gift and so much fun. But even more fun is when the whole family gets into the act! Kids imitate everything they see. If your kids see you working out, they'll want to work out, too!

There are many exercises you can do as a family. You can even make games out of exercising by setting up a little circuit in your backyard. Do some jumping jacks to warm up your body; move on to ball passing for one minute; do sit-ups for one minute, holding each other's feet; and so on. You'll see how fun it is for all your family members to sit on each other's feet and cheer each other on!

Here are some activities your whole family can do to get the heart pumping:

- ✔ Go for a walk.
- ✔ Jump rope.
- ✔ Ride bikes.
- ✔ Shoot baskets.
- ✔ Play catch.
- ✔ Swim.

Building and keeping your family strong for a lifetime

Our bodies are remarkably resilient and adapt primarily in response to the specific challenges that we give ourselves. Exercising to strengthen your family's bone density is a specific goal. As a result of numerous studies scientists have conducted, the American College of Sports Medicine (ACSM) has issued a position stand on bone health with recommendations for exercises that preserve bone. Although exercise is critically important, nutritional factors, such as the importance of calcium in the diet, is also essential to maintain bone density for life.

For growing children, calcium is an important mineral for building strong and healthy bones. That, along with exercise, is what kids need to properly mature and build strong bodies. For adult men and women to preserve bone and prevent bone loss, doing a combination of weight-bearing aerobic activities such as stair climbing, walking, jogging, or jumping activities and weight training will do the trick. Up to age 30, you want to work on building up your bone density. After the age of 40, the goal is to retain as much bone density as possible by stopping or slowing the rate of bone loss.

Any amount of weight training benefits your bones, and the more you progress to higher levels of intensity (heavier weights and fewer reps) the greater the benefits!

Chapter 21

Workouts for Baby Boomers and Beyond

When it comes to exercising and keeping a strong body, exercise is an easy and powerful way to stay young in body and mind. Research has proven that exercise can help decrease injuries, maintain your strength and stamina, and keep your bones and joints strong forever. Which means you *don't* have to give in to aging any way but gracefully — and that's good news, isn't it?

Regular exercise is, without a doubt, one of the most important things you can do to keep your body functioning as smoothly as possible. It can't turn back the clock, but it can slow it down considerably.

In this chapter, we offer some wonderful exercises that are simple and easy to do, regardless of your age.

Strength-Training Guidelines for Seniors

Weight training is among the best things you can do for your health and well-being, no matter how old you are. Having strong muscles allows you to live independently. Being able to dress yourself, shower alone, and feel comfortable going to the store to run errands are a part of enjoying a feeling of personal freedom. Training as an older adult can set you free!

In one research study, older adults who lived in a nursing home were put on a weight-training program twice weekly. Remarkably, even participants over the age of 90 improved their strength and mobility. One resident became so much stronger that he left the facility. Others were able to dress by themselves for the first time in ages.

Reaping rewards from training as an older adult

Many of the things we formerly associated with aging, we now know are simply a result of disuse. Here are some of the many benefits of regular weight training for older adults:

- ✔ Increased muscular strength and endurance
- ✔ Functional independence to enjoy a full and active life
- ✔ Improved confidence and self-esteem
- ✔ Strong bones and prevention of osteoporosis
- ✔ Balance and reduction of the risk of falls and the fear of falling
- ✔ Improvement in digestion and relief of constipation
- ✔ Improvement of glucose utilization to avoid the onset of diabetes
- ✔ Reduction of discomfort from arthritis
- ✔ Prevention of lower-back pain
- ✔ Healthy blood pressure levels

Observing safety guidelines and training tips

Weight training provides a host of benefits, but a more conservative approach is recommended for older adults — those over the age of 50. If you've trained regularly over the course of a lifetime, you may be chronologically 50, but you may have the biological health of someone who is more like a 40-year-old. Make your personal adjustments accordingly. Even for the frail elderly — such as 90-year-olds in a nursing home — the risk of being inactive is worse than the risk of injury from training.

Here are important safety guidelines for weight training and older adults:

- ✔ Get the approval of your healthcare provider first.
- ✔ Train a minimum of two days per week.
- ✔ Do one set of eight to ten exercises that challenge all the major muscle groups.
- ✔ Do 10 to 15 repetitions per set.
- ✔ Progress conservatively.
- ✔ Include a slightly longer warm-up (up to ten minutes) and gentle stretches.

Should you exercise if you have arthritis?

The big question these days is, how much exercise you should do if you're diagnosed with arthritis. Generally, if you have a flare-up in a joint, that's the time to rest and let your medication do its job. As the inflammation decreases and the pain subsides, you can gradually return to exercise. The key word is *gradually*. If you experience pain, that's your cue to stop.

However, we've come a long way from the time when people believed that if they had arthritis they shouldn't exercise. Today we know

that exercise is an important part of treating the disease. Why? Because if you don't take care of the muscles that surround the joint, range of motion will be lost and stiffness and pain will increase. The goal of people with arthritis should be to limit the progression of the existing damage in the affected joint(s), which is most effectively accomplished by strengthening and stretching the muscles that surround the joints.

✔ Do each exercise in a slow and controlled manner.

✔ Move through your active range of motion.

✔ Incorporate balance exercises.

✔ Don't do any exercise that causes pain.

As with any new form of exercise, consult your doctor before you begin a workout program. Seniors with certain conditions, such as diabetes and coronary heart disease, may have to take a graded exercise test (GXT) in which they get on a stationary bicycle or treadmill while their physician monitors their blood pressure and heart rate.

Challenging Yourself Moderately

Depending on your level of fitness, it's perfectly fine to start with no weights at all. Starting with weights that are too heavy can cause injuries, so using the resistance of your own body weight is a great way to start. As you build your strength and stamina, you'll be able to progress to using weights — but do it gradually. ***Remember:*** Slow and steady wins the race!

When you do begin adding weights to your strength workout, add a challenging amount of weight gradually — just enough that you feel like you're working out a bit harder than you were previously — because if you don't challenge your muscles, you won't get any stronger. Using 1- to 2-pound weights as you grow in strength and build a little muscle is a good way to enhance any strengthening program as your body adapts to the exercises.

The buddy system

As you get older, losing your balance and your confidence when trying new things is easier to do. Having a workout partner can help you gain back your confidence and boost your self-esteem. You have someone else to share your enthusiasm about your new workout experience and help you avoid injury. And did we mention that exercising is just a *lot* more fun when you do it in pairs? It's much easier to get motivated to go the gym or simply leave the house and take a walk if you know someone is waiting and depending on you. So, take your partner or a pick a friend and use the buddy system when you exercise to help motivate you and keep you safe at the same time!

When you do begin lifting, use a slow three seconds to push your weight into place. Hold the position for only one second, before taking three seconds to lower the weight back down to starting. And never let your weight drop! If you lower it slowly, you'll get the maximum benefit and see your muscles grow stronger faster because that's where the growth in the muscle takes place — on the downward part of the movement.

It shouldn't feel very hard to push your weight into place, but at the same time, it should feel challenging. This is where the saying "Listen to your body" comes in handy. Pay attention what you're doing and feeling throughout your workout so you can make adjustments in the amount of weight you're using.

If you can't lift a weight eight times in a row, it's too heavy and you should reduce the amount of weight you're using. However, if you can lift the weight more than 15 times in a row, it's way too light for you — increase the amount of weight you're using.

After you've determined the amount of weight that's right for you, complete 8 to 15 repetitions in a row and then wait 1 minute before doing another set of 8 to 15 repetitions of the same exercise.

A Strength-Training Routine to Help Maintain Balance

The exercises in this section are specifically designed to be accessible for anyone — even someone with physical limitations due to age or injury. None of these moves requires you to get down on the ground or to assume complicated positions. These full-body exercises are simple and straightforward to help increase your range of motion, from your head to your toes.

Hip extension

Starting with the hips and lower back, this core strengthener is a good exercise to help keep you balanced. You can use a chair or the back of a couch for assistance — just like ballet dancers do when they warm up at a ballet barre.

1. **Stand about a foot away from the back of a chair and keep your feet slightly apart as you stand tall. Hold onto the chair for balance (as shown in Figure 21-1a).**

   You can bend 45 degrees forward if that's more comfortable.

2. **Slowly extend or raise one leg behind you without bending your knee. Point your toe like a dancer (see Figure 21-1b).**

   If you bent 45 degrees forward in Step 1, maintain that position — don't bend any farther forward when you raise your leg.

3. **Hold your leg and upper-body position for 1 second.**

4. **Slowly lower your leg before repeating on the other side.**

   Alternate your legs until you've done eight to ten repetitions on each side.

Figure 21-1:
Hip
extension.

Photograph by Nick Horne

A few do's and don'ts for this stretch:

- ✔ DO keep your shoulder blades down and your upper body relaxed.
- ✔ DO keep your back straight, not rounded.
- ✔ DON'T bounce or force the stretch; keep it gentle and slowly progress into a deeper stretch.

Hip flexion

This exercise works the back, hips, and legs. It's simple and effective for strengthening your core. Any time you lift your leg off the ground, you call on your core muscles to keep you from falling.

Try this with exercise or without holding onto something, depending on your individual level of fitness.

To do this exercise, follow these steps:

1. **Stand up tall and as straight as possible (see Figure 21-2a).**

   If you need to, hold onto a table or chair for balance.

Figure 21-2:
Hip flexion.

a

b

Photograph by Nick Horne

2. **Slowly bend one knee up toward your chest, without bending at your waist or hips, and clasp your hands under your thigh (as shown in Figure 21-2b).**

   If you have trouble with balance, you can hold your arms out to your sides in the airplane position. When you get more practice, you can place both hands on your hips and then move to clasping your hands under your thigh.

3. **Hold your bent knee up for 1 second before slowly lowering your leg all the way down.**

4. **Repeat on the other leg.**

   Alternate legs until you've completed eight to ten repetitions on each leg.

A few do's and don't for this stretch:

✔ DO keep your shoulders and hips facing forward and your knees slightly bent.

✔ DO breathe through the exercise.

✔ DON'T hold the position if you feel tension or pain.

Standing side reach

Using the back of a chair for support in the standing core release allows you to reach the waist (oblique muscles) and back muscles that are difficult to release without lying on the floor. You can feel the release in your back, abs, and even the top part of your hips.

To do this stretch, follow these steps:

1. **With the back of your chair about a foot from your right side, stand with your feet about a foot apart, with your knees slightly bent and your toes pointing forward. Place your right hand on the top of the back of the chair (see Figure 21-3a).**

2. **Inhale and reach your left arm directly overhead with your palm facing inward.**

   Use the muscles in your upper back to keep your shoulder blade down. This should keep space between your shoulder and ear.

3. **As you exhale, lean to the right, keeping your right hand on the back of the chair for support and your hip and leg anchored to the floor (see Figure 21-3b).**

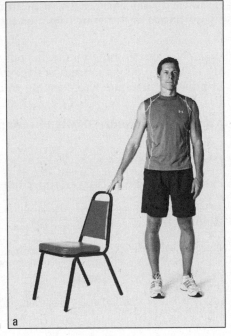

Figure 21-3:
Standing
side reach.

a   b

Photograph by Nick Horne

4. **Hold this stretch for 30 seconds or four to five slow, deep breaths.**

5. **Repeat on the other side.**

If you notice tension in your shoulders, instead of reaching with a straight arm, keep your elbow bent. The movement should come from your waist, not your shoulder.

A few do's and don't for this stretch:

✔ DO keep your shoulders and hips facing forward and your knees slightly bent.

✔ DO breathe through the stretch.

✔ DON'T hold the stretch if you feel tension or pain.

A Seated Core Routine for Strong Abs

The next two exercises modify some very popular abdominal and core exercises, making them perfect for older adults. Both of these exercises are fun and still very effective when done seated!

Seated sit-up

This exercise is a good way to work on your abdominals and lower back without having to lie on the floor and do a sit-up!

Anyone can do this exercise — it's not just for seniors. It helps you strengthen your core and helps you get up and down from a seated position without losing your balance.

To do this exercise, follow these steps:

1. **Sit tall in a chair with your hands on your knees (see Figure 21-4a).**

Figure 21-4:
Seated
sit-up.

a   b

Photograph by Nick Horne

2. **Tighten your abdominals before pressing through your heels as you straighten your legs and straighten up to a standing position with your arms extended straight out in front of you (see Figure 21-4b).**

3. **Hold for a few seconds before sitting back down in the chair as you keep your core muscles tight and engaged to help you sit back down.**

   Repeat eight to ten times.

Here are a couple do's and don'ts:

✔ DO keep your back straight and your shoulder blades down.

✔ DON'T let your knees flare out to the sides. Keep them pointing forward.

Seated core rotation

This exercise is excellent for actually increasing the rotational movement in your spine, which in turn may help you maintain flexibility in your spine by stretching out your lower-back muscles.

And what's the biggest benefit to having strong lower-back muscles? Being less prone to injury. Now that's good news for anyone! Plus, strong abdominal muscles mean stronger back muscles because these muscle groups work together to form the core of the body. The following exercise is good for both muscle groups.

To do this stretch, follow these steps:

1. **Sit up tall on a sturdy chair with your feet flat on the floor and close together and your knees at a right angle.**

2. **Anchor your left hand on the side of the chair as you place your right hand on the outside of your left thigh (see Figure 21-5a).**

Figure 21-5:
Seated core rotation.

a

b

Photograph by Nick Horne

3. **Inhale and, as you exhale, twist your torso to the left and look back over your shoulder (see Figure 21-5b).**

4. **Hold the stretch for about ten seconds.**

   Try to make a mental note of a stationary object you see that's about at eye level and look at that as you hold the stretch.

5. **Release and come back to center.**

6. **Inhale again, and as you exhale, repeat on the opposite side.**

   Find the same object you were looking at, but this time try to find another object that's past it.

A few do's and don'ts for this stretch:

- ✔ DO keep your feet flat on the floor.
- ✔ DO keep your knees and feet together and facing the front.
- ✔ DON'T force the stretch or pull too hard on the back of the chair.
- ✔ DON'T look down — find an object to look at that's at eye level.

Chapter 22

Adding Yoga and Pilates for Flexibility

*I*t's hard to find a gym these days that doesn't offer yoga or Pilates classes. Yoga and Pilates, activities that increase strength and flexibility, are the two fastest-growing programs in fitness facilities among all age groups. How are these activities different from and similar to weight training? What are the benefits of incorporating all three modes of exercise into your fitness program? How many days a week should you do each one? Will you go broke doing all these activities? Will your body collapse from exhaustion? This chapter answers all these questions and more.

Examining Yoga and Pilates

Each mode of exercise is explored in detail later in the chapter, but here's the difference between the two activities in a nutshell. Both of these exercises are mind-body disciplines. Yoga is rooted in ancient East Indian cultural traditions. In contrast, Pilates is a modern exercise practice with influence from yoga, as well as Chinese acrobatics, gymnastics, and boxing.

Harmonizing with yoga

The physical practice of yoga, known as *hatha yoga,* was developed in India more than 5,000 years ago and consists of a series of poses, known as *asanas,* that you hold anywhere from a few seconds to several minutes. Yoga moves

> ✔ Require a blend of strength, flexibility, and body awareness
>
> ✔ Promote union of body, mind, and spirit
>
> ✔ Prepare the body for the discipline of meditation and other spiritual yoga practices

Most hatha yoga styles include the same basic poses but differ in terms of how quickly you move, how long you hold each pose, how much breathing is emphasized, and how much of a spiritual aspect is involved. In the Indian tradition, all physical yoga is hatha yoga, but in the United States, different styles of hatha yoga have been given new names such as *power yoga, flow yoga,* or *hot yoga.*

Other yoga styles are named after the individual people who spread the exercise in the United States. For example, Iyengar yoga, named after B. K. S. Iyengar, is the most widely practiced style of hatha yoga in the United States; it offers more modifications for beginners and uses multiple props. Other styles, such as Bikram yoga, are for people who can already fold themselves into shapes that resemble pretzels; it's done in a very hot room.

Moving with Pilates

Pilates (puh-LAH-teez) is an exercise form named after Joseph Pilates, the former boxing and self-defense trainer who developed the Pilates technique in Germany at the turn of the 20th century. Many Pilates moves were inspired by yoga, although some were inspired by gymnastics, Chinese acrobatics, and boxing. Pilates mat classes involve a series of specialized calisthenics exercises; instead of holding the positions, as in certain styles of yoga, you're constantly moving, as in a flow or vinyasa yoga, which consists of a series of moves performed continuously, as in the sun salutation.

Private and small-group lessons are taught on machines with names such as the *trapeze table* and the *reformer.* The trapeze table looks like a four-poster bed that's been rigged for torture, with its array of springs, straps, poles, and bars. The reformer looks like a cot rigged up with assorted springs, straps, and pads; it was inspired by modifications made to cots by Joseph Pilates to provide rehabilitation exercise to people who were still in hospital beds.

Benefiting from Yoga and Pilates

Some yoga and Pilates practitioners claim that yoga and Pilates are superior to weight training because these disciplines make you stronger without creating bulky muscles. It's true that yoga and Pilates build strength without bulk — but, in reality, so can strength training with free weights or machines. The only way to end up with barrel-sized biceps is to train for it by lifting super-heavy weights and performing a minimal number of repetitions. Genetics also plays a role in how your muscles develop. So, choosing yoga or Pilates simply because you're trying to develop strength without bulk is buying into a fitness myth.

However, there are plenty of other excellent reasons to take up these alternative modes of exercise. Following is a rundown.

Engaging your whole body

Weight training tends to emphasize individual body parts; you think about working your chest muscles or your shoulders or your hamstrings. Magazines promote "The Ultimate Ab Workout" or "Eight Moves for a Better Butt." With most weight-training exercises — especially with those performed on machines — you work one or two muscle groups without involving any others.

Yoga and Pilates take a different approach and require you to engage virtually your whole body at once. For instance, when performing a thigh exercise, you don't simply straighten and bend your leg, as you would in a traditional weight-training exercise for your quads. Instead, you must

✔ Engage your butt muscles in order to sit evenly

✔ Use your abs and lower back to avoid wiggling back and forth

✔ Work your upper-body muscles to keep your back and neck in alignment

This approach is similar to the approach in core stabilization exercises discussed in Chapter 15, but yoga and Pilates are more than core conditioning.

The benefit of working so many muscle groups simultaneously is that this is the way you're likely to use them in everyday life. Lying on your stomach and arching your chest off the floor may not seem like a position you often assume during your everyday life. But if you think about it, the way you use your lower back in an exercise like this is pretty similar to the way your lower-back muscles spring into action whenever you have to screw in a light bulb that's just within your reach or when you put something back up on a high shelf.

Yoga and Pilates place particular emphasis on your "core" muscles — the abdominal, lower-back, and spinal muscles. These muscles add important value to training with yoga or Pilates because the target areas don't get much action in a weight-machine workout. When all those small, internal muscles are optimally strong, they also lend support, stability, and added strength to your weight-room activities. You may find that you can up your poundage in the weight room if you include regular yoga or Pilates sessions in your repertoire.

If you're specifically interested in strengthening your core, check out *Core Strength For Dummies,* by LaReine Chabut (Wiley), which also covers yoga and Pilates.

Increasing your flexibility

Weight training has an undeserved reputation for making your muscles tight; in reality, lifting weights can actually increase your flexibility somewhat if you go through the entire range of motion. However, strength training — even under the best of circumstances — isn't going to make a big difference in how freely your muscles and joints move. (That's why we strongly recommend stretching on a regular basis; see Chapter 16.)

Yoga and Pilates can noticeably improve your flexibility. You may never be able to fold yourself into a pretzel, but if you put time and effort into these pursuits, you'll surprise yourself by how pliable your body becomes.

Improving your balance, coordination, and concentration

Some weight-training moves, such as the squat and the lunge (and other advanced moves not included in this book), do require a fair amount of balance and coordination. But for the most part, strength training simply gives you strength. Lying facedown on a hamstring machine and kicking your legs up doesn't exactly train you to float down a flight of stairs without having to look at your feet.

But yoga and Pilates moves tend to be more complicated. Consider a Pilates move called the teaser:

1. **Lie on your back with your arms overhead and your legs straight and off the ground at a 45-degree angle.**

2. **Lift your upper body and torso off the floor and try to reach your fingers to your toes.**

This move requires more balance, strength, and flexibility than you could possibly imagine. When you first try this move, you usually tip over sideways. It can take several years just to start to perform this move with grace and fluidity. These disciplines require a lot of concentration and body awareness.

Can yoga and Pilates replace weight training?

Probably not. One of the best reasons to lift weights is to maintain and build bone density so you'll have enough bone in reserve to prevent osteoporosis later in life. Currently, no studies show whether yoga and Pilates strengthen bones. For the most part, because you're only using your own body weight and gravity for resistance, you don't work against as much resistance during a yoga or Pilates routine as you do during a challenging weight workout. But this presumes a higher level of fitness. If you're new to exercise, body weight alone may be very challenging. Evidence from numerous yoga studies shows that yoga builds muscle;

Pilates studies show that Pilates exercises effectively condition core muscles.

Although yoga and Pilates can build muscle, unless you add extra weight, yoga and Pilates exercises can't provide as much resistance as a solid weight-training program. It's important to build muscle for the same reason it's crucial to build bone: to bank it for the future when, inevitably, you'll have less of it.

For these reasons, yoga and Pilates are complementary to — not replacements for — weight training.

Fitting Yoga and Pilates into Your Fitness Program

First, accept that you can't do everything in life! You can't be a full-time investment banker *and* a professional TV critic *and* a world-class pole vaulter. There just isn't enough time in the day. By the same token, unless you're a fitness professional, you can't devote yourself to weight training, yoga, and Pilates — especially when you're also (we hope) doing cardiovascular exercise. With that said, incorporate either yoga or Pilates in your workout program. Which one? Try out both and see which one you like best.

Deciding between yoga and Pilates may take a while because so many different styles of yoga and different Pilates contraptions exist and because various instructors may conduct the same class differently. From our experience, Pilates mat classes tend to be similar nationwide, but the quality of instruction may vary widely. Yoga classes vary more because there are different styles of yoga. During this tryout period, here are some suggestions:

✔ Drop to two weight-training sessions a week and take a third day to try an alternative exercise.

✔ Take a two-week break from weight training (don't worry — your muscles won't disintegrate) and try a number of different yoga and Pilates classes and/or instructors.

After your tryout period, decide on a weight-training alternative: private Pilates lessons, a power yoga class at your gym, or a Sivananda yoga class at a studio (see "Different styles of yoga" for more information). This isn't a lifetime commitment, of course. But it's a good idea to choose one route and stick with it for at least a couple months. This gives you enough time to see whether you enjoy this type of workout and are getting benefits.

As for your weekly schedule: Lift weights twice a week and integrate yoga or Pilates twice a week. Doing any of these activities just once a week typically isn't enough for a beginner to see results and get the hang of proper technique. Studies show that participants benefit from yoga training as little as one hour once a week. So, try to fit it in twice a week, but if one is all that you can do, it's better than nothing.

Diving into Yoga

Yoga classes have become amazingly popular as people search for ways to complement the pounding and pumping they do in the gym. But this doesn't mean that yoga is easy. Yoga can be extremely demanding, both in terms of flexibility and strength. Even if you can bench-press a heavy load in the gym, you may find yourself lacking the strength to hold a yoga pose for a minute.

Here's a good rule to follow in yoga (or in life): Don't try to keep up with anyone else — go at your own pace.

Different styles of yoga

If you try out yoga at a health club or fitness facility, the best way to select a class is by choosing one that's at your level, such as beginner, gentle or restorative, intermediate, or advanced. Even if you're an experienced athlete, if you've never done yoga before, you should start in a class for beginners.

You can choose from many different types or styles of yoga:

✔ **Sivananda yoga:** Allows for a broad range of abilities from beginner to more advanced. The moves are fairly straightforward; for instance, you may practice something as simple as sitting up straight or standing with good posture. Sivananda may be a good place for beginners to start.

✔ **Ashtanga:** A style of hatha yoga known in the United States. Also called power yoga. Ashtanga is more physically demanding in terms of flexibility, strength, and stamina. You move from one posture to another without a break, and you jump from one position to another. For beginners, this may be more discouraging than invigorating.

- **Ananda:** Ananda yoga emphasizes a traditional approach to hatha yoga, keeping in mind that the purpose of physical postures is to prepare the body and mind for the rigors of meditation. Ananda yoga features the use of affirmations with each posture. The style is more flowing, soft, and gentle and is appropriate for beginners. It can be made more difficult for more experienced practitioners.

- **Kundalini:** Kundalini yoga is a style of hatha yoga that focuses on awakening and directing the subtle energy that is stored at the base of spine. You practice breathing exercises such as "breath of fire" and single-nostril breathing, in addition to meditation. This is an intense style of practice that isn't appropriate for beginners.

Most gyms and workout studios don't advertise the style of yoga practiced, and the gym staff probably won't know much about what's being taught. Your best bet is to ask the instructor what her style and teaching philosophy is. Look for a class with the word *beginner* or *novice* in the title. If you accidentally wander into a more advanced class, you may wind up feeling like one of those tangled necklaces that mysteriously appears in your jewelry box.

For more of an in-depth look at yoga, check out *Yoga For Dummies*, 2nd Edition, by Georg Feuerstein and Larry Payne (Wiley).

Finding a qualified yoga instructor

Instructors can't obtain a national yoga certification, so we can't list certain credentials to look for in a teacher. The Yoga Alliance recommends that qualified instructors have a minimum of 200 to 500 hours of training. Instructors who've met this standard can register with the Yoga Alliance. Because registration is voluntary, instructors who aren't registered may be highly qualified.

Here are some tips for choosing a yoga instructor:

- Rely on your own judgment.

- Ask for recommendations from your friends.

- Ask the instructor what type of teacher's training he has had and how many years of experience he has.

- Look for yoga instructors who wander around the room correcting class members' techniques and offering modifications for less flexible people.

Trying a couple yoga poses

The cat/cow pose (arching like a cat and rounding like a cow) helps make your back feel better, improves the range of motion in your spine, enhances strength and coordination of the muscles around your spine, and improves core muscle awareness in your entire back — all factors that make your lower back feel better and stay healthy.

To do this exercise, follow these steps:

1. **Get on the floor on your hands and knees with your hands directly under your shoulders and your knees directly under your hips.**

2. **Inhale and arch your back, lifting your tailbone and eyes toward the ceiling (see Figure 22-1a).**

3. **Hold the stretch for a few seconds, and then release the position back to neutral, and inhale again.**

4. **Exhale and contract your abdominals, rounding your back like an angry cat (see Figure 22-1b).**

5. **Hold this position for a few seconds and then release back to neutral.**

   Repeat this pose four to six times.

Figure 22-1: Cat/cow pose.

Photograph by Nick Horne

A few do's and don'ts for this exercise:

- ✔ DO pull your belly button toward your spine as if you were tightening your belt.

- ✔ DO keep the movement in your pelvis and lower back, not in your shoulders.

- ✔ DON'T tense up your shoulders and neck.

- ✔ DON'T overextend your neck while doing the old cow position.

The cobra pose strengthens the abs, back, and shoulders. It also stimulates the internal organs like the kidneys and liver in your lower-back area, to help them function better.

To do this exercise, follow these steps:

1. **Lie on the floor with your stomach down and your forearms flat on the floor. Let your forehead rest on the floor, too.**

2. **Inhale as you tighten your back and abdominal muscles, pressing your forearms against the floor to raise your chest and head (see Figure 22-2).**

Figure 22-2: Cobra pose.

Photograph by Nick Horne

3. **Exhale as you release your torso and head slowly back down to the floor to starting position.**

   Complete three times, remembering to breathe deeply each time.

A few do's and don'ts for this exercise:

✔ DO use a yoga mat or a towel support for your head to rest on.

✔ DO exhale before you extend your forearms and tighten your core muscles.

✔ DON'T forget to press the tops of your feet into the floor during this exercise.

Getting the Lowdown on Pilates

Like yoga, Pilates emphasizes correct form rather than brute strength. Many of the moves look easy but are deceptively tough. Most Pilates moves emphasize the principle of opposition: You strengthen one muscle, while you stretch the one on the opposite side of the joint. For instance, the mat class move known as *the hundred* involves pumping your arms up and down as you lie on your back with your legs lifted off the floor straight out in front of you. The purpose of the hundred is to strengthen your abs and front of thighs as you stretch out your lower back, back of thighs, and arms.

We also love that, like weight training and yoga, Pilates is progressive. Although you can't add an extra 5-pound weight plate every time an exercise becomes easy, whenever you master a move, another slightly different, slightly harder version of the move is there to take its place. It can take months to master the basics and years to become an expert.

Pilates classes and private instructors aren't tough to find in most cities. Similar to yoga, there's no national certification. The Pilates Method Alliance has created a certification examination, but many instructors may be highly qualified and experienced who haven't taken this particular examination. In order to find a good Pilates instructor

✔ Get recommendations from people you trust.

✔ Ask the instructor a lot of questions about her training, certification, and experience.

Pilates is expensive. Private lessons run from $50 to $200 a session. More and more studios and health clubs offer small group classes on the equipment for lower prices. Mat classes are a relative bargain at $12 to $25 per session, but that's still more than many monthly gym memberships. Some gyms offer Pilates classes to members at no additional charge and offer private instruction at a discount. Shop around.

If Pilates interests you, read *Pilates For Dummies,* by Ellie Herman (Wiley), for a detailed account of the exercises and benefits for your body.

If you're not sure if Pilates is for you, give the plank position a try. It works your core muscles while also working your upper body. It strengthens and lengthens your body by activating the stabilizing muscles. To do the plank exercise, follow these steps:

1. **Lie on your stomach with your hands pressed down and your fingers facing forward. Place your hands shoulder-width apart on the floor in front of you and your legs straight behind you (as shown in Figure 22-3a).**

   Your arms will be straight underneath your shoulders.

2. **Exhale as you slowly lift your body off the floor contracting your abdominals until your arms and elbows are straight (see Figure 22-3b).**

   Breathe as you contract your abdominal muscles and engage your upper body for additional support.

3. **Hold this position for a few seconds before lowering your body slowly back down to the floor.**

   Complete five to ten times, depending on your individual fitness level.

Figure 22-3: Your hands should be on the floor and in line with your shoulders.

Photograph by Nick Horne

Some do's and don'ts for this exercise:

- ✔ DO press into the floor and squeeze your glutes while you're in the plank position.
- ✔ DO keep your neck in line with your spine as you do when you're standing.
- ✔ DON'T let your back arch or sag to the floor. Keep it straight and long.

Part V
The Part of Tens

Find ten common weight-lifting mistakes to avoid in an article at www.dummies.com/extras/weighttraining.

In this part . . .

- ✔ Find ten ways to use exercise bands to tone and tighten your body.
- ✔ Discover ten ways to train with an exercise ball.

Chapter 23

Ten (Or So) Ways to Use Exercise Bands to Tone and Tighten

*B*ands and tubing can't provide as much resistance as free weights or machines, but you can develop a surprising amount of strength, muscle tone, and flexibility. In this chapter, we present ten band exercises and offer tips for using bands safely.

Note: The photos accompanying the exercises show bands, but tubing can just as easily be used instead of the bands to supply the required resistance.

Before You Start, Get an Exercise Band

Bands are particularly helpful if you want to keep up your strength and work out when you travel. You can't very well lug around a complete set of dumbbells in your suitcase. (And we hate to imagine how an airport metal detector would react.)

Bring along your training tools: band, tube, and stretch strap. Even if you're booked into a hotel that has a gym, you'll be happy to have carry-on "weights" and something to help you stretch. This way, you can easily keep up with your training and stay in shape, no matter what time zone or situation you're in.

Make sure that you use a band designed for exercising. Exercise bands cost next to nothing. You can purchase a set of three bands for less than $10 or one exercise tube for approximately $15, depending on the level of resistance (heavier resistance bands or tubes are more expensive), from manufacturers such as SPRI or Gaiam.

Buy tubing with cords or plastic or padded handles attached if you want to splurge. The handles make holding an end in one or both hands much easier. Tubing with handles may come in handy in such exercises as the band biceps curl, described later in this chapter. The handles aren't practical for exercises (such as the band butt blaster) that require tying your band in a circle; however, manufacturers do make figure-eight style and circular tubing that works well for these exercises. Because bands are inexpensive, we recommend investing in several.

In general, the shorter and/or the thicker the band, the harder it is to pull and the more resistance it provides. Bands come in several different shapes:

- ✔ Circular
- ✔ Figure eight
- ✔ Flat and wide
- ✔ Tubes (resembling surgical tubes)

Wear weight-training gloves when you use exercise bands to increase comfort for your hands.

Preparing for Your Band Workout

Experiment with different shapes, sizes, and thicknesses to determine which band you like best for each exercise. The longer the band, the better, to help increase your exercise options. You can always choke up on the band to make the resistance harder. Have all your bands within reach as you begin your workout so you don't waste time hunting under the couch for the right one.

It's a good idea to keep all your exercise equipment in one place, such as a basket in the corner of the room.

You're almost ready for your band workout. First, here are some tips for working out with bands:

- ✔ Make sure that the band is securely in place before each set.

- ✔ If an exercise calls for you to hold the end in each hand (and your band doesn't have handles), loop the ends *loosely* around the palms of your hands. Leave a little slack so as you pull on the band the rubber doesn't tighten up around your hand and cut off the circulation to your fingers.

- ✔ If an exercise calls for you to stand on the band with your feet together, place both feet on the center of the band and then step one foot out to the side so that you have about 6 inches of band between your feet. This stance prevents the band from sliding out from under you.

Bands are meant to be stretched and used for exercises. That doesn't mean that they last forever. Occasionally, your bands need replacing. Follow these suggestions for maintaining bands and knowing when to chuck the old ones and buy new:

- ✔ Frequently check for holes and tears by holding your band up to a light. If you find even the slightest tear, replace the band immediately, because it can break at any moment and may snap back at you.

- ✔ If you use the flat bands frequently and on sweaty skin, periodically rinse them in clean water, towel or drip dry, and store in a resealable plastic bag with a little baby powder. Just shake off the powder before your next use.

Getting on the Band Wagon

Integrate your favorite band exercises into your regular weight-training routine. If you plan to use a band when you travel, practice these exercises beforehand so that you don't waste time trying to figure out what to do. As with all other resistance exercises, do 8 to 15 repetitions per set and do at least one set per muscle group. (We tell you which muscle group each band exercise strengthens.) When you can perform 15 repetitions easily, make the exercise tougher by using a shorter or thicker band.

Band squat

The band squat adds resistance to the squat in lieu of free weights. This exercise strengthens your butt, quadriceps, and hamstrings. Use caution if you're prone to lower-back, hip, or knee pain.

Getting set: Hold the end of a band in each hand and stand on top of the center of the band so that your feet are hip-width apart and your hands are at your sides. Stand tall with your abdominals pulled in and shoulders square (see Figure 23-1a).

The exercise: Sit back and down, as if you're sitting on a chair. Bend your knees and lower yourself as far as you can without leaning your upper body more than a few inches forward (see Figure 23-1b). Never go lower than the point at which your thighs are parallel to the floor, and don't allow your knees to move out in front of your toes.

After you feel your upper body fold forward over your thighs, stand back up, pushing through your heels and taking care not to lock your knees. Throughout the exercise, keep your shoulders relaxed, head up, and your eyes focused directly in front of you.

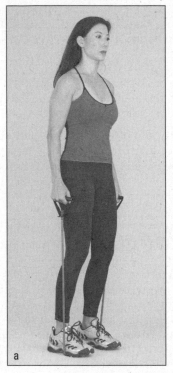 

Figure 23-1:
Band squat.

a   b

Photograph by Zoran Popovic

Band butt blaster

The band butt blaster does a better job of working your butt than many of the butt machines you find in gyms. Use caution if you have lower-back problems.

Getting set: Tie a 1-foot-long band in a circle and place it around both feet at the instep. Next, kneel on your elbows and knees. Flex your left foot. Pull your abdominals in (see Figure 23-2a).

The exercise: Keeping your knee bent, lift your right leg and raise your knee to hip height (see Figure 23-2b). Slowly lower your leg back down, taking care not to let the band go slack. Your knee should almost, but not quite, touch the floor between repetitions. Do the same number of repetitions with each leg.

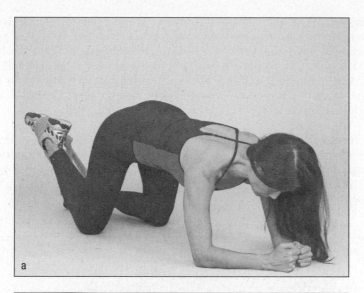

Figure 23-2:
Band butt
blaster.

a

b

Photograph by Zoran Popovic

Band outer-thigh lift

The band outer-thigh lift is a challenging exercise that specifically targets
your outer-thigh muscles.

Make sure to keep your abdominals pulled in to protect your lower back.

Getting set: Tie an exercise band (between 1 and 2 feet long) in a circle. Lie on the floor on your left side with your legs a few inches in front of you, knees slightly bent, and head resting on your outstretched arm. Place the band around your thighs, just above your knees. Bend your right arm and place your palm on the floor in front of your chest for support. Align your right hip directly over your left hip and pull your abdominals in so your back isn't arched (see Figure 23-3a).

The exercise: Keeping your knee slightly bent, raise your left leg until your foot reaches shoulder height (see Figure 23-3b). Hold the position for a moment, and then slowly lower your leg back down, keeping tension on the band the entire time. Repeat. Switch sides and do the same number of repetitions with both legs.

Figure 23-3: Band outer-thigh lift.

Photograph by Zoran Popovic

Band hamstrings stretch

Tight hamstrings are often related to improper stretching or tight quadriceps (front of your thighs). This exercise helps you gain flexibility in the back of your legs and relieve tightness in the lower back.

Getting set: Lie down on the floor with your feet flat on the floor and your knees bent, with your arms to your sides.

The exercise: Bring your right foot toward your chest and wrap an exercise band around the arch of your foot. Exhale as you extend your right leg toward the ceiling, as shown in Figure 23-4. Repeat on the other side.

Figure 23-4:
Band
hamstrings
stretch.

Photograph by Tilden Patterson

Band lat pull-down

The band lat pull-down mimics the lat pull-down you do on a machine. Like the machine version, the band lat pull-down works your upper-back muscles with some emphasis on your shoulders and biceps.

Be especially careful to follow the form guidelines if you're prone to neck discomfort.

Getting set: Sit in a chair or stand with your feet hip-width apart and hold an end of the exercise band in each hand. Raise your arms over your head with your left palm facing in and your right palm facing forward just above shoulder level (see Figure 23-5a). Your elbows should be slightly bent. Stand tall with your abdominals pulled in and your knees relaxed.

The exercise: Keep your left arm still. Bend your right elbow down and out to the side, as if you're shooting an arrow straight up into the air. Keeping your wrist straight, pull the band until your right hand is to the side of your right shoulder, the band is tight, and your right elbow points down (see Figure 23-5b). Slowly straighten your arm. Switch sides, alternating arms as you complete the set.

Figure 23-5:
Band lat
pull-down.

a

b

Photograph by Zoran Popovic

Band one-arm shoulder press

The band one-arm shoulder press strengthens your entire shoulder muscle, with additional emphasis on your triceps.

Pay special attention to your form if you have a history of lower-back or neck problems.

Getting set: Stand on top of one end of the band near the handle so that your feet are hip-width apart. Hold the other handle in your right hand and place your left hand on your hip, right palm facing forward. Raise your right hand to shoulder height so that your elbow is bent, your upper arm is parallel to the floor, and your palm is facing forward. Keep your head centered between your shoulders, pull your abdominals in, and relax your knees (see Figure 23-6a).

The exercise: Straighten your arm overhead (see Figure 23-6b) and then slowly bend your arm until your elbow is slightly below shoulder height, but no lower. After you've completed a set with your right arm, do an equal number of reps with your left arm.

Band external rotation

The band external rotation strengthens the rotator cuff muscles.

Figure 23-6:
Band one-arm shoul-der press.

Photograph by Zoran Popovic

Getting set: Tie a band around a stable object. Stand with your left side toward the tied-off end of the band. Hold the other end of the band in your right hand with your palm facing in. Bend your elbow 90 degrees (see Figure 23-7a).

The exercise: Keeping your elbow in place, move your hand a few inches away from you to increase tension in the band (see Figure 23-7b) and then slowly move it back to the starting position. After you've completed a set with your right arm, turn around and do an equal number of reps with your left arm.

Figure 23-7: Band external rotation.

Photograph by Zoran Popovic

Band internal rotation

The internal rotation exercise strengthens the rotator cuff muscles and helps to prevent shoulder injuries.

Getting set: Tie a band around a stable object. Stand with your right side toward the tied-off end of the band. Hold the other end of the band in your right hand with your palm facing in. Bend your elbow 90 degrees (see Figure 23-8a).

The exercise: Pull your arm toward you to create more tension (see Figure 23-8b). Move your arm out again. After you've completed a set with your right arm, turn around and do an equal number of reps with your left arm.

Band shoulder stretch

You will feel this stretch all around your shoulder but particularly in the front of your deltoid.

Getting set: Stand up very tall, feet about hip-width apart, holding both ends of the band in front of your thighs (see Figure 23-9a).

Figure 23-8:
Band internal rotation.

a

b

Photograph by Zoran Popovic

The exercise: Inhale as you straighten your arms and raise them overhead (see Figure 23-9b). As you exhale, move your arms farther behind your head, but don't arch your back (see Figure 23-9c).

Figure 23-9:
Band shoulder stretch.

a

b

c

Photograph by Tilden Patterson

Band triceps extension

As you might guess, the band triceps extension strengthens your triceps muscles. It's important to train your triceps because there are very few everyday life tasks that challenge these muscles.

Go easy on this exercise if you experience elbow discomfort.

Getting set: While holding onto one end of the band with your left hand, stand with your feet as wide as your hips and place your left palm over the front of your right shoulder. Hold the other end of the band in your right hand with your palm facing inward. Bend your right elbow so that it's at waist level and pointing behind you. You can lean slightly forward from your hips if you find that position comfortable, but always keep your abdominals in and your knees relaxed (see Figure 23-10a).

The exercise: Keeping your elbow stationary, straighten your right arm out behind you so the band gets tighter as you go, but don't allow your elbow to lock (see Figure 23-10b). Then bend your elbow so your hand travels back to your waist. Reposition the band to work your left triceps.

Figure 23-10: Band triceps extension.

Photograph by Zoran Popovic

Chapter 24

Ten (Or So) Ways to Have a Ball with Exercise Balls

*U*sing the exercise ball to work out is one of the most fun ways to tone your body. Because of their shape, balls are unstable and challenge your balance. The exercise ball makes you use your abdominal muscles just to sit on it. And if you don't keep your feet firmly planted on the floor, you'll fall off. This is where your balance really comes into play!

You can even substitute the ball for the bench in some of your weight-training exercises and add dumbbells. In this chapter, you gather some tips for using balls safely and discover ten basic ball exercises.

If you'd like even more ways to work out with exercise balls, check out *Exercise Balls For Dummies,* by LaReine Chabut (Wiley).

Picking Out the Right Ball

To get an effective ball workout, you must use a quality ball that is the correct size for your body. When you stand next to an exercise ball, it should be even or slightly above your knee level.

The best way to size up your ball is by sitting on it. When you sit on the ball, you should feel the same way you do when you sit on a chair. Your knees should be bent at a 90-degree angle, and your thighs should be parallel or even with the floor. Figure 24-1 provides a guide. Find your height and see which ball size you should try first. For kids who are 5 years and younger, always use a 45 cm ball.

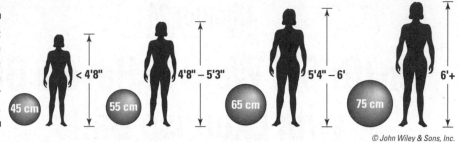

Figure 24-1: Find the right size exercise ball for your height.

Look for the following features when you're shopping for your ball:

- **Weight tested:** Manufacturers create balls that can hold up to 1,000 pounds. While the largest weight-tested ball may not be necessary for your needs, check a ball's specifications before you purchase it. Make sure that your exercise ball has been weight tested to hold at least 600 pounds or more.

- **Burst resistant:** Balls are now made of tougher materials that are more puncture resistant. Because the worst ball injuries generally occur from falls to the ground if a ball bursts, get the strongest ball possible to prevent this from happening. In addition, the more puncture resistant your ball, the longer it's likely to last in case it accidentally rolls over or into any sharp objects.

- **Slow deflation:** A ball that deflates slowly if punctured reduces the risk of injury. Deflation rate is important because injuries can occur if a ball bursts and deflates suddenly, causing you to fall to the ground. Injury risk increases if you're holding dumbbells because of the added weight and strain on your arms. If you're holding onto a weight, you don't have the use of your hands to catch yourself. A slow-deflation ball is worth the extra $5 to $10 it may cost.

Using Exercise Balls Safely

Balls require little maintenance aside from occasional cleaning and inflation. Consider the following list when maintaining and using your exercise ball:

- **Storage:** Your biggest challenge is deciding how to store your ball. If you don't have space, deflate and inflate your exercise ball in between uses. If you need to do this, buy an electric pump. The pump saves you time and relieves stress.

  Some balls have *udders* to prevent them from rolling around, like udders on a cow. This can be handy for storing it in a corner of your family room as the udders can be used to prop up the ball. Other balls come with plastic circular stands — preventing your ball from rolling. Make sure that you don't store any exercise balls near a heat source, because it can cause the ball to expand or soften and weaken the ball's surface.

✔ **Cleaning:** Clean your ball with a soft cloth or sponge and clean hot water or mild soapy water if needed. Chemical cleaners may break down and damage the ball's surface. Always use your ball on a clean dry floor. This precaution goes a long way toward keeping your ball clean and avoiding punctures.

✔ **Pumps:** Many balls sold today come with manual pumps — usually hand or foot pumps. If you're maintaining one ball and only inflating it occasionally, a manual pump should work well for you. However, if you're frequently going to inflate and deflate your ball, purchase an electric pump. If you want, you can even take yours to the gas station and use the air pump for tires — just be careful not to overinflate it.

✔ **Practice space:** Make sure that your practice space is large enough to work with a ball. The exercise area should be longer and wider than your height. Make sure that furniture with sharp edges has been cleared from the space. Remember that your balance is challenged when you work with the ball, so you may not control your movements perfectly. Keep your workout space free and clear.

Exercising on the Ball

Use your ball exercises as part of your weekly strength-training routine or rotate ball exercises in and out of your regular workouts. The variety challenges your muscles in different ways and also keeps your workouts fresh and fun. As with all other resistance exercises, perform 8 to 15 repetitions per set and at least one set per muscle group, unless indicated otherwise in the specific exercise. (We tell you which muscle group each ball exercise strengthens in this chapter.) When you can perform 15 repetitions easily, make the exercise tougher by decreasing the base of support (by picking up one foot or by bringing legs closer together) or by adding weight.

Ball bridge pose

The ball bridge pose is a great basic exercise to help strengthen your abdominal muscles, hips and lower back.

Keep your hips lifted toward the ceiling to keep your back from sagging or arching (think of an actual bridge that supports the weight of many cars).

To do this exercise, follow these steps:

1. **Sit tall on your ball with your legs at a 90-degree angle and your feet flat on the floor.**

2. **Walk your feet out until the ball is supporting your upper back, shoulders, head, and neck (see Figure 24-2).**

   Make sure to keep your hips lifted up toward the ceiling so your back and spine are straight.

3. **Hold for ten seconds, and then walk your feet back in to return to the seated starting position.**

   Complete a total of three repetitions.

Figure 24-2:
Ball bridge
pose.

Photograph by Nick Horne

A few do's and don'ts for this exercise:

✔ DO rest the back of your head on the ball during this exercise.

✔ DON'T let your hips and butt sink toward the ground. Keep your lower body tight and pressed up during the exercise.

Ball bridge lift

The ball bridge lift works your entire core area, which includes anything from your ribcage to your hips (which means your lower back, too). Because you have to use your lower legs to control the movement of the ball, this exercise may also challenge your calf muscles.

To do this exercise, follow these steps:

1. **Lie on the floor with your feet on top of the ball (see Figure 24-3a).**

   Keep your legs straight, and place your arms on the floor alongside your body for support.

2. **Exhale as you lift your hips and pelvis toward the ceiling, pressing down into the ball with your feet to maintain your balance (see Figure 24-3b).**

3. **Inhale as you slowly lower your hips back down toward the floor.**

   Complete a total of ten repetitions.

Figure 24-3: Ball bridge lift.

Photograph by Nick Horne

A few do's and don'ts for this exercise:

- ✔ DO keep your feet relaxed when they're resting on the ball.
- ✔ DO lift your hips straight up toward the ceiling and keep a straight back.
- ✔ DON'T lift your chin. Keep it tucked into your chest.

Ball push-ups

Ball push-ups target your abdominal muscles and lower back to keep you steady.

Keeping your lower legs or shins on the ball helps you balance yourself during the push-up.

To do this exercise, follow these steps:

1. **Lie with your belly on the ball and walk your hands forward until the ball rests under your legs (as shown in Figure 24-4a).**

   Make sure that you keep your hands directly below your shoulders.

Figure 24-4: Ball push-ups.

Photograph by Nick Horne

2. **Lower your upper body toward the floor, bending the elbows out to the sides (see Figure 24-4b).**

3. **Straighten the elbows and exhale as you press back up into starting position.**

   Complete a total of ten repetitions.

REMEMBER

A few do's and don'ts for this exercise:

✔ DO keep your abdominal muscles tight to help you maintain your balance.

✔ DO breathe properly — inhaling as you slowly lower your body down and exhaling as you press your body back up.

✔ DON'T arch your back. Keep it straight and in line with your head and the rest of your body.

Ball leg circles

The lifting motion of your midsection used in this exercise helps create toned abs and a stronger back. By adding the extra weight of your leg as you lift it off the ball, you'll feel a strengthening in your back muscles as well.

To do this exercise, follow these steps:

1. **Lie on the floor with your feet on top of the ball (see Figure 24-5a).**

   Keep your legs straight, and place your arms on the floor alongside your body for support.

2. **Keep your right leg on the ball and your shoulders on the floor, lift your hips, and extend your left leg toward the ceiling (as shown in Figure 24-5b).**

3. **Point your toes and use your leg to make five small circles to the right, and then five small circles to the left.**

4. **Lower your left leg back to the ball and return your hips to the floor.**

5. **Repeat this movement with the other leg.**

   Complete a total of five sets on each side.

Figure 24-5:
Ball leg
circles.

Photograph by Nick Horne

A few do's and don'ts for this exercise:

- ✔ DO keep your arms flat on the floor alongside your body for support.
- ✔ DON'T forget to contract your abs before you lift your hips off the floor.
- ✔ DON'T tense your neck and shoulders as you lift your leg off the ball.

Ball single-leg bridge

The ball single-leg bridge is a variation of the classic bridge exercise. But the ball single-leg bridge targets your lower back, abdominals, and hips, which provides you with a more toned waist. The ball single-leg bridge uses only one leg to support the weight of your entire body, so your all-important core (abs and butt muscles) gets a good workout.

To do this exercise, follow these steps:

1. **Sit tall on the ball and roll down slowly until only your shoulders touch the ball.**

2. **As you contract your abs, cross your right leg across your left thigh (see Figure 24-6a).**

Figure 24-6:
Ball single-
leg bridge.

Photograph by Nick Horne

3. **Lift your hips toward the ceiling as you contract your butt muscles (see Figure 24-6b).**

    If you find the ball moving during this exercise, place it against a wall or a heavy piece of furniture.

4. **Pause for a moment and then lower your hips.**

   Complete a total of ten repetitions before you switch legs and repeat on the other side.

A couple of do's and don'ts for this exercise:

   ✔ DO keep your hands on your hips to help steady your body.

   ✔ DON'T press your hips too high. Keep them even with your torso.

Ball core extension

In this exercise, extending your leg behind you and placing your hips over the ball works your abs, butt, and back muscles to help support your body and help you stay lifted.

Because you kneel on the floor in this exercise, you may want to place a floor mat or towel under your knees for comfort.

To do this exercise, follow these steps:

1. **Kneel with your chest on the ball and tighten your abdominal muscles.**

   Your hands will be resting on the ball for support.

2. **Slowly extend your right leg and left arm until they're opposite each other, as shown in Figure 24-7.**

   Your right hand will still rest on the ball for support. Be sure to keep your back straight and in line with your arms and legs.

Figure 24-7:
Ball core
extension.

Photograph by Nick Horne

You should be able to draw an imaginary straight line down the center of your body.

3. **Point your toes and hold that pose for a few seconds before you return to your starting position.**

   Complete a total of ten repetitions before you switch legs and repeat on the other side.

A few do's and don'ts for this exercise:

- ✔ DO keep your spine on the same plane or level with your raised arm and leg.

- ✔ DON'T arch your back when you extend your arm and leg out over the ball.

✔ DON'T arch your lower back at all during this exercise.

✔ DON'T hyperextend you neck by looking up.

Ball sit-ups

Perhaps the number-one exercise used on the ball for abdominals is the sit-up. Harder than traditional on-the-floor sit-ups and requiring more endurance, this abdominal exercise will be sure to kick your butt!

To do this exercise, follow these steps:

1. **Lie with the ball supporting your lower back and pelvis. Place your feet shoulder-width apart and keep your knees at a 90-degree angle. Place your hands behind your head and your elbows bent out to the sides (see Figure 24-8a).**

2. **Curl your body up halfway between a sitting and lying position (as shown in Figure 24-8b).**

   Keep your tailbone pressed down on the ball.

Figure 24-8:
Ball sit-ups.

Photograph by Nick Horne

3. **Slowly roll back down onto the ball, one vertebra at a time.**

   Complete a total of two sets of 10 to 15 repetitions each.

A few do's and don'ts for this exercise:

✓ DO draw your belly button toward your spine when you contract your abdominal muscles to curl up.

✓ DO exhale as you lift up.

✓ DO curl up and roll back down one vertebra at a time to keep from straining your back.

✓ DON'T pull on your neck with your hands. Keep your gaze upward as you curl up to keep your neck in line with your spine.

Ball oblique crunch

The ball oblique crunch works the muscles that run along the waist, otherwise known as the obliques. This exercise is great for men and women who want to define their waistlines and lose their love handles as they shore up their cores.

To do this exercise, follow these steps:

1. **Kneeling on the floor, position your left hip and the side of your body against the ball as you place your left arm on the ball for support.**

2. **Straighten your right leg out to the side and bring your right arm behind your head so you're touching the back of your head (as shown in Figure 24-9a).**

3. **Crunch up, bringing your right shoulder and elbow down toward your rib cage and right leg as you exhale (see Figure 24-9b).**

   Be sure to keep your left hip and side against the ball at all times to keep from slipping.

4. **Lower back down toward the ball as you slowly inhale.**

   Complete ten crunches, and then switch sides and do ten crunches on the other side.

a

b

Figure 24-9:
Ball oblique
crunches.

Photograph by Daniel Kron

REMEMBER

A few do's and don'ts for this exercise:

- ✔ DO keep the foot on your extended leg flat on the floor at all times for balance.
- ✔ DO place your foot on your extended leg against a wall if you find yourself slipping.
- ✔ DON'T forget to exhale as you crunch up, bringing your elbow down toward your knee.

Ball oblique twists

Because of the twisting motion in this exercise, your waist and your oblique muscles get a workout along with your abs.

To do this exercise, follow these steps:

1. **Lie with your back on the ball and your feet planted firmly out in front of you. Bring your arms to your chest (see Figure 24-10a).**

   Make sure you have your heels directly below your knees. Your shoulders won't touch the ball, so they're free to move from side to side.

Figure 24-10: Ball oblique twist.

Photograph by Nick Horne

2. **Starting with your right shoulder, contract your abdominal muscles as you slowly lift and turn your body toward your left hip (see Figure 24-10b).**

3. **Keep your body lifted for a moment, and then slowly lower your body to the starting position.**

4. **Repeat on the other side.**

   Continue alternating right and left side lifts for two sets of 12.

A few do's and don'ts to keep in mind:

✔ DO exhale before you contract your abdominal muscles and lift.

✔ DO rest your chin on your hands for support.

✔ DON'T rush through this exercise. Take a moment to pause at the top of the lift.

Ball exchange

This is our favorite exercise for training your abdominals. It's also good for developing hand–eye coordination, as you'll see when you start passing the ball back and forth between your arms and legs.

To do this exercise, follow these steps:

1. **Lie on your back, making sure your lower back is pressed down into the mat or floor.**

2. **Holding the ball, extend your arms and the ball directly above your head on the floor. Keep your head and neck resting on the floor (see Figure 24-11a).**

3. **Raise your arms and legs up to meet at a 90-degree angle above your torso (as shown in Figure 24-11b).**

4. **Exchange the ball by grasping it between your legs. Then bring the ball back down to the floor (see Figure 24-11c).**

   Continue exchanging the ball 10 to 12 times.

A few do's and don'ts for this exercise:

✔ DO avoid arching your back.

✔ DO keep your head and neck on the floor.

✔ DON'T forget to keep a tight grip on the ball as you pass it back and forth or exchange it.

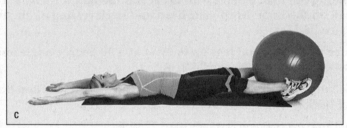

Figure 24-11:
Ball
exchange.

Photograph by Nick Horne

Index

About the Author

LaReine Chabut is a distinguished lifestyle and fitness expert, best-selling author, model, and mom. As the on-camera host of MSN's hit webseries *Focus on Feeling Better,* LaReine helped everyday people across America fit in exercise daily by taking a well-rounded approach to healthy living. As a model, LaReine has graced the covers of *Shape, Health, New Body,* and *Runner's World,* among others. She has appeared on *Chelsea Lately* on E!, *The Dr. Phil Show,* NBC, ABC, Fox News, *EXTRA,* and *Good Day L.A.*

As an author, LaReine has written *Lose That Baby Fat!* (M. Evans); *Exercise Balls For Dummies* (Wiley); *Stretching For Dummies* (Wiley); *Core Strength For Dummies* (Wiley); *Dieting For Dummies,* Pocket Edition (Wiley); *Golf All-in-One For Dummies* (Wiley); and *Yoga-All in One For Dummies* (Wiley). LaReine is most recognized as the lead instructor of *The Firm,* a series of popular workout videos that have sold over 3 million copies worldwide.

To read more about LaReine Chabut, log on to her website at www. lareinechabut.com or www.losethatbabyfat.com. To find LaReine's exercise videos, go to www.gymra.com and www.dummies.com.

Follow LaReine on Twitter at @LaReineChabut.

Dedication

For my husband, David; daughters, Bella and Sofia; and stepsons, Blake and Casey. Thanks for making this book such a family affair. My beautiful daughters, Bella and Sofia, who modeled so patiently for this and my other books; my stepson Blake, who modeled all the weight machines and was great at it; my stepson Casey, who lets me write at his desk; and last but not least, my husband David, who is perfect in every way.

Author's Acknowledgments

I am thankful to the following people for all their help and support:

- To my readers: Thank you first and foremost for reading my books.

- To my acquisitions editor, Tracy Boggier: Thank you for your enthusiasm and expertise, and for seeking me out for another *For Dummies* book and video.

- To my photographer, Nick Horne: Thank you for once again taking such beautiful photos and being so cool.

- To my video producer, Paula McKee, and Gymra: Thank you for making the most beautiful exercise videos available on the Internet, at www.gymra.com. The *Weight Training For Dummies* video came out beautifully.

- To The GYM: Thank you for letting us shoot at your new club. It is one of the best places I know to train in Los Angeles.

- To my trainer, Phong Tran: Thank you for your wealth of knowledge, expertise, and skill with all those weight machines.

- To my project editor, Elizabeth Kuball, and technical editor, Maureen Amirault: It takes a village, and you did it.

Weight Training For Dummies, 4th Edition — what a great project to be a part of. Thanks to all!

Publisher's Acknowledgments

Senior Acquisitions Editor: Tracy Boggier

Project Editor: Elizabeth Kuball

Copy Editor: Elizabeth Kuball

Technical Editor: Maureen Amirault

Art Coordinator: Alicia B. South

Project Coordinator: Patrick Redmond

Photographer: Nick Horne

Cover Image: Bottle: © iStock.com/Turnervisual; weight, apple, etc.: © iStock.com/edenexposed

Apple & Mac

iPad For Dummies,
6th Edition
978-1-118-72306-7

iPhone For Dummies,
7th Edition
978-1-118-69083-3

Macs All-in-One
For Dummies, 4th Edition
978-1-118-82210-4

OS X Mavericks
For Dummies
978-1-118-69188-5

Blogging & Social Media

Facebook For Dummies,
5th Edition
978-1-118-63312-0

Social Media Engagement
For Dummies
978-1-118-53019-1

WordPress For Dummies,
6th Edition
978-1-118-79161-5

Business

Stock Investing
For Dummies, 4th Edition
978-1-118-37678-2

Investing For Dummies,
6th Edition
978-0-470-90545-6

Personal Finance

Personal Finance
For Dummies, 7th Edition
978-1-118-11785-9

QuickBooks 2014
For Dummies
978-1-118-72005-9

Small Business Marketing
Kit For Dummies,
3rd Edition
978-1-118-31183-7

Careers

Job Interviews
For Dummies, 4th Edition
978-1-118-11290-8

Job Searching with Social
Media For Dummies,
2nd Edition
978-1-118-67856-5

Personal Branding
For Dummies
978-1-118-11792-7

Resumes For Dummies,
6th Edition
978-0-470-87361-8

Starting an Etsy Business
For Dummies, 2nd Edition
978-1-118-59024-9

Diet & Nutrition

Belly Fat Diet For Dummies
978-1-118-34585-6

Mediterranean Diet

Mediterranean Diet
For Dummies
978-1-118-71525-3

Nutrition For Dummies,
5th Edition
978-0-470-93231-5

Digital Photography

Digital SLR Photography
All-in-One For Dummies,
2nd Edition
978-1-118-59082-9

Digital SLR Video &
Filmmaking For Dummies
978-1-118-36598-4

Photoshop Elements 12
For Dummies
978-1-118-72714-0

Gardening

Herb Gardening
For Dummies, 2nd Edition
978-0-470-61778-6

Gardening with Free-Range
Chickens For Dummies
978-1-118-54754-0

Health

Boosting Your Immunity
For Dummies
978-1-118-40200-9

Diabetes

Diabetes For Dummies,
4th Edition
978-1-118-29447-5

Living Paleo For Dummies
978-1-118-29405-5

Big Data

Big Data For Dummies
978-1-118-50422-2

Data Visualization
For Dummies
978-1-118-50289-1

Hadoop For Dummies
978-1-118-60755-8

Language & Foreign Language

500 Spanish Verbs
For Dummies
978-1-118-02382-2

English Grammar
For Dummies, 2nd Edition
978-0-470-54664-2

French All-in-One
For Dummies
978-1-118-22815-9

German Essentials
For Dummies
978-1-118-18422-6

Italian For Dummies,
2nd Edition
978-1-118-00465-4

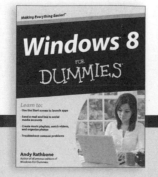   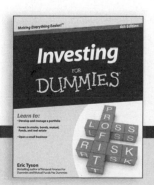

Available in print and e-book formats.

Available wherever books are sold. **For more information or to order direct visit www.dummies.com**

Math & Science

Algebra I For Dummies,
2nd Edition
978-0-470-55964-2

Anatomy and Physiology
For Dummies, 2nd Edition
978-0-470-92326-9

Astronomy For Dummies,
3rd Edition
978-1-118-37697-3

Biology For Dummies,
2nd Edition
978-0-470-59875-7

Chemistry For Dummies,
2nd Edition
978-1-118-00730-3

1001 Algebra II Practice
Problems For Dummies
978-1-118-44662-1

Microsoft Office

Excel 2013 For Dummies
978-1-118-51012-4

Office 2013 All-in-One
For Dummies
978-1-118-51636-2

PowerPoint 2013
For Dummies
978-1-118-50253-2

Word 2013 For Dummies
978-1-118-49123-2

Music

Blues Harmonica
For Dummies
978-1-118-25269-7

Guitar For Dummies,
3rd Edition
978-1-118-11554-1

iPod & iTunes
For Dummies, 10th Edition
978-1-118-50864-0

Programming

Beginning Programming
with C For Dummies
978-1-118-73763-7

Excel VBA Programming
For Dummies, 3rd Edition
978-1-118-49037-2

Java For Dummies,
6th Edition
978-1-118-40780-6

Religion & Inspiration

The Bible For Dummies
978-0-7645-5296-0

Buddhism For Dummies,
2nd Edition
978-1-118-02379-2

Catholicism For Dummies,
2nd Edition
978-1-118-07778-8

Self-Help & Relationships

Beating Sugar Addiction
For Dummies
978-1-118-54645-1

Meditation For Dummies,
3rd Edition
978-1-118-29144-3

Seniors

Laptops For Seniors
For Dummies, 3rd Edition
978-1-118-71105-7

Computers For Seniors
For Dummies, 3rd Edition
978-1-118-11553-4

iPad For Seniors
For Dummies, 6th Edition
978-1-118-72826-0

Social Security
For Dummies
978-1-118-20573-0

Smartphones & Tablets

Android Phones
For Dummies, 2nd Edition
978-1-118-72030-1

Nexus Tablets
For Dummies
978-1-118-77243-0

Samsung Galaxy S 4
For Dummies
978-1-118-64222-1

Samsung Galaxy Tabs
For Dummies
978-1-118-77294-2

Test Prep

ACT For Dummies,
5th Edition
978-1-118-01259-8

ASVAB For Dummies,
3rd Edition
978-0-470-63760-9

GRE For Dummies,
7th Edition
978-0-470-88921-3

Officer Candidate Tests
For Dummies
978-0-470-59876-4

Physician's Assistant Exam
For Dummies
978-1-118-11556-5

Series 7 Exam For Dummies
978-0-470-09932-2

Windows 8

Windows 8.1 All-in-One
For Dummies
978-1-118-82087-2

Windows 8.1 For Dummies
978-1-118-82121-3

Windows 8.1 For Dummies,
Book + DVD Bundle
978-1-118-82107-7

Available in print and e-book formats.

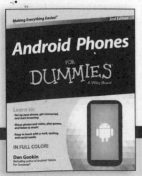

Available wherever books are sold. **For more information or to order direct visit www.dummies.com**